WITHDRAWN

HARVARD LIBRARY

WITHDRAWN

Transatlantic Anti-Catholicism

PALGRAVE MACMILLAN TRANSNATIONAL HISTORY SERIES

Akira Iriye (Harvard University) and **Rana Mitter** (University of Oxford)
Series Editors

This distinguished series seeks to: develop scholarship on the transnational connections of societies and peoples in the nineteenth and twentieth centuries; provide a forum in which work on transnational history from different periods, subjects, and regions of the world can be brought together in fruitful connection; and explore the theoretical and methodological links between transnational and other related approaches such as comparative history and world history.

Editorial board: **Thomas Bender** University Professor of the Humanities, Professor of History, and Director of the International Center for Advanced Studies, New York University **Jane Carruthers** Professor of History, University of South Africa **Mariano Plotkin** Professor, Universidad Nacional de Tres de Febrero, Buenos Aires, and member of the National Council of Scientific and Technological Research, Argentina **Pierre-Yves Saunier** Researcher at the Centre National de la Recherche Scientifique, France **Ian Tyrrell** Professor of History, University of New South Wales

Published by Palgrave Macmillan:

THE NATION, PSYCHOLOGY AND INTERNATIONAL POLITICS, 1870–1919
By Glenda Sluga

COMPETING VISIONS OF WORLD ORDER: GLOBAL MOMENTS AND MOVEMENTS, 1880s–1930s
Edited by Sebastian Conrad and Dominic Sachsenmaier

PAN-ASIANISM AND JAPAN'S WAR, 1931–1945
By Eri Hotta

WOMEN, GENDER, AND POSTWAR RECONCILIATION BETWEEN NATIONS
By Erika Kuhlman

1968 IN EUROPE: A HISTORY OF PROTEST AND ACTIVISM, 1957–1977
Edited by Martin Klimke and Joachim Scharloth

THE CHINESE IN BRITAIN, 1800–PRESENT: ECONOMY, TRANSNATIONALISM, IDENTITY
By Gregor Benton and Terence Gomez

THE IDEA OF HUMANITY IN A GLOBAL ERA
Bruce Mazlish

TRANSATLANTIC ANTI-CATHOLICISM: FRANCE AND THE UNITED STATES IN THE NINETEENTH CENTURY
By Timothy Verhoeven

TELEGRAPHIC IMPERIALISM: CRISIS AND PANIC IN THE INDIAN EMPIRE, C. 1850–1920
D. K. Lahiri-Choudhury (forthcoming)

EUROPEAN HISTORY IN AN INTERCONNECTED WORLD
By Matthias Middell, Michael Geyer, and Michel Espagne (forthcoming)

COSMOPOLITAN THOUGHT ZONES: INTELLECTUAL EXCHANGE BETWEEN SOUTH ASIA AND EUROPE, 1870–1945
Edited by Kris Manjapra and Sugata Bose (forthcoming)

IRISH TERRORISM IN THE ATLANTIC COMMUNITY, 1865–1922
By Jonathan Gantt (forthcoming)

Transatlantic Anti-Catholicism

France and the United States in the Nineteenth Century

Timothy Verhoeven

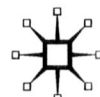

TRANSATLANTIC ANTI-CATHOLICISM
Copyright © Timothy Verhoeven, 2010.

All rights reserved.

First published in 2010 by
PALGRAVE MACMILLAN®
in the United States—a division of St. Martin's Press LLC,
175 Fifth Avenue, New York, NY 10010.

Where this book is distributed in the UK, Europe and the rest of the world, this is by Palgrave Macmillan, a division of Macmillan Publishers Limited, registered in England, company number 785998, of Houndmills, Basingstoke, Hampshire RG21 6XS.

Palgrave Macmillan is the global academic imprint of the above companies and has companies and representatives throughout the world.

Palgrave® and Macmillan® are registered trademarks in the United States, the United Kingdom, Europe and other countries.

ISBN: 978–0–230–10287–3

Library of Congress Cataloging-in-Publication Data is available from the Library of Congress.

A catalogue record of the book is available from the British Library.

Design by Newgen Imaging Systems (P) Ltd., Chennai, India.

First edition: May 2010

10 9 8 7 6 5 4 3 2 1

Printed in the United States of America.

Contents

Series Editors' Foreword vii

Acknowledgments ix

Introduction: Father Hyacinthe in America 1

1 The Transatlantic Case against Catholicism 19
2 Catholicism, Slavery, and the Family—The Mortara Affair 57
3 Natural or Unnatural? Doctors and the Vow of Celibacy 75
4 Neither Male nor Female—The Jesuit as Androgyne 103
5 The Captivity of Sister Barbara Ubryk 129

Conclusion: Father Hyacinthe and the Vatican Council 159

Notes 177

Selected Bibliography 211

Index 225

Series Editors' Foreword

One of the pleasures of studying transnational history is the discovery of manifold, yet hitherto little-suspected, connections across national boundaries. Timothy Verhoeven's research on nineteenth-century anti-Catholicism has yielded ample evidence to show constant engagements and mutual influences among American and French opponents of the Catholic Church.

As his book notes, anti-Catholicism has many roots, but the negative responses to the church in the United States and France in the nineteenth century suggests some shared political and intellectual foundations. In both, the principle of separation of church and state was emphasized as a way to ensure national independence and to reduce, if not eliminate altogether, influences of potentially subversive religious organizations, especially the Catholic Church. In particular, the church's rule of celibacy was condemned as scientifically unsound, harmful to both individuals and to society, and even conducive to national decay. Such an argument was buttressed by medical research that seemed to point to dire consequences of enforced sexual abstention. That two countries as different in many ways as the United States and France should have shared such opinions and movements points to the existence of strong Transatlantic connections.

Historians have mostly examined these connections in relation to reform movements such as those that aimed at the emancipation of slaves, the disenfranchisement of women, or world peace. In the Palgrave Macmillan Transnational History Series, we have published a study of Irish terrorism as a transnational movement, spreading from Ireland to continental Europe and to North America, but Verhoeven's book offers the first scholarly treatment of anti-Catholic ideas and activities as a Transatlantic phenomenon. Among the fascinating details offered by the book is its discussion of the question of celibacy. In a sense, there was a transnational discourse on sexuality in which there was constructed a sharp distinction between male and female beings, but in which their sexual relations (normally as married couples) were considered normal, even normative. The Catholic vow of celibacy, therefore, was considered by its opponents unnatural and subversive of both natural order and social order.

The nineteenth century is typically put in the context of the birth of the modern nation state, a phenomenon that suggests bounded national identities and interests. Yet the borders were never exclusionary, and there was virtually complete freedom of movement of ideas, particularly those that contributed to strengthening transnational connections. At the same time, however, anti-Catholicism was also anti-universalism in that the Catholic Church's authority extended throughout the world. As the author demonstrates, the Catholics, especially Jesuits, were seen by their opponents as enemies to the independent nation. The Jesuit priest was frequently depicted not only as straddling the divide between man and woman, but also as existing in the fringes of the national community, as someone who did not fit into the emerging modern state, or, even worse, as an agitator among the mobs who were potentially subversive of the state. Thus anti-Catholicism had both transnational and national undertones. To understand the complex engagement between transnationalism and nationalism is another objective of transnational history, and this book serves that objective admirably.

AKIRA IRIYE
RANA MITTER

Acknowledgments

Many people contributed to the research and writing of this book. I would first like to thank Dr. David Goodman and Professor Charles Sowerwine at the University of Melbourne, Australia, for their advice and expertise in the drafting of the book. Earlier versions of chapters were read by Dr. Susan Foley and Emeritus Professor Colin Nettelbeck, and both made important contributions. An Embassy of France in Australia travelling fellowship awarded by the Australian Academy of the Humanities allowed important archival work to be carried out in France and in Switzerland. I was also the fortunate recipient of a short-term fellowship from the Library Company in Philadelphia, and wish to express my gratitude to all the staff for their ideas and assistance. The Library Company's rich collection of medical textbooks was a particularly valuable resource.

My parents, Martin and Wallis, have been a welcome and ongoing source of support. I would also like to thank my wife, Jana, for her unstinting enthusiasm and encouragement, as well as her great help in producing the final version of the manuscript. Finally I dedicate this book to Mark and Luise who, I hope, will enjoy reading it one day.

Introduction: Father Hyacinthe in America

On October 19 1869, the front page of the *New York Times* was almost entirely devoted to a visitor from abroad who seemed an unlikely candidate for such attention: a French Carmelite monk called Father Hyacinthe. The interest generated by Hyacinthe's arrival was enormous. A crowd gathered at the dock to greet him, then followed him to his hotel where, the *Times* reported, porters were kept busy running written requests for interviews up to his room. On October 21, Hyacinthe posed for the famous photographer Mathew Brady, and his portrait quickly became one of the most popular in Brady's gallery. Many leading religious and literary figures shared this curiosity toward the French monk. Over the next two months Hyacinthe would meet with, amongst others, Harriet Beecher Stowe, famed ministers Henry Ward Beecher and the Reverend Leonard W. Bacon, poet Henry Wadsworth Longfellow, historian Charles Francis Adams, and the Governor of Massachusetts, William Claflin. The publisher George P. Putnam took advantage of Hyacinthe's fame to rush into print, with the Frenchman's consent, a translation of his sermons and addresses. For the former Consul and American minister to France, John Bigelow, Hyacinthe's reception in America was nothing less than sensational. "Every source of information," Bigelow later wrote, "was ransacked for details of his life; his hotel was thronged; he was interviewed by reporters; he was deluged with invitations; shop windows and illustrated journals were radiant with his portrait."[1] This Carmelite monk had become a star.

Hyacinthe owed his fame in America to a dramatic act of rebellion against his own church. Just weeks before his arrival in New York, Hyacinthe had resigned from his Carmelite order. On September 21, a letter to his Carmelite superior explaining his resignation appeared in *Le Temps*, before being reprinted in newspapers throughout France the following day; by October 5, it had reached the front pages of the American press.[2] In the letter, Hyacinthe launched a bold attack on the Vatican. The church, he lamented, had deliberately turned its back on the progressive values and spirit of nineteenth-century civilization. "I protest," he wrote, "against the divorce as impious, as it is insensate...between the Church, which is our eternal mother, and the society of the nineteenth century, of which we are the temporal children, and towards which we also have duties and regards." For Hyacinthe, the Vatican's complete intolerance for secular humanism, and its unwillingness to attempt any conciliation between religion and science, had weakened the church's influence. Hyacinthe ended his letter by pleading for a church more tolerant of dissent and more willing to embrace the political, intellectual, and social developments of its age.

On both sides of the Atlantic, Hyacinthe's letter created a sensation. Commentators expressed their amazement at Hyacinthe's temerity in so openly challenging the Vatican. The *Moniteur Universel* described the letter as "one of the religious events of this era."[3] One of the most prominent French republicans and anticlericals, Charles Sauvestre, applauded the letter, noting that public opinion was sure to be moved by such an act of defiance. For *La Tribune*, Hyacinthe's resignation proved that the church could never accommodate any priest with "the impertinence to have talent and to put it at the service of an idea of progress."[4] The American press quoted many of these French reactions, and then added its own. In an assessment that was typical of the secular press, the *New York Herald* called the letter a "bombshell."[5] Such language, commentators remarked, had not been heard since the Middle Ages; they likened Hyacinthe to the great religious reformers of the past. The *New York Times* declared that "The fire which burned in the hearts of the most memorable reformers of history animates Father Hyacinthe, and will yet compel him to do a work which will live after him." That work might be nothing less, commentators suggested, than a new Reformation. In the annals of religious reform, the name Hyacinthe might, the *New York Herald* conjectured, "be as great a name as that of Luther."[6]

For his American supporters, then, Father Hyacinthe was far more than a disgruntled monk. He was the herald of a great religious schism. Yet what is particularly striking about his reception in the United States is the manner in which his rebellion against the Vatican was understood in gendered terms. By casting off the authority of the church, Hyacinthe was seen to have recovered not just his independence and his integrity, but his very manliness. The *Independent* of New York, for example, labeled Hyacinthe's letter the "immortal manifesto" of a priest who has "too great a Christian manhood to keep him the submissive slave of the Pope."[7] Such language was repeated throughout his stay. A host of American commentators congratulated Hyacinthe for having reclaimed his masculinity. With Hyacinthe listening in the audience, Henry Ward Beecher praised him as "the great European exponent and advocate of the independence of Christian manhood."[8] From the perspective of the *Chicago Tribune*, the transformation was stunning; "the man," it declared, "had appeared under the priest."[9]

A reading of Hyacinthe's posture and countenance indicated to contemporaries that such a shift had indeed occurred. Hostile descriptions of priests invariably emphasized a number of physical features. In an outward sign of the submission of their souls to the Catholic hierarchy, priests were imagined as slouching, furtive figures, their bent bodies and downcast eyes revealing their unmanly state of dependence and submission. In contrast, Hyacinthe showed all the exterior signs of masculine independence. His features, described by one paper as "round and plump," contrasted with the "thin" and "weazened" face which betrayed a religious fanatic; Hyacinthe's countenance, the paper concluded, had "all the sensibilities of a man."[10] The signs of manliness seemed, in fact, obvious. As one observer after another emphasized, he walked with his body straight and his head held upright, and regarded others with a direct and frank gaze. In an article describing the crowds flocking to study the photograph of Hyacinthe in Brady's gallery, the *Independent* concluded that "the monk and the man are at war, and the man has prevailed."[11]

If any doubts as to Hyacinthe's masculine virtues remained in the minds of Americans, they were dispelled by his apparent opposition to ecclesiastical celibacy. This understanding was slightly odd, for Hyacinthe had never directly expressed any opposition to celibate vows. Admittedly, in his sermons he had often praised family life and marriage as noble and Christian institutions. Yet such eulogies of domesticity on the part of Catholic clerics were not unprecedented, and by no means entailed a rejection of ecclesiastical celibacy. For proof that Hyacinthe envisaged a more radical position, his supporters looked to one sentence in the famous letter of resignation. In that sentence, Hyacinthe had protested against what he termed "that opposition, more radical and more frightful still, to human nature." The formulation was vague, and did not specify the celibate vows. But the belief that the celibate state was "unnatural" was, as we shall see, pervasive on both sides of the Atlantic, and Hyacinthe's supporters read his statement as a coded attack on celibacy. This became clear in the response to the only public speech that he gave during his stay at a benefit for the French Benevolent Society in New York on December 9. The opportunity to see Hyacinthe attracted some of the leading figures of New York society. Tickets were sold out two days in advance, and the audience was composed, in the words of one newspaper, of the "intelligence of the city."[12] One of the spectators, the noted children's author Elizabeth Prentiss, recorded in her journal the curious sight of the monk lecturing to such a group; the "very elite of intellectual society," she wrote, "[were] gathered around one modest, unpretentious little man." Another member of the audience to record his impressions was the poet William Cullen Bryant. Any reference by Hyacinthe to the abuses of Catholicism, Bryant wrote, was "clapped vehemently."[13]

After the speech, Hyacinthe's admirers celebrated what they perceived as a brave attack on ecclesiastical celibacy. In its review of the occasion, the *New York Times* reported that Hyacinthe "could not avoid branding celibacy as a 'cowardice' and speaking in most earnest words of the great error of his Church in Europe, in separating the daily practical life of the world from the life of religion."[14] Hyacinthe, as another paper informed its readers, had "assaulted the doctrine of celibacy as taught and practised" in the Catholic Church.[15] Had Hyacinthe, though, launched such a direct assault on one of the fundamental rites of the Catholic Church? A reading of Hyacinthe's words does not quite support such a conclusion. Hyacinthe had indeed labeled celibacy as "cowardice," but added the following, curious qualification—"if it does not glorify marriage." For his audience, however, there seemed to be little ambiguity. Hyacinthe's opposition to celibacy appeared unequivocal, and as a consequence he could no longer hope for any reconciliation with the church. "His theological goose," as the *Daily Cleveland Herald* put it, "is cooked."[16]

In coming to this conclusion, American commentators were unaware of an intriguing personal dimension to Hyacinthe's attitude on this question. At the time that he toured the north-eastern states, Hyacinthe was in love. On June 17, 1867, Hyacinthe met an American widow, Emilie Meriman, who had come to France several years earlier with a letter of recommendation from her pastor, Henry Ward Beecher, followed by a short note from President Abraham Lincoln. "I have no personal acquaintance with the lady of whom Mr. Beecher has written above," Lincoln wrote, "but his commendation is a good voucher with me, and should be, I think, with others."[17] Hyacinthe and Meriman became friends, and in 1868 he converted her to Catholicism. Their friendship, however, soon turned to love. In a journal entry dated August 5, 1868, Hyacinthe made the following confession regarding his relationship to Meriman: "Up to now, I had known friendship, I had not known LOVE."[18] But what sort of love was Hyacinthe talking about? From the evidence of his journals and their letters, it seems almost certain that the relationship throughout 1869–1870 remained chaste, and that Hyacinthe conceived their love in spiritual rather than physical terms. He refers repeatedly, for example, to Meriman as the "wife of his soul."

His journal describes a man wrestling with the contending forces of his love for Meriman and his obligation to uphold the vow of celibacy. In March 1869, for example, Hyacinthe wrote, *"How happy I would be, and how blessed, if this woman were my wife."* But in what was perhaps a sign of his inner turmoil, Hyacinthe immediately qualified the sentiment: "She won't be my wife, in the sense that men give to that word." His American supporters apparently remained unaware of his relationship to Meriman. Yet many detected signs of his struggle. In his journal for the period of his stay in America, Hyacinthe records a conversation with John Bigelow. In his memoirs, Bigelow would later claim that at this time he did not know of Meriman's existence.[19] Nevertheless, from the evidence of this entry of November 28, 1869, it seems that Bigelow, like so many Americans, considered Hyacinthe to be an opponent of ecclesiastical celibacy. "Not only," Hyacinthe wrote of the meeting, "would he not be shocked to see me married one day, but he would be shocked if it were otherwise, for it would be cowardice not to bring my acts into line with my convictions." All this remained hidden from the American public. By the time of his return to France on December 11, 1869, Hyacinthe had given little sign of having resolved either his external struggle against the Vatican, or his emotional struggle over Emilie Meriman.

* * *

The visit of this French monk to America was the culmination of three decades of cross-border exchange between opponents of the Catholic Church in the two nations. In recent years historians have sought to move our understanding of the past out of what Daniel T. Rodgers has termed the "analytical cage" of the nation-state. Rather than the single-nation approach which has tended to dominate historical scholarship, historians are now far more conscious of the movement of ideas, books, and people across the Atlantic and between the European states which marked the nineteenth century. At the same time, arguments for the distinctiveness of certain national traits, developments, or ideals have increasingly been treated with skepticism, at least in the absence of a comparative framework. In the United States, where a resilient and deep-rooted belief in national uniqueness has tended to produce narratives which emphasize America's differences with other nations, this movement to internationalize the past has been particularly strong. The assumption that the United States has taken a vastly different historical trajectory to that of other industrialized nations has resulted, for many critics, in a history that obscures or ignores not only the common elements across a range of societies, but also the international flow of ideas and people in which Americans, as much as Europeans, were active participants.[20]

European historiography has its own approaches to the past which challenge the primacy of the nation-state. In France, the early *Annalistes* moved well beyond the events of a single nation by emphasizing the longue durée, the broad economic and social processes occurring across centuries and affecting a wide geographic area. The early *Annalistes* were also highly aware of the benefits of a comparative approach. In an important essay, Marc Bloch described the advantages of the comparative frame of reference, as well as the criteria for the fruitful adoption of such an approach.[21] More recently, the schools of *Transfergeschichte* and *histoire croisée* have explored, for example, the manner in which German and French systems of education influenced each other, and other facets of the "entangled" history between those two nations.[22]

On the subject of opposition to Catholicism in the nineteenth century, however, historians have only rarely looked past the borders of the nation-state. In the United States, historians have consistently located anti-Catholicism in certain quintessentially American traits and circumstances: as an enduring strain within American political culture dating back to the Puritan settlement, a response to waves of predominantly Catholic immigration, or an expression of a broader American propensity to imagine vast and sinister conspiracies threatening the body politic.[23] A new wave of studies has linked anti-Catholicism to conventional and widely held beliefs about gender and domesticity. Historians have mounted a powerful case that the church's perceived violation of the prevailing ideals of femininity, masculinity and family drove much anti-Catholic sentiment.[24] Yet even when conceding the influence of foreign works in the United States, scholars have continued to insist on the uniquely American shape of anti-Catholicism. Jenny Franchot's *Roads to Rome: the Antebellum Protestant Encounter with Catholicism* typifies this limited approach. Although conceding that one of the features of anti-Catholic discourse was "its ability to cross national, class, and ethnic boundaries," Franchot's consideration of international influences on American anti-Catholics goes little further than a brief discussion of the reception of the French historian Jules Michelet's polemic against the Catholic confessional, and the lesson provided by Mexico, whose apparent political instability and economic stagnation was viewed by many Americans as an outgrowth of its Catholicism.[25]

Scholars of French anticlericalism have also rarely moved beyond a national framework. Some historians have argued that anticlericalism should be understood as an authentic and comprehensive system of belief.[26] In other accounts, anticlericalism appears as merely a strategic tool for binding together an otherwise fractured republican movement, a smokescreen to deflect criticism away from the limited social and economic reforms undertaken by republican governments.[27] A related disagreement concerns the extent to which the beliefs and attitudes of the church and its opponents diverged. The conflict between anticlericals and the church is sometimes presented as a clash between two opposing camps whose vision of French history and society was essentially irreconcilable.[28] On the other hand, in the fields of morals and gender in particular, the similarities between the two sides have seemed more striking than the differences.[29] Yet whatever their conclusions, all of these interpretations remain anchored in a purely national viewpoint.

Partial attempts to understand anti-Catholicism and anticlericalism as transnational phenomena have been made. Susan M. Griffin's *Anti-Catholicism and Nineteenth Century Fiction* offers a comparative analysis of the use of anti-Catholicism by major American and British novelists. While acknowledging at certain points the international reception of key French works such as Eugène Sue's *Le juif errant*, Griffin does not consider in any detail the influence of French authors on American attitudes to Catholicism. In the field of European anticlericalism, calls for a more systematic comparative or transnational approach have not been lacking. The French historian René Rémond, in assessing opposition to the political pretensions of the church, once suggested that, "The time has come to take a wider view, crossing political frontiers and transcending national particularisms."[30] But the articles which followed this call for a broader approach reflected instead the continuing dominance of the nation-state as the key frame of reference, for each was devoted to one particular nation. In their recent work *Culture Wars: Secular-Catholic Conflict in 19th Century Europe,* Christopher Clark and Wolfram Kaiser make a stronger case for the interconnectedness of the various battles between the church and secularist movements in nineteenth-century Europe. Wolfram Kaiser in particular presents an overview of the manner in which anticlerical sentiment "penetrated local, regional and national spaces."[31] Yet despite its promise, the book itself contains the same failing as previous efforts. Aside from its first two chapters, the bulk of the book is devoted to the culture wars in single nations only, and the interconnections between them are largely ignored.

The movement which sought to curtail the social and political influence of the Catholic Church in the nineteenth century would seem, however, the ideal candidate for a transnational study. To begin with, the Church itself was a transnational organization. We should, of course, be wary of repeating one of the standard attacks on the Church: that its members were indifferent to national sentiment and blindly followed the orders of their ultimate master, the pope. However, through its ability to dispatch funds and personnel across borders, the church was an organization which in many ways transcended national boundaries. The cross-border links within the church became clear in moments of crisis; following their expulsion from Switzerland in 1847, for example, many Jesuits fled to the United States. American opponents of Catholicism, then, could hardly ignore the global reach of their enemy, or pretend that the battle could be won on national soil alone.

Yet another imagined feature of Catholicism which clearly favored an international response was its allegedly unchanging nature. For its critics, Roman-Catholicism's identity had been forged in the Middle Ages when a ruthless and ambitious papacy had overthrown the egalitarian and communal spirit of the primitive church. The beliefs and character of an individual pontiff were, in this view, irrelevant; regardless of the nation and the era in which it operated, the Vatican had no choice but to stick to the same outmoded and sinister principles. Of course, opponents of the church in France and the United States often warned that their nation was a privileged target of Catholic subversion. But the balancing assumption, that the church took a near-identical form in whichever country it infiltrated, fostered an intense international traffic in anti-Catholic literature. After all, accurate and credible descriptions of the menace posed by Catholicism need not be local in origin. A native of New York or Massachusetts who suspected the convent of concealing a range of awful crimes behind its walls, or who found the prospect of Jesuitism flourishing in the United States troubling, might just as easily look to a French as to an American source in his or her effort to understand the workings of such Catholic bodies. As we shall see, this is precisely what occurred, and on a vast scale.

There were solid reasons, then, for opponents of Catholicism to look beyond national borders for ideas, support, and inspiration. The aim of this book is to examine such linkages between opponents of Catholicism in two nations, France and the United States. Why these two nations? After all, the connecting network joining opponents of Catholicism extended across a series of countries and continents. American convent atrocity stories were published in the United Kingdom and Australia; the Italian renegade priest and anti-Catholic lecturer, Alessandro Gavazzi, created scandal in both the United States and Britain; the historian Jules Michelet's denunciation of the Catholic confessional was published in Belgium, Spain, the United Kingdom, the German-speaking states, Australia and Hungary. Such examples could be multiplied indefinitely; the traffic in anti-Catholic literature and ideas in the middle decades of the century paid little heed to national borders or linguistic barriers.

Yet within this international circuit of anti-Catholic ideas and literature, the linkages between France and the United States were particularly strong. Importantly, these bonds were formed not in spite of, but because of the differences between the two societies. The position of the Catholic Church itself constituted a major point of divergence. The church in France was by far the largest congregation and, though no longer the official state religion under the terms of the 1801 *Concordat*, a significant social and political force. From the perspective of French republicans, Catholicism loomed as a serious obstacle to the creation of a democratic and secular state. In the United States, on the other hand, the church was a largely immigrant organization operating in an environment of religious disestablishment and Protestant dominance. Given this fundamental difference in the status of the church, opposition to Catholicism in the two nations could hardly be identical.

Such differences, however, proved a spur rather than an obstacle to the cross-border movement of ideas and literature. American anti-Catholics certainly mined the works of Protestants in Britain and Germany for descriptions of the evils of Catholicism. Yet polemical texts from a majority-Catholic country like France had the great advantage of a familiarity with the enemy that works from Protestant nations could not match. As we shall see in chapter 1 of this study, the testimony of French writers, with their first-hand experience of the church, was highly prized in the United States. Of course, some American reviewers frowned upon the reputation for irreligion enjoyed by some French intellectuals. Yet though at times lamenting an absence of Protestant spirit, reviewers also pointed to the significant advantage of these works, namely, their authenticity and credibility. The works of Jules Michelet, Edgar Quinet, and a host of other French authors had emerged from a long knowledge and unrivalled intimacy with the alleged wiles of the church. From the French perspective, difference could also be understood as an advantage rather than as a barrier. French anticlericals looked with envy across the Atlantic where a dynamic young Republic appeared to have triumphed over the church. Their interest in the United States stemmed from an awareness that, on the question of church-state relations, the two nations had very little in common. America was worthy of emulation because it appeared to have succeeded where France seemed to be failing.

For the historian interested in cross-border movement and exchange, France and the United States represent an interesting challenge. Both nations displayed a strong and vital sentiment of national uniqueness. In the United States, social commentators boasted of the advanced nature of American political institutions and social customs. No other nation, in this view, had taken such a bold step into the future. The contrast with countries such as France seemed clear: American government was more democratic; American women were more independent; American workers were more resourceful. "This nation," declared the historian John Lothrop Motley in 1869, "stands on the point toward which other people are moving."[32] The notion of exceptionalism is not an invention of modern scholars; throughout the nineteenth-century, many Americans were imbued with a belief in their nation's unique role as a harbinger of the modern age. France, too, had its own version of exceptionalism founded on its mission to spread the principles of 1789 throughout the world. France was thought the key battleground between the forces of reaction and revolution, a battle whose outcome would be decisive for all other nations. Nineteenth-century republicans were particularly convinced of France's unique position in the world. France, in their view, was not just a nation, but the incarnation of humanity's best hopes. As Jules Michelet wrote, "our history alone is complete. Take the history of France; with it you know the world." The history of France, he concluded, was "that of humanity as a whole."[33] This sense of their nation's importance underlay much of their opposition to Catholicism. If the church were to triumph in France, republicans argued, it would sweep over the civilized world. In the contest with Catholicism, Edgar Quinet warned, "if this country [France] gives herself up, the spirit of death would pounce upon the West."[34]

However, such sentiments of uniqueness and difference should not overshadow the evidence of an equally strong interest in the experience of the other. Contemporaries were just as ready to proclaim that they were living in an international age, an age of movement, interconnection, and exchange. In the field of hostility to Catholicism, the French and American belief in national uniqueness proved no obstacle to a dynamic interchange of ideas and books across borders. In fact, the presence of a common enemy appeared to smooth over these perceptions of national difference. In their battle with a mutual enemy, French and American opponents of the church found ample shared ground on which to construct a Transatlantic case.

The case against Catholicism is also an interesting example of the manner in which transnational discourses operated under the cover of nationalism. The perceived need to defend the homeland was at the heart of opposition to Catholicism. French and American opponents of the church imagined the agents of Catholicism ceaselessly at work undermining their national institutions and their social values. Indeed, it was the church's alleged indifference to the claims of the nation which made it such an appalling enemy. Yet for contemporaries, there was no contradiction in looking abroad for intellectual support so as to better defend the nation. Polemical works attacking Catholicism convey a strong sense that the fate of nations was intertwined. In part, this was due to the belief that the church, when rebuffed in one nation, would shift its focus to another. But there was a more fundamental reasoning here—namely, the conviction that in an age of connection and movement, only a coalition of allies could defeat an enemy such as Catholicism. As its opponents were only too aware, history provided ample proof of the church's capacity, when defeated in one nation, to regroup within the shelter of another, and resume its attack.

Opposition to Catholicism is not the only example of a transnational discourse serving national purposes. Anti-Semitism is another. We can see many parallels between anti-Semitism and aspects of anti-Catholic thought, particularly anti-Jesuitism. Like the anti-Jesuit, the anti-Semite imagined a vast conspiracy led by the most cunning and resourceful of opponents. In both cases, the enemy was cosmopolitan, a figure incapable of feeling true patriotism because bound to wider allegiances. Both, too, were held to wield subtle weapons, mounting their attack not through armies but through the subversive manipulation of prominent institutions and social values. Admittedly, the fear of the enemy's financial power dominated the anti-Semite's imagination to a far greater extent than the anti-Jesuit's. It is interesting to note, too, that hostility to Catholicism in the nineteenth century could engender greater sympathy for Jews. This was clear in the Mortara Affair, the subject of chapter 2 of this study, where the Vatican's removal of a Jewish boy from his family sparked an international protest movement in which opposition to the church blended easily with solidarity for the persecuted Jewish minority. Yet both shared this fundamental similarity: in the face of an enemy considered international in nature, a transnational discourse with strong nationalist overtones emerged.

* * *

This study is focused on the period 1840–1870. Though occurring before and beyond this period, the flow of ideas and literature through this Transatlantic channel was particularly vibrant in the middle decades of the century. International opposition to the church was electrified by a series of mobilizing events. The papacy of Pius IX (1846–1878) witnessed a slew of initiatives which not only dismayed many liberal Catholics, but also exacerbated hostility to the church. Some of the most significant were the Dogma of the Immaculate

Conception (1854), which proclaimed Mary free from the stain of original sin, the Syllabus of Errors (1864), which condemned many of the basic tenets of nineteenth-century society, and the First Vatican Council (1869–1870). This was also the era in which the doctrine of Ultramontanism came to dominate the church in both France and the United States. Ultramontanism denotes a number of shifts in worship and doctrine, amongst which a more sentimental piety centered on Vatican-approved miracles and devotions such as the Sacred Heart, a suspicion toward national variations within Catholicism, and above all a stress on the primacy of the papacy in matters of teaching and church administration. The rise of the Ultramontanes, which was confirmed in the adoption of papal infallibility in 1870, created some dissension within the church.[35] Outside the church, however, Ultramontanism fuelled a growing suspicion that the Vatican had come under the control of a faction which was fundamentally at odds with the central values of the age. At the same time, the belief amongst the church's opponents that Catholicism sought to replace reasoned faith with childish superstition was confirmed, in their eyes, by the crowds of pilgrims flocking to the sites of the Marian apparitions at La Salette (1846), Lourdes (1858), and Pontmain (1871).

In the same period, the ongoing question of the status of the Papal States maintained an international focus on Catholicism's alleged quest not merely for spiritual, but also for political domination. This issue was, of course, particularly pressing for France, whose troops had restored Pius IX in 1849, and whose garrison continued to maintain papal control over Rome from 1860, when the bulk of the Papal States were claimed by the Piedmontese government in the name of Italian unity, until the final withdrawal of 1870. But though less directly concerned, the American public and press showed a keen interest in the Italian question. The pope's refusal to cede control of his remaining territory to a nationalistic movement proclaiming the eminently modern principles of national unity, democracy, and capitalism was seen in America as manifest proof of the fundamental schism between the church and the age. In 1860, for example, a letter from Pius IX to Napoléon III, in which the pontiff characterized the principles espoused by the advocates of Italian unity as immoral, was widely published in the American press. As the *New York Times* reminded its readers, the pope's condemnation of the forces of Italian unification could just as easily be extended to another nation which was the product of a nationalistic revolution, the United States.[36]

It is remarkable, however, that so few accounts of American anti-Catholicism acknowledge the crucial role played by such Vatican initiatives in stoking suspicion and animosity toward the church. Father Hyacinthe's visit to the United States is an obvious example.

Apart from a brief account in a doctoral thesis written by a student at the American Catholic University in 1941, Hyacinthe's visit has been ignored by every scholar of American anti-Catholicism.[37] Even John McGreevy, whose analysis of the interplay between Catholic and American ideas of freedom is in many ways sensitive to the influence of international ideas and events, gives the first Vatican Council, perhaps the most significant and controversial religious event of the age, little more than a paragraph.[38] Scholars of French anticlericalism have not made the same mistake. The rise of the Ultramontane movement, for example, and the controversies surrounding its most provocative and prominent secular supporter, the journalist and editor of the *Univers*, Louis Veuillot, have long been recognized as decisive factors. Yet as much as historians of American anti-Catholicism, these scholars have failed to seize the opportunity to engage in a comparative study of the reactions to these papal initiatives in France and elsewhere. Were these reactions identical, or did they vary to any degree? If so, what factors might account for these variations?

A focus on the middle decades of the century also supports the increasing recognition of Second Empire France as a crucial formative period for republican politics. In the field of nineteenth-century anticlericalism, the decades prior to the advent of the Third Republic have received comparatively little scholarly attention. Since the Third Republic witnessed the legislative enactment of much of the anticlerical program, from the expulsion of the Jesuits in 1880 to the separation of church and state in 1905, a focus on the latter decades of the century is understandable. Nevertheless, as a growing number of studies have pointed out, the Second Empire was a key period in the evolution of both liberal and republican thought. The ideas underlying the Third Republic did not emerge from a vacuum, but had been developed and elaborated through the years of opposition and marginalization under Louis-Bonaparte. For Sudhir Hazareesingh, "the 1860s represented a defining moment in the conflict between Church and State, preparing the terrain for the battles which would lead to the 1905 separation."[39] This study thus constitutes part of this historiographical trend toward a greater appreciation of the political and intellectual developments in the decades immediately preceding the Third Republic.

* * *

In addition to transnationalism, a second major theme of this book is gender. The manner in which Americans conceived Father Hyacinthe's revolt in terms of manliness and marriage was emblematic of the broader case against the Catholic Church. In both France and the United States, Catholicism was portrayed as such a sinister, even malefic force because it was understood to threaten the prevailing ideals of femininity, masculinity, and family life. Of course, the case against Catholicism was not confined to these issues. In both nations, Catholicism was attacked on the grounds that it violated the scientific and rational principles which were seen as a hallmark of the nineteenth century. But the issues which inspired so much of the animosity toward the church were far more personal. Even a cursory reading of the literature dedicated to exposing the evils of Catholicism in both nations reveals a preoccupation with the status of wives and mothers, the security of masculine privilege and the sanctity of the home. Such literature is filled with images of priests or Jesuits craftily usurping the authority of fathers, of young girls being tricked into entering convents and then subjected to merciless sexual and physical abuse, of families torn apart by the agents of the church. For its opponents, the church's larger aim of fomenting social disorder and undermining national freedom began with an assault on individual happiness.

Even the great international controversies surrounding the Vatican were often construed in terms of femininity, masculinity, and domesticity. One of the grounds of opposition to the Dogma of the Immaculate Conception, for example, was the power it appeared to ascribe to a feminine figure. By elevating Mary to the status of a divinity, opponents of the Dogma argued, the church was throwing down a challenge to the conventional view of female authority as circumscribed and hidden. The Mortara Affair is another example. In that case, the removal of a Jewish boy from his family provoked a storm of outrage that centered on the church's apparent intolerance for the cherished values of domesticity and the sanctity of the home.

It is not surprising, then, that in their effort to conceptualize the nature of Father Hyacinthe's revolt against the Vatican, Americans turned to a language of masculinity and family. Nor is the preoccupation with Hyacinthe's views on celibacy surprising, for the celibate vows were thought responsible for producing the sexual crimes which so dominated the imagination of opponents of the church. Chapter 3 examines a neglected aspect of this debate over celibacy, the role played by medical writers for whom the priest and nun were ideal test-cases to determine the physiological effects of sexual abstinence. As I have noted, American scholars, though operating strictly within a national frame, have detected such gender concerns within the anti-Catholic movement. In France, however, there has been less recognition of the central role played by gender in driving the anticlerical campaign. Historians of French anticlericalism and the principle of *laïcité* have continued to depict the complaint against Catholicism as largely a matter of freeing the state from religious interference. In an isolated essay first published more than thirty years ago, the historian Theodore Zeldin pointed to the prominence of questions of gender and family within French anticlericalism. In particular, Zeldin analyzed the fear amongst French anticlericals that the Catholic confessor might attain a special influence over wives and mothers.[40] Remarkably few historians, however, have built on Zeldin's insight. Hostility toward the convent, a regular theme in the writing of republicans and liberals, remained almost entirely neglected until the recent publication of Caroline Ford's *Divided Houses*.[41] Ford's analysis, however, does not offer either a comparative or transnational approach.

This study, then, refers extensively to the set of gender ideals labeled "separate spheres." Opponents of the Catholic Church referred again and again to their belief that men and women were endowed with a set of opposite and complementary qualities. Women, in this view, were governed by the sentimental virtues of the heart; men possessed all the traits of reason and of the intellect. This bifurcated view of male and female nature underlay the ascription of the private sphere to women, and the public sphere to men. Such views were crucial to the case against Catholicism. A central argument put by campaigners against the church on both sides of the Atlantic was that Catholicism was a dangerous transgressor of this dividing line between the sexes. Chapter 4 examines one such transgressor of gender boundaries, the androgynous Jesuit, a figure uniting the characteristics of both men and women. Then, in chapter 5, we turn to one of the most feared of all Catholic institutions, the convent, a site of imagined misery and captivity where all of a woman's innate qualities were brutally and remorselessly stripped away. Whether in the shape of the androgynous Jesuit or the captive nun, Catholicism was accused of undermining the social order that was based, to a large degree, on the maintenance of gendered spheres.

The ideal of separate spheres thus provides a crucial tool for understanding the depth of anti-Catholic hostility in the nineteenth century. It must be acknowledged, however, that historians on both sides of the Atlantic have increasingly cast doubt on the usefulness of the separate spheres model as a guide to the lives of men and women in the past. Criticism has emerged from different quarters. For some scholars, the model tells us very little about the experiences of women who were neither white nor middle-class.[42] A second line of criticism suggests that even in relation to white, middle-class women, a public/private framework of analysis obscures rather than reveals large elements of female experience. By assuming women to be largely anchored in the domestic setting, historians have failed to appreciate, in this view, their prominent public presence. In recent years, there has been more attention to the public nature of female activism, as well as the manner in which the two spheres, public and private, were intertwined. As Michelle Perrot has argued, the private sphere was never entirely feminine, and the public sphere was never entirely masculine.[43]

Yet the campaign against Catholicism suggests that the separate spheres ideology has not outlived its usefulness as a tool for understanding nineteenth-century society. The ideal of equilibrium between gendered domains was both a means of understanding the threat from Catholicism, and a strategy for mobilizing popular opinion against the church. Both men and women in the nineteenth century rushed to defend the separate spheres model against its perceived enemy, the Catholic Church. The case against Catholicism in fact reveals the extent to which so many of the fundamental questions of nineteenth-century society were suffused with gender. At first glance, the question of the Catholic Church's power for good or evil appeared to have little connection with the role and identity of men and women. Yet these gender issues were at the heart of the campaign against Catholicism.

Finally, a word about sources. This is a study of representations. My interest is not to correct inaccuracies in the historical record, but to assess the manner in which historical events were understood and presented. On the question of nuns who were allegedly abused in convents, I have not attempted to determine if a nun was truly ill-treated or if her story was little more than an invention. Whether accurate or not, such stories were generally believed, and it was this willingness to accept such stories rather than their degree of truthfulness which gave them their power. In other words, I am tracing reactions and perceptions. To that end, my principal sources have been newspapers, pamphlets, novels, tracts and correspondence rather than archival material.

Father Hyacinthe's visit to the United States came at the end of three decades of intense Transatlantic traffic in ideas, books, and people. The process, as we shall see, was never entirely smooth. Affirmations of national uniqueness were heard on both sides of the Atlantic. Americans in particular reveled at times in the contrast between their own, as they saw it, progressive and democratic civilization and a backward, even immature France. Yet we should not allow such claims to mask the equally important channels of exchange and reciprocity, the sense of acting as privileged allies within a dense international network. A shared commitment to a fundamental set of gender ideals provided the conceptual framework through which opponents of the church in both the United States and France understood the nature of the Catholic enemy. But the two nations were also bound by an intense trade in ideas and information. Tracing this cross-border flow provides the point of departure for this study.

1
The Transatlantic Case against Catholicism

In 1837, the celebrated inventor and painter Samuel F.B. Morse edited and published a book entitled *Confessions of a French Catholic Priest*. Morse, the author of several anti-Catholic tracts, explained in his preface that he had agreed to publish the narrative of the anonymous priest because it provided a unique, first-hand account of the anguish and guilt endured by the Catholic clergy. The *Confessions* recounts the story of a young man who, though entering the priesthood for devout and pure reasons, soon finds himself wrestling with the restraint imposed by his celibate vows. His fellow priests, less sincere in their vocation, freely indulge in the opportunities for sexual license which, the author explains, are abundant in the confessional box. Unwilling to give in to temptation yet surrounded by corrupted peers, the priest comes close to insanity before salvation arrives in the form of Protestantism. A chance encounter with the writings of the Protestant reformers allows the priest to see the errors of the Catholic faith and to reconcile the demands of the flesh with the callings of the spirit. Having abandoned the priesthood, and fearing retribution at the hands of the Church, the ex-priest then flees his native France for the United States, hoping, as Morse recounted, to awaken Americans to the dangers posed by the Catholic clergy.

For Morse, the example of France proved how serious these dangers were. On both sides of the Atlantic, Morse argued, Catholicism had adopted the same sinister methods. There was, he wrote, "an identity of modes" as well as an "identity of object, namely, the DESTRUCTION OF LIBERTY."[1] To emphasize the degree to which allies of the Revolutionary era were once again engaged in battle with a common enemy, Morse placed a quotation from the great French friend of the American Republic, the Marquis de Lafayette, on the title page of the book. During a visit to Paris four years earlier, Morse claimed, Lafayette, ever concerned for the health of the Republic he had helped to establish, had given him the following warning: "American liberty can be destroyed only by the Popish clergy."

In the decades following the publication of the *Confessions*, French anticlerical works poured into the United States. One of the richest sources was French Protestants. The French-speaking Calvinist Jean-Henri Merle d'Aubigné's four-volume *History of the Reformation in the Sixteenth Century* was a huge bestseller across the English-speaking world, and quickly became the standard historical work on the topic. The connections between the d'Aubigné family and America were not only literary; Merle d'Aubigné's older brother Guillaume emigrated to the United States in 1816, established himself as a successful businessman, and remained there until his death in 1868.[2] D'Aubigné's book was an unsparing attack on papal domination. By the middle ages, the "holy and primitive equality of souls" which marked the early church had been swept away, usurped by a "spiritual king" and his caste of priests on one side, and beneath them "servile flocks reduced to a blind and passive submission." This was the tyrannical, ambitious church, d'Aubigné wrote, that now loomed over modern society.[3]

The *History* had an enormous appeal which cut across regional and social distinctions, attracting large numbers of readers among men and women, clergy and laypeople, northerners as well as southerners. One of the book's publishers, the *American Tract Society*, wrote that no work "is better adapted for general circulation, at the present time, in every part of our country, unfolding the wiles of popery."[4] It was in fact through the *Society*, and particularly its network of colporteurs, that d'Aubigné's work was able to reach such a broad audience. According to d'Aubigné, the Society had written in 1844 to inform him that, in addition to the 75,000 copies sold by other publishers, some 24,000 had been sold by its colporteurs. Through this system the Society could reach readers in isolated areas of the country, areas where, as d'Aubigné noted, the "pope ceases not to send active emissaries." Abridged versions of the *History*, as well as further works by d'Aubigné, soon appeared in America. In the preface to the *History of the Reformation in the Time of Calvin*, the fifth volume of his narrative, d'Aubigné in fact declared that the example of America had been present in his mind during its writing, for no other country better exemplified the two major themes of the work, political and evangelical liberty.[5]

In 1846, the publishers James Harper and Brothers contracted Reverend Robert Baird to provide a translation of d'Aubigné's speeches and sermons. Baird was an ideal candidate for the task. In 1835, he had traveled to Europe, and stayed there for nine years.

Much of the time was spent in France, where he met most of the leading Protestants, and became their main source of information about the progress of their faith in America. In 1837 he published an anonymous work on the separation of church and state in America; this was followed in 1844 by a two-volume, detailed examination of the beliefs, practices and expansion of the many religious faiths in his native country, *De la religion aux États-Unis d'Amérique*. Upon his return to America, he corresponded with d'Aubigné, and acted at times as the author's spokesman in America. It is not surprising, then, that he was engaged to translate d'Aubigné's speeches. Given the success of his previous works, Baird bet on the translation winning a large audience. According to the contract, he waived an upfront payment, receiving instead ten percent of the trade-list price of all copies sold.[6]

Fictional descriptions of the oppression suffered by the Huguenots at the hands of the French Catholic Church were popular in America. The Protestant theologian Félix Bungener wrote a series of works on church history and the religious controversies of the day. Like many French Protestants, Bungener was a keen student of American society, and in 1865 published a biography of Abraham Lincoln. Bungener's most popular work, though, was a series of fictionalized accounts of the persecution of Protestants and the spread of religious skepticism from the reign of Louis XIV to the end of the eighteenth century. In the second, which was published in America under the title *The Priest and the Huguenot*, Bungener wrote that Catholicism was the "easiest of all religions," making few demands on its adherents: "You receive your luggage at your birth; you are in nowise responsible for what it does or does not contain."[7] The translator of Bungener's work was Mary Engles Potts, the eldest daughter of George Potts, a Presbterian pastor. Fluent in French, German and Italian, Mary Potts was also gifted musically; Robert Schumann dedicated his *Bunte Blätter* (Opus 99) to her in 1851. She had met Bungener during her honeymoon in Europe, but her career as a translator was brief—she died in July 1858 at the age of thirty-one.[8] The book contained vivid descriptions of Protestant defiance and suffering—for example, the 1762 "martyrdoms" of Pastor Rochette as well as Jean Calas, the latter accused of murdering his son who intended, according to rumor, to become a Catholic—as well as the spread of infidelity in the form of the *Encyclopédistes*. The *New York Times* praised *The Priest and the Huguenot* as "a valuable contribution to our literature [which] will be permanently and widely read"; the *Methodist Review* predicted that both theological students and the general reader would flock to the book.[9]

Another French pastor, Napoléon Roussel, wrote many articles for the English and American religious press in which he denounced the practices of Catholicism in his own country. In 1855, Roussel published *Catholic Nations and Protestant Nations Compared*, a detailed survey which began with the proposition that religion, rather than race or climate, was the key factor in setting the course of a nation. In three key areas—wealth, knowledge and morality—encompassing data as diverse as agricultural productivity, the number of newspapers and journals, and illegitimate births, and ranging across both Europe and the Americas, Roussel's work concluded that societies grounded in Protestantism had far outstripped their Catholic counterparts. One reviewer described it as "an excellent book of reference" which made an "appalling" case against Catholicism yet without indulging in the "diatribes" and "furious declamations" so common in anti-Catholic works.[10]

The argument that Protestantism fostered national progress whereas Catholicism produced decline was challenged by a number of Catholic writers. One 1842 work, *Protestant and Catholicity Compared in their Effects on the Civilization of Europe*, by Father Jaime Balmes, was translated into several languages, and offered Catholics a strong counter-argument. In its attack on religious authority, the Reformation, Balmes wrote, was a precursor to Robespierre and the violence of the French Revolution. Far from spreading liberty and progress, the Reformation, Balmes concluded, had opened the way to political instability and the rise of absolutist regimes.[11] The Bishop of Louisville, and later Archbishop of Baltimore Martin John Spalding, also directly challenged the equation between Catholicism and national stagnation. The relative poverty of the laboring masses in England compared to their counterparts in France was proof, he wrote, that Protestantism was no guarantee of wealth, while the economic backwardness of Catholic Ireland was a result not of religion but of English and Protestant oppression.[12] Despite such claims, however, the linkage between progress and Protestantism was one of the recurring arguments in the case against Catholicism.

For many French Protestants, in turn, the United States figured as an exemplary society which, by fully realizing the emancipatory potential of the Protestant creed, had created a powerful mix of religious zeal and political and social liberty. The historian René Rémond has charted the upsurge of articles about America in *Le Protestant* from the 1830s, a trend he attributes in part to the influence of Robert Baird, a crucial mediator of information.[13] But rather than simply relying on second-hand information, many French Protestants went to see America for themselves. César Pascal was one of many French pastors to visit the United States; like Félix Bungener, he wrote an account of Abraham Lincoln's life in the aftermath of the President's assassination. For Pascal, the pervasive spirit of independence, initiative and love of liberty which he witnessed in America were built squarely on a Protestant foundation. Furthermore, Pascal was convinced that Catholicism could never thrive in such an atmosphere of liberty. During his visit in 1870, Pascal heard a very strange rumor that Pope Pius IX might flee to America following the take-over of Rome by Piedmontese troops. Few Americans appeared to take the rumor seriously. Even if true, however, Pascal confidently predicted that a basic incompatibility between the papacy and the great Protestant Republic made any such scheme impossible. In particular, he wrote, "the lively air of liberty, of inquiry and of the Gospel" which characterized American society could only be fatal to the papacy.[14]

In the eyes of many French Protestants, then, no society better demonstrated the social, political, and moral benefits conferred by an attachment to the Protestant rather than the Catholic faith. The relative merits of Protestantism and Catholicism were made clear in the account of another noted Protestant visitor to the United States, Jean Henri Grandpierre. For Grandpierre, who toured the United States in the early 1850s, a simple comparison between Catholic Canada and Protestant New England settled the question of Protestantism's superiority. In the latter, Grandpierre observed all the hallmarks of an advanced civilization: factories, railways, and steamships. Having crossed into the Catholic province of Quebec, Grandpierre found himself, in his own words, "in a different world." A people he described as "ignorant and wretched" and "without energy or industry" lived in an untamed and uncultivated wilderness, their houses more akin, he lamented, to the huts of African tribes than those of European settlers.[15]

It is perhaps not surprising that Protestants on both sides of the Atlantic would agree on the superiority of their faith over Catholicism. But the Transatlantic case against the Church extended far beyond this Protestant channel. On the question of Catholicism, French anticlericals with little connection to Protestantism, and even with a reputation for irreligion, were just as acceptable to American readers. By far the most influential French author, and almost the only one whose popularity has been acknowledged by scholars of anti-Catholicism in the United States, was the republican historian Jules Michelet.[16] Virtually all of Michelet's works were translated and published in America. Reviewers praised his major historical narratives, especially his monumental *History of France*, as the most complete and authoritative yet written. Michelet himself was made aware of the success of the work by a correspondent from New York, Charles Jules Hempel, who informed him in April 1845 that everyone there was reading it.[17] Ralph Waldo Emerson was just one famous American who read Michelet's *History*. A charming testimony comes from Emerson's eldest daughter, Ellen Tucker Emerson. Her father, she would later recollect, "brought home Michelet's books and others from the Athenaeum, and would let me sit by him and look over while he read them to me—scraps of French history, they were, which made me love it."[18] In fact, Emerson's journals show that he returned again and again to Michelet's *History*; he borrowed Volume 14, for example, from April 4 to May 22 1866, and volume 2 later that year.[19] Nor was admiration for Michelet restricted to the North. Southerners such as the poet, novelist, and historian William Gilmore Simms praised Michelet's skill as a historian, and Edwin D. Leon described him as "brilliant," while several Southern women recorded their admiration of his work in their journals.[20]

Emerson would perhaps have hesitated, however, to read all of Michelet's works to his young daughter. Two books in particular in which he set out his theory of the nature and role of women, *L'Amour* (published as *Love* in 1859) and *La Femme* (published as *Woman* in 1860), provoked a great deal of criticism in America. Many reviewers objected to Michelet's insistence that women were at the mercy of their bodies, constantly rendered frail and ill by the menstrual cycle. Michelet was widely accused of exaggerating the physical weakness of women as well as their dependence on their husbands; as one reviewer dryly observed, "The wonder inevitably is, what kind of women M. Michelet has been in the habit of seeing."[21] Yet though characterizing woman as close to an invalid, Michelet at the same time exalted her spiritual power, her gifts of intuition and sentiment which elevated her above men. Woman, in Michelet's bifurcated view, was "higher, and yet lower, than man."[22]

Though never winning unanimous praise, Michelet's descriptions of women were popular with leading members of the American literary elite as well as with the public. Harriet Beecher Stowe quoted Michelet in works such as *The Chimney Corner* (1868) and *Oldtown Folks* (1869). The poet Henry Wadsworth Longfellow read *L'Amour* in French, describing it as "poetic and physiological—a wonderful book in its way. I am glad he has had the courage to say such things." Longfellow concluded that "The cause of Woman has never been so ably pleaded before."[23] The preacher and abolitionist Theodore Parker was less enthusiastic, noting in his journal that the book "contains much nonsense of a romantic character, and gives a quite incomplete notion of woman." Still, he went on, "the book also has great excellences."[24] Public interest was just as high. Less than thirty days after its release, *Woman* had sold almost twenty thousand copies.[25]

How exactly were these works of Michelet translated and published in the United States? The publisher of both *Love* and *Woman* was George W. Carleton, an illustrator and author of several travel accounts. A short account of the publication of Michelet's books is contained in a preface to *Love* written by its translator, Dr. John W. Palmer. According to Palmer, the "intense interest" created by the publication of *L'Amour* in France and in England "seemed to have created a call for its immediate production in this country."[26] For Palmer, the key word here was no doubt "immediate." To understand why, it is necessary to appreciate the legal and economic factors governing the American publishing world of the nineteenth century. Under the 1790 Copyright Act, only works written by citizens or residents of the United States were protected under copyright, a situation which would continue, with only minor amendments, until 1891. In fact, an 1831 amendment to that Act specifically exempted foreign authors from protection. For some time publishers had observed what was known as a "courtesy copyright," which gave sole rights to the first reprinter of a foreign work. However, the profusion of small publishing houses, and the intense competition thus generated, soon led to the abandonment of courtesy copyrights, and pirated works from abroad flowed into the United States.

In this situation, the only advantage a publisher could gain was to be the first in the marketplace. Publishers went to extraordinary lengths to obtain advance copies of books before their competition. Agents were employed in England to send the earliest sheets of new novels across the Atlantic by the fastest ships available. On arrival in America, the work would be rushed directly to the printer, which would run its presses until the copy had hit the market. The emphasis on speed and capturing the market for a brief period is expressed in a letter by the leading Philadelphia publishers Carey and Lea in 1823:

> We have rec'd *Quentin Durward* most handsomely and have the Game completely in our hands this time. In 28 hours after receiving it, we had 1,500 copies sent off and ready to go...In two days we shall publish it here and in New York and the Pirates may print it as soon as they please. The opposition Edition will be out in 48 hours after they have one of our copies but we shall have complete and entire possession of every market in the Country for a short time.[27]

The absence of copyright protection doubtless facilitated the interchange of books between nations in the nineteenth century, and helps to explain the profusion of French anticlerical works in the United States. It is worth noting, however, that rather than simply pirating an existing British translation, American publishing firms generally went to the trouble and expense of producing their own translations of French anticlerical works. The history of the publication of Michelet's *La Femme*, which is contained in the recollections of the leading publisher J.C. Derby, is a case in point. According to Derby, the success of *Love* led Carleton to publish an English-language version of *Woman*. Palmer was paid 1,000 dollars for the translation, but the emphasis was very much on speed. Palmer was given only seventy-two hours to translate the book, and furthermore was to be penalized ten dollars for every hour past that time limit. According to Derby, however, Palmer managed the feat of delivering the more than 450 pages of manuscript ready for the compositors and printers within the time allotted.[28]

Palmer, of course, did not require Michelet's approval for these translations, though it perhaps helped sales if an English-version of the work could be advertised as "official." Merle d'Aubigné, for example, urged his American readers to purchase only the edition of his works published by Carter and Brothers, the edition "from which alone he derives some advantage."[29] Establishing a relationship with the author was nonetheless important, for it enabled the publisher to receive advance copies of the manuscript. It seems to have been this consideration in particular which led Dr. Palmer to write to Michelet. On February 17, 1860, Palmer advised Michelet that he had sent his translation of *L'Amour* to his French publishers, Hachette, the previous November, and that he hoped it had met Michelet's satisfaction. Palmer also informed Michelet that *Woman* had just appeared on the American market, and expressed the desire that "should it be your intention to produce another work, in continuation of the subject," Michelet would "see fit to instruct your publishers to furnish me with early sheets, before publication and before binding." Palmer further promised to ensure that a payment would be sent to Michelet's publishers.[30]

Michelet responded to Palmer's letter on March 17, 1860. He congratulated Palmer on the quality of his translation, and thanked him for publicizing his work in both America and England. "I know," Michelet concluded, "how much these great nations are sensitive to the religions of the home and of the family."[31] Further letters passed between the two men. On April 26, Michelet recounted his personal ties to America. Michelet's father-in-law had lived for a long time in Louisiana, and was, according to Michelet, a naturalized American.[32] An account of his American experience appeared in the opening section of *L'Oiseau*, a work which Palmer had also translated (*The Bird*). In September, Palmer wrote back to Michelet, describing the difficulty of translating Michelet's "poetic and subtile [sic]" prose, and thanking him for his praise.³³ Just days later, Palmer wrote again, this time after having read in the press that a sequel to *Love* and *Woman*, entitled *L'Enfant*, was almost ready for publication. Michelet had not mentioned this in his correspondence, and now Palmer wrote with some alarm, begging Michelet "to send me a *very early* copy in sheets, before publication—*the first* that can be got from the printers." Palmer concluded by declaring "I will spare no pains to do you credit, and increase your popularity in this Country."³⁴ There is no record, however, of Michelet responding to this plea.

Judging by his correspondence, Michelet seemed acutely interested in the publication of his works in the United States. In 1856, he sought advice on the best means of publicizing his books in both England and America from Théodore Karcher, a French socialist living in exile in London. Karcher offered to write reviews of Michelet's work for English newspapers and journals, including the *Times*, the *Westminister Review*, and *Blackwood's Magazine*. Such prestigious publications, Karcher continued, were also widely read in the United States. To ensure a greater audience there, Karcher recommended the *New York Tribune*, the *Washington Era*, and Putnam's *New Monthly Magazine*, as well as several German-language publications in New York.³⁵ Some months later, in May 1857, Karcher, who was also the European correspondent for the *New York Tribune*, wrote to inform Michelet that his review of *La Ligue et Henri IV* had recently appeared in that newspaper, as well as another in the *Pionier*, a German-language journal. Such publicity, according to Karcher, would inevitably lead bookshops and publishers to produce translations of Michelet's works.³⁶ Karcher declared himself willing to accept "all literary, artistic and political reviews which he [Michelet] would like to see reach America."³⁷

It was through his more explicitly anticlerical works, however, that Michelet exerted a decisive influence over American opponents of Catholicism. Particularly influential was his alarming portrayal of the power wielded by the Catholic confessor in *Du prêtre, de la femme et de la famille*, which was published by J.M. Campbell of Philadelphia in 1845 under the title *Spiritual Direction and Auricular Confession*. For Michelet, the confessor's influence over wives and daughters was a fatal threat to the authority of the male head of household. In a famous scene, Michelet evoked this rivalry between patriarch and confessor during a family dinner. The husband sits down to dine with his mother, wife, and daughter, and talks to them proudly of modern advances in education, science, and technology. His mother, however, shakes her head, his wife contradicts him, and his daughter silently disapproves. The husband soon realizes that his family's inability to share his enthusiasm for the modern age is due to the invisible presence at the table, the Catholic confessor, who has molded all these women in his own regressive and outmoded ideals, and made them servants of a backward church. The husband's progressive spirit will find no echo in the women of his family, and his authority over them has been lost.[38]

Unlike later works by Michelet, there is no translator listed in J.M. Campbell's 1845 edition of *Spiritual Direction and Auricular Confession*. For this reason, it is reasonable to surmise that, as with other pirated books, the American publisher simply copied the British translation which had appeared the same year. This British version, translated by Charles C. Cocks for the publisher Longmans, also appears in the holdings of many American libraries. Cocks had an intriguing and varied career. A long-time resident of Bordeaux, he would later write what would become the most influential guide to the wines of the region, a work which remains a reference for wine-lovers today.[39] On March 13, 1845, he wrote to Michelet informing him of his intention to translate *Du prêtre*, and asking him to add some explanatory notes as a means of increasing its success in the market. Whether it found an American translator or not, the book was popular in the United States, where it won acclaim from a range of American reviewers. The *Princeton Review* praised *Spiritual Direction and Auricular Confession* for portraying "in lively colors the degradation and misery consequent on the dominion of the priesthood."[40] The *Methodist Quarterly Review* declared that the book contained "the profound historical and logical analysis, and earnest, thrilling appeal of a man who... has deeply pondered and keenly felt a horrible evil."[41] The secular press gave Michelet's denunciation of the confessional box as much attention as Protestant journals. A long and favorable review of the work which had initially appeared in the British *Foreign Quarterly Review* was reprinted in two American publications.[42]

A range of American writers drew on Michelet's denunciation of the power of the confessor. One of the most popular writers on domesticity in this period, John Angell James, quoted at length from Michelet to demonstrate the dangers which the Catholic priest posed to the American home.[43] More avowedly anti-Catholic writers made great use of Michelet's polemic. In his bestselling *Auricular Confession and Popish Nunneries*, the renegade ex-priest William Hogan directly quoted large segments of Michelet's writings on the confessional and the influence of the priest. Works of popular fiction with a clear anti-Catholic purpose such as *The Arch Bishop, or Romanism in the United States* (1855) by Orvilla S. Belisle and *Secrets of the Convent and the Confessional* (1872) by Julia McNair Wright also borrowed from Michelet.[44] In the battle against Catholicism, even respectable and high-minded reformers relied on Michelet's work. Catharine Beecher, the educational reformer and leading proponent of female domesticity, was just one prominent American who recognized her debt to Michelet. Beecher attacked the textbooks used in Catholic schools which, she alleged, deliberately distorted historical facts and ignored scientific theories. The purpose of such practices was, Beecher alleged, to prevent Catholic students obtaining the knowledge and critical faculties which might allow them to question the dominance exerted by their priests. Beecher's authority on this matter was not a fellow Protestant, but Jules Michelet; as she wrote, "the recent writings of Michelet set forth this practice as indisputable."[45]

How did the Church itself react to the appearance of such books? Although a comprehensive account of the Church's response falls outside the parameters of this study, it is worth noting that the Church was not an inert, passive victim of such attacks. Defenders of the Catholic Church in America mounted a fierce campaign against Michelet's book. In the words of the then Bishop of Louisville, Martin John Spalding, "if Satan himself could appear upon earth, clad in bodily form, armed with the appliances of pen, ink, and paper, he could not have written a worse book."[46] The most influential Catholic intellectual in the United States, the journalist and editor Orestes A. Brownson, was just as scathing. Michelet's book, Brownson wrote, was "a compound of ignorance, infidel malice, prurient fancy, and maudlin sentiment."[47] Such condemnation was typical of the Church's energy in defending itself. Unfortunately, however, these attacks appeared to do little to diminish the reputation of the book in the minds of most Americans. In 1867, more than twenty years after its first appearance, the New York Times noted that Michelet's book on the confessional "plays an important part today."[48] Ten years later, a retrospective study of Michelet's works continued to praise *Spiritual Direction and Auricular Confession*. The book was, the author noted, "a marvelous study on the clerical domination, remarkable for the sagacity and keenness of its moral analysis."[49]

Another book co-written with Michelet's fellow republican and lecturer, Edgar Quinet, was almost as influential. Entitled simply *Des Jésuites*, the book comprised a series of lectures delivered by the two historians at the *Collège de France* in 1844. The lectures themselves had created a sensation in France. Students crowded into the halls to hear Michelet and Quinet, working in tandem, deliver a detailed and savage indictment of the principles and ambitions of the Society of Jesus. The Jesuits, Michelet and Quinet argued, embodied no other principles than permissiveness, hypocrisy and a thirst for power, and posed a deadly threat to society and government. In October 1844, even before it had been translated into English, the book-length edition of the lectures was being commended to American readers.

In a long analysis of their work, the *North American Review* praised Michelet and Quinet for exposing the sinister workings of the Jesuits. The Jesuits, the *Review* warned, were "spreading, and silently acquiring strength in the United States"; this expansion threatened, in the *Review's* words, to spread religious hostility and violence across the country. In fact, the *Review* envisaged nothing less than a Jesuit-inspired descent into medieval intolerance and persecution. "Many, whose eyes are open to the fact," the *Review* concluded, "see in our future history *auto-da-fes* and inquisitions."[50] Of course, some readers may have found such warnings exaggerated. But for proof of the seriousness of the threat, the *Review* looked to France where, it reported to its readers, the very word Jesuit had become a "word of terror." For those Americans keen to prevent their nation also falling under the Jesuit yoke, the *Review* suggested, Michelet and Quinet's work provided a vital guide to the nature of their enemy.

Once translated into English under the title *The Jesuits*, large numbers of American readers were able to obtain Michelet and Quinet's attack on the feared Society. As was so often the case, the translation came about because of individual initiative. In the case of *The Jesuits*, the translator was a man who enjoyed a long and eccentric literary career, Charles Edwards Lester. At various times a lawyer, Presbyterian minister, abolitionist, newspaper correspondent, as well as American consul at Genoa, Lester was a figure of some controversy in the literary world. Having attended the 1840 antislavery conference in London, Lester then infuriated many American abolitionists when, in a book entitled *The Glory and Shame of England*, he argued that Southern slaves enjoyed better living conditions than the majority of English factory workers, or as he termed them, operatives. "I would sooner see the children of my love born to southern slavery," Lester wrote, "than to see them subjected to the blighting bondage of the poor English operative's life."[51] Such comparisons were regarded as treasonous by Lester's fellow abolitionists. A review which appeared in William Lloyd Garrison's *Liberator* described the book as "trash," a work deserving "condemnation and contempt."[52] But abolitionists were not the only group to accuse Lester of placing financial gain ahead of literary integrity. The *New York Times*, for example, described one of Lester's publications, a journal entitled *The Herald of the Union*, as little more than a paid advertisement in the guise of a literary journal; the publication was, the *Times* declared, "devoted to the most elaborate exposition of the private business of every man willing to pay roundly for the same."[53]

Lester's interest in Michelet and Quinet's book, however, perhaps sprang from a more sincere aversion to the Jesuits. He appears to have maintained some contacts with the nativist American Party—several newspaper articles list him as a member of the Party's 1856 Convention. Furthermore, under the pseudonym of Helen Dhu, he would publish a popular and melodramatic tale of Jesuit intrigue, *Stanhope Burleigh: The Jesuits in our Homes*. It is perhaps not surprising, then, that he would take upon himself the task of translating *Des Jésuites*, as well as another book by Quinet, *The Roman Church and Modern Society* (1846). As he explained in a letter to the two men, dated November 1, 1846, he wished "my countrymen to see & feel how the Reformers of France & Europe were working." We Americans, Lester declared, "are not Englishmen—but their conquerors...we love Frenchmen better than Britons."[54] On February 26, 1847, Michelet responded to Lester's letter. Apologizing for the delay in replying, a delay caused, as he explained, by the death of his father, his own illness, and the need to finish another work, Michelet praised Lester's translation as "excellent."[55]

Widely reviewed in both the secular and religious press, *The Jesuits* had, according to the 1851 *Encyclopaedia Americana*, reached a "vast circulation."[56] The *United States Democratic Review* described Quinet and Michelet as heroes "contending in the sacred cause of human liberty."[57] Many reviewers saw the book as a practical guide to an organization which was increasingly menacing American society. One Methodist journal found the book a valuable reminder of the evils of Jesuitism for those politicians oblivious to its spread within America.[58] The Jesuits, as the *Biblical Repository and Classical Review* warned its readers, "are in the midst of us, and too often we know it not...What they [Michelet and Quinet] have written is exceedingly valuable at the present time."[59] The *Albany Spectator* similarly warned of thousands of Jesuits "exerting their deadly influences here" and urged that "this work, which has been their terror in the old world...let *it* meet them here." For the Cincinnati *Evening Journal*, the very familiarity of Michelet and Quinet with Catholicism made the book of such value as an exposé of Jesuit intrigue. If Catholicism "be the corrupt and rotten edifice described by these men who have grown up in her bosom, and who live in the midst of her influences, the blows of assailants so able and bold will shake her walls." The book's lessons, in short, were not considered to be limited to France and French affairs. Michelet and Quinet's work, as the *New York Evangelist* declared, "is as well adapted to the designs of the Jesuits here as there."[60]

Such reviews highlight the key selling point of French anticlerical works: their credibility. In the United States, the thirst for credible testimony of the Church's iniquity from those most familiar with its spirit and workings led opponents of Catholicism to turn to a range of French sources, including literary works. The most popular fictional attack on the Jesuits was undoubtedly Eugène Sue's bestseller *Le juif errant*, which told the story of a plot by the Society to destroy the Protestant Rennepont family and steal its immense fortune. Under the title *The Wandering Jew*, Sue's novel was serialized in the *New World: A Weekly Family Journal of Popular Literature, Science, Art and News* in 1844. This was a "mammoth" newspaper, so called because it printed enormous amounts of text in very small print on poor-quality paper. Costing just a few cents, such papers were very popular, especially with subscribers, and often contained complete novels in just one edition. Sue had already won fame both in France and abroad for his bestselling *Les Mystères de Paris*. The archives of its American publisher, James Harper and Brothers, records that Charles H. Town was paid 500 dollars for its translation in December 1844.[61] But it was the *Wandering Jew*, a work which, according to the *New York Herald*, more than any other work of imagination had "so widely embraced social life in all its different aspects," that would become a publishing phenomenon.[62]

Replete with scenes of murder, violence and seduction, and filled with a varied and exotic cast of characters, including a Javanese prince, a Siberian animal-tamer and a Napoleonic general, Sue's novel became a huge success. The American public eagerly awaited each installment of the book; as even one of its critics was forced to lament once the final chapter had appeared, "This slowly continued serial has reached its close at last, after having kept nine-tenths of the community, during long months, on the utmost stretch of curious expectation."[63] The end of serialization, however, hardly abated the public appetite for Sue's story; once published in book form, sales were enormous. The fervor surrounding Sue's novel was witnessed by an English traveler, Sir Charles Lyell. In a conversation with one of the novel's publishers, the nativist James Harper, Lyell learned that 80,000 copies had been sold in the first few months of publication. Sue's book seemed, in Lyell's judgment, to be inescapable: "It had so often been thrust into my hands in railway cars, and so much talked of, that, in the course of my journey, I began to read it in self-defence."[64]

The American translator of Sue's work was another colorful figure, Henry William Herbert. An Englishman by birth, Herbert contributed to literary journals and magazines, wrote works of fiction aimed squarely at the mass market, and when short of money, took on tasks such as translating foreign works and even finishing the novels of other writers. He enjoyed greater success under the guise of Frank Forester, a popular writer on sporting topics. Following the failure of his second marriage, Herbert committed suicide in 1858; his final note was then widely published in the American press. Herbert translated Sue's novel for Jonas Winchester's *New World Press*. His letters from the period give little detail as to the circumstances of the translation, beyond noting the financial strain to Herbert caused by the bankruptcy of the publisher in July 1844. In a letter to John Louis O'Sullivan, co-founder of the *Democratic Review* and reputed inventor of the phrase "Manifest Destiny," Herbert complains that the *Wandering Jew* "has kept me enslaved the last year and more," but that it was "drawing to a conclusion."[65]

The Wandering Jew contained many controversial elements. Part of the message of the book was that the principle of association rather than competition should form the basis for industrial society, a proposition that sparked both acclaim and hostility. The novel attracted further criticism for its suggestion that marriage oppressed and degraded women; one scene in particular, in which the heroine, Adrienne de Cardoville, openly repudiates the indissolubility of marriage, outraged some American critics. In fact, one of the book's greatest critics was its own translator, Henry William Herbert. Having worked for such a long time on the book, Herbert discovered, in his own words, that the book was "utterly subversive of social morality, destitute of religion, and adverse to Christianity."[66] But the core of the novel's fame and success was its attack on the Jesuits, and its greatest fictional legacy was the most sinister Jesuit of all, Rodin. The mastermind of the plot to destroy the Rennepont family, Rodin is the key character in the novel, a figure whose deviousness, ambition and energy appear almost limitless. Rodin was without doubt the nineteenth-century's most notorious and captivating fictional representation of the Jesuit. "We feel," wrote one reviewer in a testament to the popular enthrallment with Rodin, "that he is a creeping and venomous reptile, yet like the rattlesnake, gifted with a power to fascinate and destroy."[67] For a generation of American readers, the murderous Rodin became not only the ultimate figure of Jesuit intrigue, but also a yardstick against which all forms of cunning and hypocrisy could be measured. Commenting on an unrelated case of fraud, the *Boston Daily Atlas* in 1846 marveled at a plot which was "as deep laid a scheme of villainy as the jesuitical Rodin of Eugene Sue could ever have conceived." Sue's novel had become, in short, not only an American publishing phenomenon, but an exposé of a Society widely understood to be one of the deadliest enemies of the Republic, a work which, in the words of one reviewer "should be in the hands of every American citizen."[68]

The influence of French authors was even more apparent on one of the most sensitive questions of church-state relations, education. The issue of public schools was at the heart of Catholic-Protestant animosity in America in the middle decades of the century, and the flashpoint was the drive, led by Archbishop John Hughes of New York, for the Church to obtain public funding for its parochial schools. Several factors underlay this ambition: a desire to preserve religious and social solidarity, as well as an effort by the church to adapt to the broader cultural emphasis on education in America. One of the primary reasons, though, was the Protestant bias of the public school system. Catholics objected strongly to the use of the King James Bible in classrooms, as well as to the anti-Catholic bias of school textbooks, a charge which the scholar Ruth Miller Elson has found to be justified.[69] Critics of the Church responded that these objections, and the campaign to establish separate, state-funded schools, masked a deeper Catholic ambition to fragment and destroy the public school system. Although in parts of the Midwest and West Catholic schools were welcomed as they were often the first, and sometimes only schools for children, in the eastern states the prospect of taxpayer-funded Catholic schools was attacked as divisive and sectarian. What the Church feared, for its critics, was not Protestant bias, but the schooling of Catholic children in the enlightened principles of republican government.

For proof of these claims, and as a cautionary warning about the perils of Catholic-run education, some Americans turned to the work of the leading French republican Charles Sauvestre. In 1867, Sauvestre had published an inquiry into the strength of the religious orders in France, including their dominant position in the education system, entitled *Les congrégations religieuses dévoilées*. Writing in *Putnam's Magazine*, Henry C. Lea, the author of a magisterial history of sacerdotal celibacy, summarized Sauvestre's conclusions for an American readership. "In their schools," Lea reported, "more than half of the children of France are educated; by their confessors a large proportion of the faithful are ruled." The lesson of Sauvestre's work, Lea wrote, was that the monastic system was far more difficult to eradicate than was commonly believed: "As long as it continues to respond to a want in the human soul, it will flourish, and the world will yet have to undergo a long course of education before that want will cease to be felt."[70] More direct testimony of the social degradation induced by Roman-Catholicism and the growth of convents came to Americans from the pen of the scientist and popular republican, Francois-Vincent Raspail. In a letter that was reprinted in, among others, the New York *Herald* and *Harper's Weekly*, Raspail deplored the hypocrisy concerning religion in his native France. The French nobility maintained the exterior signs of religious observance, he alleged, while freely indulging in the most sinful behavior. Attendance at Mass, he continued, was regarded in the same light as attending theatre, a chance to show off one's dress and to charm one's social equals. Raspail saved his most venomous words for convents which, he wrote, "are real houses of infamy and degradation." Within them, a "vast army of over 100,000 persons" lived, "all the time engaged in disseminating infamy and in corrupting women."[71]

Within this flow of works from France to the United States, even controversial works emanating from within the Church itself were prominent. In 1863, a novel entitled *Le maudit* by the *Abbé* *** created a sensation in France. The novel recounted the career of Julio de la Clavière, the *curé* of St Aventin. It begins with an attack on the Jesuits—Julio's aunt, a wealthy woman, has been manipulated by her Jesuit confessor into bequeathing her fortune to the Society rather than her nephew and her niece, Louise. The hero, Julio, whose frankness of character and honesty has already put him at odds with the town's Jesuit priests, inspires even further enmity when he publishes the confessions of the town's Archbishop, which contain an account of the Society's treacherous dealings. Banished to a remote mountainous town, Julio's duel with the Jesuits continues—in revenge for Julio legally disputing the validity of his aunt's will, the Society tricks Julio's sister into joining a convent, and much of the novel is taken up with the story of her eventual rescue. Finally Julio becomes the editor of a liberal Catholic paper, publicly opposes the temporal power of the papacy and dies under the ban of the Synod.

Again, the Church itself responded forcefully to the appearance of the book. As speculation about the identity of its author raged, *Le maudit* was denounced in the French Senate by Cardinal Donnet, and placed on the Vatican's index of forbidden literature. The *Revue du monde catholique* was forthright in its condemnation. The author was not, alleged the *Revue*, a priest at all, but a free-thinker intent on scandalizing Catholic opinion and creating as much publicity as possible. As for its readers, any person who enjoyed such a book, the *Revue* concluded, would go directly to hell.[72] Amidst the controversy, sales soared. Within a year of its publication, *Le maudit* had sold around 20,000 copies. A correspondent for the anticlerical paper, *Le Temps*, testified to the book's success: "I wanted to obtain it during these last days, and it was in vain that I requested it at four bookshops, which had already exhausted their stock and re-ordered new copies."[73] A sequel, *La religieuse* (1864), created almost as much controversy with its frank portrayal of the abuses hidden behind the walls of the convent, including a scene in which a nun is whipped and then imprisoned in an underground cell.

The author of both works was a priest named Jean-Hippolyte Michon, but despite many attempts on the part of both admirers and detractors of the novels to unearth his identity, it remained a secret.[74] Both works by Michon soon appeared in the United States, where they received thoughtful and extended reviews. *Le maudit*, which was translated and published in the United States as *Under the Ban* in 1864 and again in 1865, was described by a reviewer in *Harper's New Monthly Magazine* as "a vehement protest against and fierce attack upon the ecclesiastical system of France." The *New York Times* commended the book's "unsparing exposure of clerical abuses." Like Michelet and Quinet's attack on the Jesuits, *Under the Ban* was deemed a salutary lesson in the evils of Catholicism for a complacent American public. "For the American reader," a reviewer in *Harper's Weekly* declared, "it has an extraordinary interest, and for every reader a profound warning." The religious press in America celebrated this fictional attack on celibacy and the Jesuits, with one critic declaring that "a more thorough onslaught upon Ultramontanism, monarchism, and sacerdotal sin it has never been our good fortune to read."[75] The anonymous priest behind these works, another reviewer declared, was a better writer than leading Protestant minister, Henry Ward Beecher.[76]

At times, the route between France and America passed through other nations, particularly the United Kingdom. As we have seen in the case of Michelet's *Du prêtre, de la femme et de la famille*, translations of some important French works were imported directly from London. Another example was a two-volume work by the noted philanthropist and industrialist Charles-Philibert de Lasteyrie, the *History of Auricular Confession*. Lasteyrie savaged the confessional as sanctioned neither by Scripture nor by the practice of the early Church, a medieval imposition which had fostered moral and social corruption. The confession, he argued, offered sinners an easy forgiveness, and priests a temptation to sexual vice which few, Lasteyrie concluded, were prepared to resist. This book was not published in the United States, yet it appears in a range of library catalogues, and seems to have gained a significant American readership. Popular anti-Catholic writers cited Lasteyrie's book and surveys of key theological texts described it as authoritative. One such survey by Howard Malcolm, a president of the *American Tract Society*, included Lasteyrie's book in the section listing works devoted to exposing the evils of confession, followed by the comment "A tremendous blow."[77]

The web of books and ideas linking opponents of the Church in France and the United States was also often formed from works originating in third countries. On the question of convents, a memoir by an Italian ex-nun, Enrichetta Caracciolo, reached an international audience that included France and the United States. Daughter of a marshal in the Neapolitan army, Caracciolo had been, by her own account, forced into the convent of St Gregorio at the age of eighteen by her mother. In her nine years there, she found the "morals of the age of the Borgias...and the brutalized ignorance and superstitions of the populace at the epoch of the auto-da-fé."[78] Her account of idle, superstitious and ignorant nuns fighting each other for the attention of confessors, and others driven to insanity by their radical seclusion from the world, was translated and published in France as *Les mystères des couvents de Naples* in 1864, and went through three editions within a year. In its entry on convents, the Larousse *Grand dictionnaire* made the book the centerpiece of its analysis of the evils fostered by the growth of the convent system in the modern age.[79] Caracciolo's book was translated by the publisher Justus Starr Redfield, who had taken up the post of United States consul at Otranto, Italy, in 1861, and was published in three editions, attracting a series of positive reviews. The San Francisco *Daily Evening Bulletin* characterized her revelations as "startling."[80] The *New York Observer and Chronicle* declared that the book "ought to open the eyes of the world to the danger of exposing the young to the vices of these moral pest-houses."[81]

* * *

In examining the transmission of these attacks on Catholicism between the United States and France, an immediate imbalance becomes clear. Throughout the middle decades of the nineteenth century, Americans were enthusiastic readers of French works which set out the allegedly depraved and backward nature of Catholicism. Few American anti-Catholic texts, however, found their way to France. Some key works, such as the bestselling series of letters to Archbishop John Hughes by the Reverend Nicholas Murray, were translated and published in France, but their impact beyond a circle of Protestant readers appears negligible. Most American attacks on Catholicism simply did not appear in France. In the United Kingdom, on the other hand, bestselling American works, such as the famous tale of convent abuse, *The Awful Disclosures of Maria Monk*, were published in multiple editions.

What factors might account for this imbalance? To begin with, the far more active censorship regime in Second Empire France would have barred the majority of American polemics against Catholicism. In part, too, the lack of French interest was one facet of a broader disdain for American cultural productions. As Henry Blumenthal has argued, with some notable exceptions few American literary works found a French audience. In 1848, the abolitionist and activist Julia Ward Howe witnessed this dismissive attitude firsthand. Attending a lecture in Paris by the noted critic Philarètes Chasles, she was dismayed to hear him describe America as a country of absolutely no interest from an intellectual viewpoint.[82] More fundamentally, French anticlericals, for whom the Catholic Church was an enemy which was only too familiar, had little need to seek documentary evidence of Catholicism's purportedly sinister nature from across the Atlantic.

The absence of any significant movement of American anti-Catholic works into France did not, however, signify a lack of influence, for the United States in fact became a vital source of inspiration for French opponents of the Catholic Church. To begin with, many French anticlericals seized on the example of America to argue that Protestantism nourished social and economic progress while Catholicism stifled it. The economic dynamism of the United States compared with its Catholic neighbors in Central and South America was seen as proof that Protestantism was the religion most conducive to development. This argument appeared most natural to Protestant republicans and liberals such as Eugène Pelletan and Agénor de Gasparin. Pelletan, one of the best-known and most prolific writers and publicists of the Second Empire, and an implacable opponent of the regime, wrote at length of the glory of America, its alluring mix of liberty, progress and piety, all of which, he argued, stemmed from its Protestant origins. In fact for Pelletan it was only Protestantism, and not Catholicism, which could have furnished the settlers to colonize the wilds of the New World. A Catholic man, Pelletan argued in *Les dogmes, le clergé et l'état* (1844), needs a church and a priest to direct him; a Catholic woman, he thought, could never brave the possibility of dying without a priest by her side. Protestants, on the other hand, needed no such guidance, and were filled with the individual initiative and self-reliance which made the feat of conquering such a vast continent possible.[83]

The work of another prominent French Protestant, Count Agénor de Gasparin, had a direct influence on American opinion. Gasparin, who obtained information for his study of America from, among others, Robert Baird and the Secretary of State in the Lincoln administration, William Seward, had led a varied career as a legislator and statesman during the July Republic, and then as a writer and champion of various social causes, from the abolition of slavery to the reform of laws governing marriage. As for so much of the French intellectual liberal and republican elite, de Gasparin regarded slavery as the great moral blot on an American society which he otherwise greatly admired. The election of Lincoln, which he interpreted as initiating the abolition of slavery, cleared away this obstacle to his enthusiasm for America, and he quickly became a dedicated and enthusiastic advocate for the North in the Civil War. In 1861 he published *Les États-Unis en 1861: Un grand peuple qui se relève*, followed in 1862 by *L'Amérique devant l'Europe, principes et interêts*. In electing Lincoln, he wrote, America had saved itself from the sin of slavery and the capitulation to expediency; a great people had thrown off material self-interest and moral compromise to fight for the cause of emancipation. The two books also contained de Gasparin's theory of the origins of American liberty. Perhaps not surprisingly, he placed religion at the top of the list of American virtues: "that energetic Christianity, those self-sustaining churches, that absence of administrative tutelage and centralization, that individual liberty...which are the astonishment and sometimes scandal of the Old World."[84]

In 1861 Mary L. Booth read *Les États-Unis en 1861: Un grand peuple qui se relève*, and immediately persuaded the publisher Charles S. Scribner to arrange a translation. Booth was a journalist, feminist and historian who would translate some forty works, including those of Blaise Pascal and Victor Cousin. As we have seen in the case of Michelet's translators, Scribner agreed to publish the work, but insisted on a short deadline—in this case, though, for fear that the Civil War would end before the work could be published! Working twenty hours a day, Booth had the translation ready within a week. Through her contacts with de Gasparin and other French writers, Booth went on to translate other pro-Northern French works, such as Augustin Cochin's *The Results of Slavery* (1863) and *The Results of Emancipation* (1863).[85] These displays of solidarity on the part of French intellectuals had a great impact on Northern opinion. In a speech to the Senate in 1862, Charles Sumner praised Gasparin for his "impassioned love of liberty and enlightened devotion to our country."[86] On August 1 1862, President Lincoln wrote to Booth to thank her for translating the work.[87] De Gasparin had in fact written to Lincoln on July 18 to assure him of continued European support for the North; the reply praised de Gasparin in the following terms: "You are much admired in America for the ability of your writings, and much loved for your generosity to us, and your devotion to liberal principles generally."[88]

Admiration for America was not a purely Protestant phenomenon. Prominent anticlericals who never formally embraced Protestantism, such as Charles Renouvier, Jules Simon, and Edgar Quinet, also argued that the prosperity and political liberalism of the United States were built on a Protestant foundation. For Edgar Quinet, the contrast between the fate of Catholic and Protestant nations was clear. In *Des Jésuites* Quinet had directly attributed the decline of the southern European states in the modern era to the Society of Jesus. For Quinet, the divergent economic path of North and South America was yet more proof of the economic and social stagnation induced by Roman-Catholicism. In *L'Enseignement du peuple* Quinet argued that the "growing fortune of the heretical United States" shone out when set against the "servitude of Catholic democracies and monarchies in the states of the South." States governed by Catholicism, Quinet concluded, were doomed to perish.[89] The liberal Édouard Laboulaye, though himself a devout Catholic, also saw the Puritanism of the New England settlers as the origin of American democracy. Catholicism, a religion founded on the principle of authority and which demanded total submission from its adherents was far more likely, Laboulaye argued, to provide subjects for a monarchy than independent and spirited republicans for a democracy. Puritans, Laboulaye concluded, who were required to interpret the Bible themselves, and who knew their religious fate to lie in their own hands, already possessed the souls of republicans.[90]

A similar argument was put by another renowned observer of American life, the economist Michel Chevalier, who traveled throughout the United States between 1833 and 1835. In a series of letters first published in the *Journal des Débats*, Chevalier argued that Protestantism, with its faith in individual judgment and initiative, provided the essential framework for democratic and republican political systems. On the other hand, the hierarchical spirit of Catholicism, which suppressed all expressions of individual reasoning, could foster only monarchies. For this reason, Chevalier maintained, any attempt to institute democracy in a Catholic nation was bound to fail; a populace unaccustomed to the exercise of individual judgment would be incapable of showing the self-restraint and discipline demanded of citizens in a democratic system. Democratization in Catholic societies, in Chevalier's judgment, could only result in anarchy.[91] Chevalier subsequently extended the field of his comparison to economic progress, and reached a conclusion similar to that of so many of his contemporaries: Protestant nations, and in particular the United States, had clearly outstripped Catholic nations. For proof, Chevalier contrasted the continental expansion and swelling population of the United States with the decline of his native France, a country which, he lamented, had once been at the head of modern civilization. In a sign of the close attention paid by many Americans to foreign perceptions of their country, both the religious and secular press in the United States quoted at length, and with some satisfaction, Chevalier's comments.[92]

Not content with lauding the material progress and political liberalism fostered by Protestantism, some French liberals and Republicans advocated American religious doctrines. In particular, the brand of Unitarianism associated with William Ellery Channing enjoyed widespread popularity among the intellectual elite of the Second Empire. Channing was a liberal theologian who rejected the Calvinist emphasis on innate depravity and predestination; his God was a figure of love and compassion rather than wrath, a God whose benevolence could be comprehended by human reason. This sort of religion, with its articulation of human goodness and its grounding in rationality, appealed immensely to many French intellectuals, including leading anticlericals. It must be remembered that anticlericals did not necessarily deny the validity of all forms of religious faith. Particularly in the 1840s and 1850s, many French liberals and republicans who had abandoned the Catholic Church nevertheless maintained a conviction that religiosity was a vital element in individual happiness and social harmony. Religion did, however, have to be compatible with modern principles, and this was the core of Unitarianism's appeal. In contrast to the medieval spirit they detected within Catholicism, liberals and republicans found Channing's Unitarianism to be far more amenable to the tenets of modern civilization.

The man most responsible for propagating Channing's ideas in France was the liberal Édouard Laboulaye, professor of comparative law at the *Collège de France*, and one of the most fervent French admirers of the United States in the period of the Second Empire.[93] Laboulaye, who is now chiefly remembered for devising the idea of presenting the United States with a statue celebrating liberty, lectured and wrote extensively about American history and political institutions. Laboulaye regarded the United States as a model of social and political liberty, and strove throughout his career to persuade his fellow citizens to learn from the American example. His reputation as a great friend of America extended across the Atlantic; the translator Mary L. Booth thought Laboulaye's knowledge of the United States was "perhaps greater than that of any other man in Europe."[94] In addition to his scholarly works, Laboulaye also authored a novel, *Paris en Amérique*, under the pseudonym René Lefebvre. The book describes the experiences of a Frenchman who takes an opium pill and awakes to find himself a resident of the United States. The Frenchman is bewildered at every turn by the contrast between his own values and the norms of the society in which he finds himself. His nineteen-year-old daughter studies anatomy and strolls the streets without a chaperone, his wife eschews servants and prefers to maintain the household herself, and the Frenchman is even enrolled into a volunteer fire brigade. Though light in tone, the message of the book was clear—the United States had constructed a progressive social and political model which France could only envy. The book was also immensely popular, going through eight French editions just one year after its publication in 1862, and thirty-five by 1887. It was also published in eight English editions.

For all his admiration of the United States, however, Laboulaye never set foot there. His knowledge of America came from his own extensive reading, and a circle of American acquaintances. One of the most important was Robert Walsh, American Consul in Paris from 1844 to 1851, who remained there until his death in 1859. From Walsh's private library, Laboulaye was able to read studies of American history, society, and politics by authors such as George Bancroft, Richard Hildreth, and Channing. Laboulaye also corresponded with historians and intellectuals such as Bancroft, who had been elected a correspondent of the Institute of France in 1848, and the political scientist and jurist Francis Lieber.[95] In June 1858 he called on another acquaintance, Senator Charles Sumner, during the latter's visit to Paris. Sumner, who was still suffering from the beating inflicted on him in the Senate by Preston Brooks, was confined to bed. Laboulaye, as Sumner's memoirs record, "desired to know something about Channing."[96] Another American Consul with whom Laboulaye formed a close relationship was John Bigelow, who took up the post in 1861, and found in the Frenchman an influential and committed supporter of the Northern cause.

Laboulaye translated many of Channing's works and helped to initiate a wave of enthusiasm for Unitarianism among French intellectuals. Protestants such as Eugène Pelletan, who included a chapter on Channing in the second volume of his *Heures de travail* (1854), were among the most enthusiastic advocates of Unitarianism. But Channing's doctrines attracted interest from a broad range of French writers and activists.[97] Edgar Quinet, for instance, praised Channing for striving to harmonize religion with both democratic political principles and a commitment to rational inquiry. In a letter to another of Channing's admirers, Eugène Sue, who had proposed an association for the advancement of Unitarianism in France, Quinet argued that the philosophy expounded by Channing was similar to that which he and Jules Michelet had put forward at the *Collège de France*. "I was astonished and proud," Quinet wrote to Sue, "to see that we were saying almost the same thing at the same time, on opposite sides of the ocean."[98] Another admirer of Channing was the novelist George Sand. Writing to her son Maurice, who had joined Prince Joseph Napoléon on his visit to the United States in 1861, Sand described Channing's works as encapsulating the heart and intelligence of America. Though rejecting the individualism at the core of his philosophy, Sand nonetheless applauded the "beautiful ideal" of a society founded on love and tolerance that Channing sought to realize.[99] The republican Jules Simon also publicly endorsed Channing's philosophy of religious tolerance. During a debate in the *Corps Législatif* in 1868 on the abrogation of the law which made attacks on religion and public morality an offense, Simon related an anecdote about the United States. There too, he said, a journalist was convicted for criticizing religion, in this case a Protestant church. Rather than approving this act, however, a group of Protestant ministers signed a petition to Congress demanding that such laws be repealed, and insisting that religion required no other protection than the truth of its doctrines. Who, Simon asked, was the first to sign the petition? It was Channing, the "illustrious apostle of tolerance."[100]

Not all French intellectuals shared this admiration for Channing. Ernest Renan offered a more ambivalent review of Channing's philosophy in the *Revue des Deux Mondes*. Though praising his pragmatic and socially active conception of religion, Renan argued that Channing's theology, like America itself, was too utilitarian in nature, lacking the critical sharpness and the poetic beauty which distinguished true religion. The literary critic Philarète Chasles, whose dismissive attitude to American culture had so angered Julia Ward Howe, also attacked Channing's lack of intellectual depth, and his propensity, in Chasle's view, to try to satisfy all parties and to please all readers.[101] Nonetheless, there was a considerable vogue among French intellectuals for Channing's philosophy. Channing's appeal even extended to leading free-thinkers with little sympathy for organized religion. The economist and co-founder of the *Société Démocratique des Libres Penseurs*, Henri Baudrillart, as well as republican free-thinkers such as Léon Gambetta and Henri Allain-Targé, joined the acclaim for Channing.[102]

Channing also attracted admiration for his attacks on Catholicism. Although most of his French admirers stressed the tolerance at the core of Channing's philosophy, a tolerance which stood in direct contrast to what they perceived as the spirit of religious zealotry animating Catholicism, a few took note of Channing's own expressions of hostility towards the Catholic Church. The economist and political scientist Émile de Laveleye, a regular contributor to the influential *Revue des Deux Mondes*, approvingly quoted one such attack. Channing, as Laveleye informed his readers, had described Catholicism as a religion rooted in the Middle Ages which would inevitably fall before the modern triumph of free inquiry and individual rights. Furthermore, as Laveleye reported, Channing was convinced that Catholicism could only ever be an aberration in the most progressive and liberal society on earth, the United States.[103]

Of course, not all French anticlericals were attracted to either Unitarianism or Protestantism more generally. In his book *La démocratie*, the free-thinker Étienne Vacherot argued that, though American Protestantism was undoubtedly far more congenial to modernity than either Catholicism or English Anglicanism, it contained the great flaw of all religious systems, namely, an element of dogmatic authority that prevented the full realization of democracy.

French travelers to the United States were nearly unanimous in condemning aspects of the social control exerted by the Protestant churches, notably the laws prohibiting commercial activity on the Sabbath. The socialist Pierre-Joseph Proudhon, a fierce enemy of all forms of organized religion, ridiculed writers such as Sue for suggesting that France adopt Unitarianism.[104] The republican Henri Allain-Targé, though expressing his admiration for Channing, dismissed the argument put by Quinet, Laboulaye and others that the democratic virtues of the United States stemmed from Protestantism. Their real source, he argued, was the Enlightenment values of the Founding Fathers; as he wrote in a letter to his father, "the founders of the United States were all free-thinkers, men of the eighteenth century."[105]

Nevertheless, even those French anticlericals with little or no attachment to Protestantism praised the United States for having solved the problem posed by Catholicism. The American example appeared especially instructive on the question of convents. As we shall see, the imagined crimes concealed behind the convent walls dominated the anti-Catholic mind. In both France and the United States, calls were made for the mandatory state inspection of convents, and even the abolition of institutions deemed to be out of step with the values of an open and enlightened age. For many French anticlericals, the solution to the growth of convents was to be found across the Atlantic. Charles Sauvestre, whose investigations into the expansion of Catholic orders had been relayed to the American public by Henry C. Lea, argued that the availability of well-paid and respectable teaching jobs for single women in the United States had effectively undercut the appeal of convents. Unlike France, where impoverished young women often had little choice but to seek refuge in the convent, Sauvestre claimed, American society gave its young women a secular alternative: "In America, young women do not lock themselves up in convents; they find an honorable and lucrative profession in teaching." Sauvestre went on to quote what was, in his view, the stunning number of 18,915 female teachers in the state of New York in 1861.[106]

Education was another field where the contrast between America and France seemed stark. French anticlericals were infuriated by the growth in the Church-run school system which had occurred after the adoption of the Falloux Law in 1850. That law, by allowing religious orders such as the Jesuits to open schools, and by exempting teaching nuns from the obligation to obtain the official qualification, the *brevet*, opened the way to an expansion of Church-run schools. To counteract the Church's role in shaping the next generation of French men and women, all French republicans agreed upon the urgency of establishing a universal, state-run educational system. Not surprisingly, the United States was held up as a model to emulate. One admirer was the journalist and writer Xavier Eyma, who visited the United States in 1845 and used his travels as the basis for a series of books, becoming an acknowledged expert on America and its institutions. Eyma argued that this emphasis on popular education, the pillar of American democracy, was inherent in the Puritan faith of the settlers of New England. From the first day of the establishment of New England, he wrote, education and democracy developed hand-in-hand, each assuring the success of the other whenever America expanded its geographical reach.[107] In 1865, Émile de Laveleye praised the American commitment to public education as a lesson for all other nations, including France. In virtually every aspect, from the curriculum to the training of teachers to the state of the school buildings, the American system, de Laveleye reported, was exemplary.[108]

The lesson was particularly striking in the field of female education. By 1865, 55.8% of all French female primary pupils were taught by teaching nuns, a situation which disturbed not only the republican opposition but some members of the government.[109] The idea that the Church was shaping the future wives and mothers of the nation in its own spirit appalled many republicans and liberals. In 1867, the Minister for Instruction, Victor Duruy, who as a young man had acted as Jules Michelet's secretary, attempted to create a nationwide system of free primary schools for girls; the resulting decree of April 10, 1867 stipulated that all communes with over 500 inhabitants must create such schools. One clause in the decree, however, effectively blunted its impact—communes could escape the obligation by pleading financial hardship, a course adopted by the vast majority. Duruy also tried to expand the state system of teacher training schools for women, and introduced public secondary schools for young women in forty towns and villages. Such measures were attacked by the Church. When a secular secondary school for girls was announced for the city of Orléans, its Bishop, Félix Dupanloup, savaged the plan in a series of four pamphlets. Such schools would promote immorality in their students and upset family relations, Dupanloup charged; and in a famous phrase, he assured his readers that French girls were happy to be educated "on the knees of the Church."

As part of his efforts to reform the education system, Duruy sent Célestin Hippeau to the United States to examine firsthand the American public schools. One of Hippeau's first reports, published in the *Revue des Deux Mondes*, concerned the education of American girls.[110] In 1870, Hippeau published the findings of his research trip in a book entitled *L'instruction publique aux États-Unis*. The keystone of the American education system, Hippeau proclaimed, was democracy: "The idea on which public education in the United States is based is consistent with the democratic principles to which everything is subordinated in the most truly free nation on earth." This democratic spirit permeated every aspect of the education system, from its decentralized administration to its funding through local initiative to the acceptance that knowledge should be spread among all classes. The goal of the system, Hippeau concluded, was to instill democratic principles in its citizens, and the enormous sacrifices borne by the North in the Civil War proved the degree to which the system had succeeded.[111] The feminist and republican Olympe Audouard, who visited America in 1868, thought the American system of primary education far superior to the French in almost every aspect. Unlike France, she wrote, children of all social origins mingled in American schools, and democratic sentiments were implanted in the hearts of future citizens. She was particularly impressed with the spread of gender equality through the encouragement of women teachers, co-education and the possibility for women to enter institutions of higher learning. "If we want progress," she concluded, "if we want to march with our century, we must copy America."[112]

Particularly admirable, in the view of French republicans and liberals, was the determination with which Americans barred religion from the classroom, a practice which prevented the growth of sectarian rivalries and ensured the development of a patriotic citizenry. Xavier Eyma praised the American system for banning all religious instruction in public schools. In 1870, *La Démocratie*, a journal edited by the pro-American freethinker Charles-Louis Chassin, drew a similar lesson from the American model. "American education," he wrote, "begins by eliminating religious instruction"; this measure not only saved time in class, but freed scientific teaching from the need to appease religious sensitivity.[113] Hippeau, too, noted that the country where religious sentiment appeared the most vital was also the one which most strictly barred religious intolerance from the classroom. However, such a policy was, Hippeau warned, coming under increasing attack, and the most hostile party was the Catholic Church. "Catholicism," he wrote, "energetically complains about this system."[114] Émile de Laveleye also highlighted the fact that the only church which opposed this principle of secularism in American schools was the Catholic Church. According to de Laveleye, the Church's hostility to public schools was based on the fear that any exposure of young Catholics to the spirit of free inquiry would undercut the principle of passive obedience at the heart of Catholicism.[115] De Laveleye and Hippeau were not alone in arguing that the Catholic hierarchy sought to undermine the American public school system. In a campaign that he judged directly analogous to that undertaken by the Church in France, Charles Sauvestre reported that the Archbishop of New York, John Hughes, was determined to sabotage the non-Catholic education system. Hughes, according to Sauvestre, had "placed himself at the head of a crusade which aims to withdraw children from national schools, and to place them in exclusively Catholic schools."[116]

The powerful influence of the American educational system extended to the man who would lead the Third Republic's introduction of universal, state-run education, Jules Ferry. In a speech before the *Société pour l'instruction élémentaire* in April 1870, Ferry outlined his program for a future education system in France. The key theme of his speech was equality. Without equal access to education, Ferry declared, a true democracy was unattainable; the existence of two classes in society, the educated and uneducated, was a fatal barrier to the spirit of solidarity which was at the heart of democracy. Education, Ferry declared, should be both free, and oriented towards practical and modern arts such as mathematics, natural history, and of course the inculcation of a truly patriotic sentiment in its students. For a picture of what such an education system would look like, Ferry, who had read Hippeau's report, turned to the public schools of America. The system there, Ferry told his audience, was free, comprehensive—seven million children taught at the primary level, versus only five hundred thousand in France—and generously funded. Finally, Ferry continued, the core principle of the American system was liberty, a liberty which stemmed from its administration by local communities rather than a national administration. Ferry finished by considering the state of female education. America, he argued, had achieved gender equality in education, thereby proving that women, as much as men, could be educated to be intelligent, modern and above all patriotic contributors to society. France, in contrast, had failed to shake the education of its future mothers from the grip of the Church, to the detriment both of the nation and of the men whose wives, having been indoctrinated in the regressive spirit of Catholicism, remained alien to them. As "the bishops know too well," Ferry concluded, "he who controls the woman controls all, firstly because he controls the child, then because he controls the husband."[117]

We can, of course, question the accuracy of many of these French descriptions of the American public schools. The stated goal of Horace Mann and other proponents of public schools was not a secular but a non-sectarian school system; a proper grounding in Christian morals was, for Mann, a proper and vital ambition for any public school. Hippeau, de Laveleye, Sauvestre, and others appear not to have noticed the role of religion in the American classroom, nor the complaints of Catholics that this emphasis on Christianity masked a bias towards the Protestant creed. Yet for an anticlerical movement which had ceded so much ground to the Catholic Church in the realm of education, the United States shone as an example of what could be achieved: a republic molding its citizens, including its young women, in the values and spirit of a progressive and democratic era. In an article for the republican *Siècle*, which was reprinted in the Boston *Daily Advertiser*, one of its editors Edmond Texier compared American and French girls he had met in Paris, and alluded to Dupanloup's claim that girls should be educated on the knees of the Church. When you talk to American girls, Texier wrote, "you find out that the time which our French *belles* pass on their own knees or on the knees of the Church have been spent by the fair Americans in acquiring a variety of knowledge of which those educated on the Dupanloup system have but very vague notions indeed—such as languages, arts, science, history... The fact is, America raises women, and France dolls."[118]

On another crucial question for French anticlericals, the separation of church and state, the great advance made by the United States was just as hard to ignore. French commentators had long been fascinated with the model of religious disestablishment offered by America. Well before the advent of the Second Empire, French writers and intellectuals were studying the consequences for both church and society of a constitutional structure which recognized no official religion and, in theory at least, offered no state support to any particular creed. Gustave de Beaumont, who accompanied Alexis de Tocqueville on his visit to the United States in 1831, offered a detailed and perceptive study of the role of religion in American public life in an appendix to his novel, *Marie*, which was first published in 1835. In some states, he noted, religion and law remained mixed—in Massachusetts, for example, where the state only recognized Christianity, or in Maryland, where an office-holder was required to be Christian. He also recognized the prejudice, both in society and in law, against atheism. These exceptions aside, de Beaumont concluded, state laws mandated a strict neutrality regarding religious faith, a provision which, far from tempering religious enthusiasm, appeared to invigorate it.[119]

The leading French advocate of what became known as the American principle of separating church and state was the liberal Édouard Laboulaye. In his opening series of lectures at the *Collège de France* in 1849, he praised what he termed the absolute freedom of religion which was guaranteed by the American Constitution, a freedom which contrasted with the intermeshing of church and state in France under the *Concordat* of 1801. Americans, Laboulaye argued, were not obliged to financially support ministers of a religion which was not their own; in France, on the other hand, the state salaries paid to priests represented, for non-Catholics, a form of tyranny.[120] Throughout his career Laboulaye used the experience of America to rebut the most common arguments made against disestablishment. To those who argued that an absence of state control would unleash inter-religious hostility, Laboulaye pointed to America which, as he wrote in his 1865 program for the Liberal movement, maintained a spirit of religious tolerance despite its "thirty or forty churches." Nor had disestablishment, as Laboulaye pointed out, led to an increase in religious skepticism. In fact, the separation of the spheres of religion and state had clearly benefited both. This was even true, as Laboulaye liked to argue, for the Catholic Church in America. "In which country," as he asked, "are the most churches, hospices and Catholic schools constructed? In which country are priests best-treated, most respected and most influential?"[121] The answer, of course, was America, "the country of liberty."

In the first decade of the Second Empire the ties between church and state were increasing. The Church had strongly supported the coup d'état carried out by Louis-Napoléon, and, in the eyes of anticlericals, won significant concessions in return. By the 1860s, however, relations between the Vatican and the regime were coming under greater strain. Napoléon III's support for Italian unification, a process which could only be achieved by the dismantling of the large Papal States, was the most significant point of conflict.[122] Anticlericals seized on this growing animosity to make louder their calls for the adoption of what was often termed the "American" principle of religious neutrality. In a speech to the International Association for Progress in the Social Sciences in 1863, the freethinker Frédéric Morin proclaimed "Let us...carefully separate the temporal and the spiritual, following the example of the United States, where each religious community exists freely and the government never thinks of interfering with them."[123] The Protestant Agénor de Gasparin, long an advocate of the separation of church and state, praised its implementation in America as bringing a number of practical benefits. Among these was an absence of distractions. In contrast to the French government, which was continually embroiled in political controversies concerning religion and the Vatican, the American government, de Gasparin wrote, was free to focus on more important issues.[124] The radical Ulric de Fonvielle, who had volunteered to fight in the Northern army, wrote from America that religious issues never bring their "venom" into political questions; churches on both sides had played no role, he thought, in the onset of the Civil War.[125]

Such views continued to be expressed well after the War's conclusion. In 1868, Jules Ferry looked to America to find what he termed "active, radical, self-mastering" democrats. These democrats, he wrote in Eugène Pelletan's *La Tribune*, "don't have a national Church, don't have a roman question and, not having Cardinals in the Senate, leave everything in its proper place: science in schools, preaching in churches, politics in legislatures."[126] By 1869, and the approach of the first Vatican Council, these calls for the separation of church and state were becoming even more insistent. Another of the French to volunteer for the Northern army, the political radical, atheist and future Communard Gustave Cluseret, advocated that France establish "a free Church in a free State, such as it exists in the United States."[127] In the same year the editorial committee of the *Siècle* called for "the immediate abolition of the Concordat, the immediate separation of the State and of Churches, *and the establishment of the American system in religious matters.*"[128]

Of course, the principle of the separation of church and state was not exclusively construed as a blow against the Catholic Church. A number of liberal French Catholics drew on the American experience to argue that Catholicism could thrive without the patronage of the state. The prerogatives of the French state over religious matters were, in their view, as much a hindrance as an aid to the spread of Catholicism. As early as the 1830s, Henri-Dominique Lacordaire, at that time already a leading figure in the circle of the influential priest and author Félicité Lammenais, had written several articles in which he praised the freedom from state interference enjoyed by the Catholic Church in the United States; the flourishing state of the church there was clear proof, for Lacordaire, that the separation of church and state would be favorable to Catholicism.[129] Alexis de Tocqueville had observed that Catholicism prospered in the absence of state support in the United States, and that Catholic priests were some of the most avowed defenders of democratic institutions. Subsequently, other liberal Catholics, including Charles Montalembert, Emile Jonveaux, and Augustin Cochin, extolled the American model of separating temporal and spiritual powers. Montalembert expressed his admiration for the religious liberty in the United States in his famous 1863 address "A Free Church in a Free State," and even planned to visit America.

From the perspective of French anticlericals, however, the separation of church and state appealed above all as an indispensable step on the path to a modern, democratic France. First, to a degree far greater than any other church, the Catholic Church was understood to be intrinsically motivated by the desire to unite the temporal and spiritual powers. For anticlericals, there seemed abundant proof both abroad and at home that this was indeed the Church's ambition.

Though not restoring a national church, the *Concordat* of 1801 recognized Catholicism as the religion of the great majority of French people, and the dominant position of Catholicism in French life was clear. As the liberal Lucien Prévost-Paradol, briefly French consul to Washington, argued in his 1868 program for reform, *La France nouvelle*, it was the Catholic Church, much more than the Protestant or Jewish faiths, which was, "through our traditions, through its history, through its ancient and tight relations with the people, our national Church."[130] Abroad, the tenacity with which the Vatican resisted all efforts to loosen its grip on the Papal States was regularly cited as proof of its thirst for temporal authority. Perhaps the most compelling affirmation of Catholicism's intrinsic quest for worldly power, at least in the eyes of its opponents, was the Syllabus of Errors of 1864. One of the most controversial Church documents of the age, the Syllabus was a list of "condemned propositions." Number fifty-five of these beliefs declared anathema was: "the Church ought to be separated from the State, and the State from the Church."

In the eyes of French liberals and republicans, there thus seemed little doubt as to which Church would suffer most from the adoption of a secular regime. The separation of church and state was, in this argument, an inoculation against the threat from Catholicism. For proof of the healthy body politic which would ensue from such a system, French anticlericals looked, of course, to America. As Émile de Laveleye argued, the American Constitution had effectively shorn Catholicism of its capacity to do harm. The church in the United States, Laveleye asserted, shared the same despotic and regressive tendencies as in other nations. But only in America, where the state offered no official patronage to any Church, had Catholicism become a relatively benign institution.[131]

This assumption that American republican institutions and social practices had effectively blunted Catholicism's despotic ambitions explains one of the oddities of French anticlerical writings about the United States, the absence of any depictions of popular hostility to the Catholic Church. Aside from a few isolated examples, French opponents of Catholicism consistently portrayed the United States as a society where religious animosity was almost non-existent, and Catholics were subject to little discrimination or antagonism. There were, of course, exceptions. Michel Chevalier, whose visit to America coincided with the destruction by a group of Protestant men of the Ursuline convent in Charlestown, Massachusetts in 1834, noted the hostility towards Catholics in the New England states, but thought the attitude of the populace far kinder elsewhere.[132] Gustave de Beaumont also narrated the burning of the Charlestown convent, and the hatred felt by many in the North towards Catholicism.[133] The republican Charles Sauvestre reported an attack on a Jesuit seminary in Missouri. However, far from criticizing such an action, Sauvestre labeled it a praiseworthy example of popular violence employed as a corrective to improper concentrations of power.[134]

Nevertheless, the majority of anticlericals presented the United States as a society in which the application of certain enlightened principles, from the separation of church and state to the maintenance of a public education system, had made inter-religious hostility almost redundant. Few anticlericals detected any significance in the rise of the anti-Catholic Know-Nothings in the early 1850s. The journalist, author and music critic for the republican *Siècle*, Oscar Comettant, wrote several accounts of American society. In one, *L'Amérique telle qu'elle est*, his fictional visitor to the United States, Marcel Bonneau, derided the Know-Nothings' policies as "narrow, destructive and self-interested" and expressed some relief that they were unable to "stand for long against the good sense of the majority."[135] The Protestant Jean-Henri Grandpierre, whose visit to the United States coincided with the rise of the Know-Nothings, stressed the lack of religious persecution in the United States. "There cannot be cited a single instance," Grandpierre claimed, "of persecution or intolerance against the religion of the minority, either on the part of the citizens or of the government."[136] Admittedly, the Church itself took far more notice of the Know-Nothings. But at least among liberals and republicans, the United States stood as a model of religious harmony. The philologist and professor of French literature at the *Collège de France*, Jean-Jacques Ampère, who visited the United States in 1851, claimed that Catholicism in the United States was "the object of no malevolent prejudice."[137] Another French traveler to the United States, the young journalist Ernest Duvergier de Hauranne, observed that though there was some hostility between Protestants and Catholics, the general climate of religious liberty prevented this antipathy developing into hatred.[138] The question of the relations between church and state had been, de Hauranne noted, resolved in the United States, and all religions had benefited.

* * *

In the middle decades of the century, American readers could choose from scores of French attacks on the Catholic enemy. Whatever their focus, from the alleged temporal ambitions of the Vatican to the spread of foreign convents, Americans turned to French sources for a guide to the nature of the threat. Such a choice was perfectly natural. Whether in the guise of a renegade priest or a republican intellectual,

French writers enjoyed a strong credibility which stemmed from their familiarity with the nature of the adversary. From the French perspective, there seemed little reason to seek information about the church from a majority-Protestant society like the United States. In this exchange, America was thus the debtor nation. But there was nonetheless a strong element of reciprocity in this relationship, for America had other lessons to offer French opponents of the church. As Édouard Laboulaye argued, the ties between France and America were not merely a legacy of the Revolutionary era. "A secret instinct," he wrote, "tells us that there the problems concerning our own future are tackled and solved."[139] One of these problems was the role of Catholicism. As French travelers, social commentators and political activists suggested, America, in contrast to France, seemed to have succeeded in the urgent task of subduing the political and social influence of the church. Of course, the praise was never unanimous. The Protestantism of American society jarred with many positivists and free thinkers; French travelers almost uniformly condemned the influence of pro-temperance and pro-Sabbath activists. Yet few anti-clericals could resist concluding that the church, which seemed such a threat to the achievement of a modern, progressive nation, had been made benign in the atmosphere of American liberty.

What do these exchanges tell us about the broader story of intellectual borrowing and interaction between France and the United States? One lesson concerns chronology. In his study of the social progressive movement in the late-nineteenth and early-twentieth centuries, Daniel T. Rodgers argues that American reformers drew heavily on overseas experience and ideas. However, Rodgers maintains that such international borrowings were only possible in a brief time span—from the last decades of the nineteenth century, when Americans first adopted an international perspective, to the end of World War II, when the United States emerged as a superpower. In the middle of the nineteenth century, Rodgers claims, Americans were still so convinced of their nation's exceptional position that all political or social ideals originating from the Old World were automatically rejected as unsuitable or irrelevant.[140] Such a periodization, however, ignores the international consciousness of Americans at mid-century. On the evidence of their eager consumption of French attacks on Catholicism, Americans in the middle decades of the century were far more open to European influences than Rodgers gives them credit for.

On the French side, Thomas A. Sancton has made a forceful case that the Civil War was a crucial turning point in the attitude of the French Left toward the United States. Much of the French Left, he argues, was hostile to America in the first decade of the Second Empire. The American model of federalism, bicameral legislatures and an independently elected President were, according to Sancton, considered inapplicable to French history and circumstances. French socialists, in turn, rejected the materialism, the laissez-faire individualism and the stress on self-help which they saw as dominating American life. French liberals and republicans were also virtually unanimous in condemning American slavery. It was only with the onset of the Civil War that, according to Sancton, the image of America was rehabilitated, and by the end of the decade a broad pro-American sentiment could be said to characterize liberals and republicans.[141] My own research suggests that, at least on the questions which mattered most to anticlericals, from education to church-state relations to the role of convents, the positive influence of America was far more consistent across the middle decades of the century than Sancton suggests. Well before the Civil War, French travelers and writers were praising American policies and attitudes on these questions, and advocating their application in France.

The evidence of this American influence also challenges some of the more extreme theories of French anti-Americanism. In a recent study, Philippe Roger argues that French opinion of the United States has been overwhelmingly hostile since the early nineteenth century.[142] Roger's analysis, however, ignores the swathe of pro-American opinion in France, a sentiment which was clearly on display in the French admiration for the manner in which the United States appeared to have tamed the Catholic Church. This turn toward the United States on the part of French republicans was entirely natural. It is worth recalling the anomalous position of the American republic in the mid-nineteenth-century world. In an age where only a handful of republics existed, the United States could hardly inspire anything less than wonder on the part of French republicans. In economic, military and diplomatic terms, America at mid-century was far from a world power. But for many French writers and commentators, the prospects of the republic across the Atlantic were of immense significance. As Xavier Eyma, one of the more prominent French commentators on America declared, "There is no other country which we talk about as much as North America."[143]

On the American side, too, there was much appreciation for these positive French assessments of their nation. Indeed, in contrast to what they perceived as the disparaging and hostile tone of many English observers, Americans often explicitly expressed their preference for French descriptions of their nation. During his lifetime, Alexis de Tocqueville's analysis of the United States was already heralded by Americans as among the truest and most favorable accounts of their society and its institutions. In 1856 the *North American Review*, for example, offered the following assessment of de Tocqueville's merits as an observer of American life:

> Tocqueville is no new name to us on this side of the Atlantic, and when we reflect upon all the bad faith and all the narrow-minded prejudice that have been expended upon European pictures of American society, (especially where the painters have belonged to our own Anglo-Saxon race,) we cannot but feel grateful to the intelligent Frenchman who at all events earnestly strove to do justice to us in every respect.[144]

In a work published in 1864, Henry T. Tuckerman denounced what he called the "prejudiced style of most English writers," and even argued that Americans had more in common with the French than with the English.[145]

The interchange of books and ideas between opponents of the Church formed the basis of what might be termed the Transatlantic case against the Church. In their battle with a mutual enemy, French and American opponents of the Church found ample shared ground on which to construct such a case. Yet another development which served a crucial role in solidifying this sense of transnational solidarity was the actions of the Vatican itself. Of all the controversies around the Vatican in the middle decades of the century, none had a greater impact than the Mortara Affair.

2
Catholicism, Slavery, and the Family—The Mortara Affair

In 1858, the fate of a boy called Edgardo Mortara sparked an international controversy that, more than any other single issue before the convening of the first Vatican Council, exposed the divide between supporters and opponents of the Vatican. The story began in the city of Bologna, which at that time formed part of the papal domains. On the evening of June 23, two officers of the military police demanded entry to the apartment of a Jewish family named Mortara. Having verified the identity of the family members, one of the policemen, Marshal Pietro Lucidi, revealed the purpose of their visit. The papal government had recently learned that six-year-old Edgardo Mortara had undergone a Catholic baptism. The consequences, Lucidi explained to the boy's parents, Momolo and Marianna, were immense. As a Catholic, Edgardo's salvation would be at risk if he were to remain in the custody of his Jewish parents. Canon law dictated that Edgardo now be instructed in the rites and sacraments of the Catholic faith. For this reason, Lucidi concluded, he had been ordered to remove the boy from the care of his family that very night.[1]

Despite their shock, the boy's parents immediately began to interrogate Marshal Lucidi. None of the family members had heard anything of the purported baptism. What proof was there that it had actually taken place? Who had carried it out? When? In response, Lucidi would only repeat that he had been ordered to take Edgardo away. Momolo Mortara persisted with these questions, however, and soon other members of the family began to arrive at the scene. Faced with a growing protest, Lucidi relented. The execution of the order could be delayed, he conceded, so as to allow Momolo time to seek more information from the papal administration. The next day Momolo obtained an interview with the inquisitor of Bologna, Father Feletti. Like Lucidi, Feletti refused to give any details about the circumstances of the baptism. The administration was satisfied, he informed Momolo, that a valid baptism had been performed on Edgardo, and there was only one possible course of action: a Catholic boy could not remain in the custody of a Jewish family. The father's pleas for the order to be rescinded left Feletti unmoved. On the evening of June 24, Marshal Lucidi, accompanied by several other officers, returned to the Mortara apartment, placed Edgardo in a carriage, and without informing the family of the boy's destination, drove away.

In the weeks after the removal of Edgardo, the family managed to obtain answers to many of the questions regarding the secret baptism. Edgardo, they discovered, had been baptized by Anna Morisi, a Catholic servant who had been employed by the family for several years. While still a baby, Edgardo had become gravely ill and, fearful for his salvation in the event that he died, Morisi, only fourteen years old at the time, had baptized him. Unfortunately for the Mortaras, Anna subsequently revealed her actions to a fellow servant, who in turn informed a priest. His parents also learned the location of their son—the House of the Catechumens in Rome, an institution whose goal was the conversion of Jews and Muslims to Catholicism.

In August 1858, scattered reports of these events in Bologna began to appear in the American press. Public interest in the Mortara case, however, soared in September and October as a result of a series of protest meetings organized by local rabbis. From that point, the Mortara Affair became one of the great controversies of the day. In November, the *Philadelphia Public Ledger* printed nine articles; from mid-November to mid-December, the *Chicago Tribune* printed sixteen; in December the *New York Times* published twenty. Virtually all of this press commentary was a mixture of condemnation and fury at the abduction, as it was commonly labeled, of Edgardo Mortara. The *National Era* described the case as an "outrage that would have been in keeping with the spirit of the Roman Catholic world in the sixteenth century."[2] The *New York Herald* opined that "a grosser infringement of the natural rights of the parent over the child, or a more despotic exercise of ecclesiastical authority, has never been committed."[3] A series of public meetings composed of Jews and non-Jews was held across the country to protest the Vatican's actions and to demand a strong diplomatic intervention from the American government. When the Buchanan administration, citing the principle of noninterference in the domestic affairs of other countries, rebuffed these efforts, the response from much of the press and the public was scathing. The *New York Times* branded the administration's position a humiliating betrayal of America's mission in the world:

> Happily for humanity...several of the governments of Europe, with whom benevolence is not merely a by-word, or the cause of human progress a sham...have already done what it will be the shame of the American people if our Government leaves undone...If...we are destined to see the European powers taking the lead in the assertion and defence of principles which it is peculiarly the province of the American people to assert and defend, they will not forget to whose stupid obstinacy they owe the exclusion.[4]

To capitalize on the widespread hostility to the actions of the Vatican, a play entitled *Mortara; or, the Pope and His Inquisitors* soon appeared.

In France, the reaction to the Mortara Affair was even more intense. Aside from the pro-Catholic paper *L'Univers* which, through its pugnacious editor, Louis Veuillot, waged a vociferous campaign in defense of the Vatican, the press response was overwhelmingly hostile. An editorial in the *Journal des Débats* described the actions of the papal government as "odious," and "an overturning of justice and universal morality."[5] The liberal *Revue des Deux Mondes* denounced "the apologies both odious and ridiculous which have been shamelessly offered in defense of an act which not only breaches natural moral law but which, if it had been committed in France, would have been punished by our courts as a criminal act."[6] An anonymous pamphlet described the case as "one of the most serious which can occur"; not only had the rights of the Mortara family been ignored by the Vatican, but the removal of the boy also represented "a violation of the rights of humanity itself."[7]

This condemnation in the press was accompanied by a determined effort on the part of the Imperial government to persuade Pius IX to return the boy to his family. Napoléon III had been urging the pope to modernize the government of the Papal States for some time; he found the removal of Edgardo Mortara from his family not only repugnant in itself, but also a provocative and public rejection of his call for modernization. In his appeals to the pontiff, the French emperor disposed of more than his status as the leader of the most influential Catholic nation. In 1849, after all, French and Austrian troops had suppressed the Roman Republic and restored the pope to his seat at the Vatican. In 1858, papal authority over cities such as Bologna was still largely dependent on the presence of a garrison of French troops in Rome. Much of the French press decried the pope's refusal to give up Edgardo Mortara as an act of ingratitude and suggested that the role of the French troops in reinforcing papal authority had made France an accomplice to the crime. In the *Journal des Débats*, Prévost-Paradol reminded readers that the confinement of Edgardo Mortara was occurring "at several paces from our soldiers since, after all, it is our flag which flies over Rome; and when you thus defy good sense and humanity, it is the protection of our armies that you abuse."[8]

The American press closely followed these efforts of the French government to overturn the Vatican's decision. The *Philadelphia Public Ledger* described the emperor as "indignant" at the Vatican's actions.[9] The *New York Times* and other papers noted the protests made by the French ambassador at Rome, the Duc de Gramont, to Pius IX, a diplomatic initiative that contrasted with the apparent passivity of the Buchanan administration.[10] The French public, as the press informed its readership, was in such an uproar that the Imperial government would have to respond; according to one widely circulating rumor, if Pius IX continued in his obstinacy, French troops might even liberate Edgardo from the House of Catechumens. As in so many of the great international controversies surrounding the Vatican, the American press, in this instance also, relied on French sources for the details of significant developments. The first comprehensive American report about the baptism performed on Edgardo Mortara came from the *Siècle*.[11] The same paper was cited by *Harper's Weekly* to discredit the claim that the baptism had been made necessary by the boy's severe illness. Quoting an interview with the family's doctor that had appeared in the *Siècle*, the American journal argued that the boy's life was never at risk.[12] American readers also relied on the French press for descriptions of the conditions surrounding the boy's stay at the House of Catechumens. The *New York Tribune*, for example, reported the contents of a letter that had been published in the *Journal des Débats*. Contradicting the Vatican's assertions that Edgardo's parents had unrestricted access to their son, the letter claimed that, apart from one supervised meeting in which Edgardo had pleaded to be allowed to return home, the doors of the House of Catechumens had remained barred to Momolo Mortara.[13]

The plight of the Mortara family captured public attention on both sides of the Atlantic. Yet it is worth considering what made the Mortara Affair such a great controversy. Of course, it is easy to imagine that the removal and sequestration of a child would create such levels of outrage. But this was not the first such case. In 1817, there was a similar case in Ferrare involving a six-year-old girl who had been baptized by a servant; analogous cases were also reported in Ancone in 1826, Modena in 1836, and Reggio d'Emilia in 1844.[14] Nor was the practice of separating children from their parents unknown in the nineteenth century; as we shall see, defenders of the Vatican were quick to point to the sale of slave children in the American South. Why, then, did the case of Edgardo Mortara become such an international scandal?

One reason was its timing. The removal of Edgardo Mortara occurred at exactly the moment when calls for Italian unification were growing louder and the status of the Papal States was everywhere coming under increasing scrutiny. In the months leading up to the Mortara Affair, the international press had been reporting rumors that the French government intended to form an alliance with Piedmont to achieve Italian unification, a goal which, it was assumed, necessarily entailed the dissolution of the independent papal domains.[15] The depiction of the papacy as an obstacle to the cherished goal of Italian unity was common in both the United States and France. In the final months of 1858, as the American press printed article after article on the Mortara Affair, an advocate of Italian unification calling herself Madame Mario was drawing large crowds in New York. The Papal States, she told her audiences in a series of lectures reprinted in the press, were "the great stumbling block to the freedom of Italy."[16] While the climate of political censorship in France made such overt actions in favor of Italian unification more difficult, a similar message was contained in the writer and journalist Edmond About's best-selling account of the Papal States, *La question romaine*, which was published in the immediate aftermath of the Mortara Affair. About's book, which was subsequently translated and published in America, described the Papal States as economically backward and politically oppressive, a feudal remnant that the tide of Italian unification would mercifully dissolve.[17]

The Mortara Affair thus became an ideal opportunity to denounce the abuses that necessarily ensued when, as in the Papal States, temporal and spiritual powers were joined in one government. The Mortara tale was equally, in its way, a captivity story: the fate of the boy held against his will in the mysterious House of Catechumens and forbidden, according to much of the press, any contact with his parents, evoked the troubling stories of young girls confined in convents. Much of the press also seized on the case to ridicule Catholicism's irrational belief in the transformative power of miracles. The idea that a Jewish boy could be filled with the light of the Holy Spirit merely through the sprinkling of a few drops of water by an uneducated servant girl seemed further proof that Catholicism valued superstition over rational inquiry. In this context, the Mortara Affair was hardly an isolated case. Just a few months before Edgardo's removal, reports detailing claims of an apparition by the Virgin Mary outside a village in France called Lourdes had begun to appear.

All these factors contributed to the public anger over the Vatican's decision. Yet what really drove the backlash against the Vatican was a sense that the very sanctity of the home was under threat. The removal of Edgardo was depicted as a sensational attack on one of the basic principles of the age, the right of mothers and fathers to freely raise their own children. Parental prerogative was repeatedly invoked as a natural and fundamental right that the claims of religion could not override. For the *New York Herald*, a clear and straightforward principle was at stake: "The right of the parent to guardianship over the infant is a natural right, somewhat older than the Roman Church. Any attempt to infringe upon that right, while it is duly and properly exercised, is an outrage upon the civilization of the age, and no special pleading whatever can justify it."[18] The *New York Times* agreed that parental rights were at the heart of the case: "A parent who is not a criminal has the right to the care and jurisdiction of his children. This is a natural law, with which no divine law whatever clashes."[19] By removing Edgardo Mortara against the wishes of his parents, the church had, for the majority of commentators in the United States, violated one of the most basic tenets of nineteenth-century civilization, the authority of parents over their children.

In the United States, much more than an abstract principle was seen to be at stake in the Mortara Affair. As many commentators warned, Protestant children residing in the Papal States were also at risk of abduction by the Vatican if surreptitiously baptized by a Catholic. In a potentially more disturbing allegation, anti-Catholic writers began to insinuate that even children living in the United States might be at risk. The sensitive point here concerned the large number of Catholic servants in major American cities. In an article published in several newspapers, the ex-priest William Hogan, whose virulent attacks on Catholic convents and confessionals were best sellers in the antebellum period, alleged that Catholic servants were, just as Anna Morisi had done, baptizing Protestant babies throughout the United States. "I would not be surprised," Hogan was quoted as declaring, "if one half of the children of Boston are now baptized Roman Catholics."[20] Other writers claimed that Catholic nurses were smuggling Protestant babies to priests to have them baptized. Describing this purported practice, the Boston *Daily Evening Transcript* observed that "quite a flutter has ensued in maternal bosoms since the development of the Mortara Affair."[21] Even among those Americans who might have considered such claims outlandish, there was a discernible belief that the actions of the Vatican threatened the security of families well beyond the borders of the Papal States. As the *New York Observer* grimly warned, "Every family is indirectly threatened in the affair of young Mortara."[22]

For the French liberal and republican press, the underlying issue in the Mortara case was also this apparent conflict between the natural rights of parents and the claims of the Catholic Church. In a series of editorials, the *Journal des Débats* denounced the church for privileging canon law, which ruled Edgardo's baptism to be valid and his removal from his Jewish family thus not only justified but imperative, over natural law that guaranteed the prerogatives of parents over the upbringing of their children. Avoiding the theological question of the validity of the baptism performed by Anna Morisi, the paper declared that, even if canon law justified such acts, the natural law of parental authority took precedence in a civilized society: "If canon law is, on this point, in disagreement with moral and civil law, if it authorises the enormities that are justified in its name, we can only say: Too bad for canon law."[23] One of the most popular newspapers of the day, *La Presse*, was equally clear about the basic issue at stake in the affair: "Removing a child from his parents...is certainly one of the greatest attacks which can be committed against the liberty of human conscience and against paternal authority."[24] If such a case were to arise in France, the paper concluded, not only would the civil tribunals immediately restore Edgardo to his parents, but those responsible for his removal would also be tried as kidnappers.

What particularly shocked and infuriated American and French opinion was the aggressive manner in which the Vatican had intruded into the domestic realm. In disrupting the tranquility of the Mortara home, the Vatican had touched a particularly sensitive nerve. On both sides of the Atlantic, the home was more and more viewed as private and independent. As a number of scholars have argued, the dominant model of the family in the nineteenth century stressed its detachment from market relations and public life. In their survey of the evolution of the American family, Steven Mintz and Susan Kellogg write, "By the 1830s, Americans had come to define the family as essentially a private place, distinct from the public sphere of life. It was a shelter and a refuge, a contrast to the outside world."[25] The family's stability as a unit, as well as the happiness of its members, was thought to derive from this isolation. Boundaries, then, in some sense defined the modern family. Given this conception, the Vatican's interference in a private family appeared a particularly disturbing violation of a fundamental social ideal.

At the same time, much more was at stake than simply domestic privacy. In both France and the United States, the family was seen to play a crucial role in maintaining social stability. Mid-century social commentators repeatedly emphasized that the family was the cornerstone of the state. Domestic tranquility, in this view, was the essential precondition for social stability; contentment in the private sphere, it was assumed, would bind individuals to the prevailing political order and forestall efforts to stir up social discord. As the French philosopher Paul Janet succinctly affirmed in his popular treatise on the family,

"Order in the family is order in society. Disorder in the family is disorder in society."[26] The family was equally a crucial training ground where future citizens received their first and most valuable lessons in civic responsibility. By so callously destroying the happiness of the Mortara family, the Vatican appeared intent on undermining that domestic harmony that was the very foundation of the state.

The argument on which French and American defenders of the Mortara family based their campaign—a shared conception of domesticity—may appear surprising in the light of the national stereotypes that prevailed at the time. On the question of domestic happiness, many French observers referred to the United States as a model. In a paean to what he called "this young and strong" nation that was advancing into the future "with giant strides," the Protestant Eugène Buisson identified the source of American vitality in its "domestic mores."[27] Such views were typical of a broader French admiration for American domestic arrangements. In many mid-century French accounts, the United States figured as a land governed by domestic harmony. Marriages were more equitable, the authority of parents over children more reasonable, and the respect of children for parents more freely given.

American observers of France, however, portrayed the French home in a very different manner. In scores of sermons, travel accounts, and novels, nineteenth-century Americans agreed that French society was governed by a moral dissipation that precluded the development of true domestic feeling. Infidelity, in this view, was the rule rather than the exception in French marriages; the relations between parent and child, in turn, were governed by blind authority and obedience rather than trust and respect. It is a measure of just how ingrained this perception was that even the few dissenting voices that were raised were forced to concede the futility of revising public opinion. The author Edwin Lee Leon was exceptional in arguing that "neither in England nor in America is the marriage vow kept more inviolate" than in France. Yet even Leon doubted that many Americans would ever abandon their conviction that, for the French, "there is *no home*, properly speaking...marriage being with them only the convenient cloak for license, and every French-man and woman disregarding the divine and human precepts which make it a solemn and binding sacrament."[28] The Mortara Affair failed to overturn this almost reflexive American belief in French immorality. But at least in relation to Catholicism, such views coexisted with an equally strong sense of acting in unison with fellow defenders of the family across the Atlantic.

Defenders of the Mortara family on both sides of the Atlantic were, however, confronted with a major difficulty. As we have seen, opponents of the Vatican argued that, in removing a boy from his family, the church had infringed a fundamental social principle, the autonomy of the home. Yet at the same time, many of these same critics were coming to accept that another major institution had not only the right but also the responsibility to supervise and regulate the inner workings of the home. That institution was the state. More and more, a concern for the proper molding of future citizens was cited to justify state regulation of the home.[29] As early as 1839, the Pennsylvania Supreme Court had established a precedent for the forcible removal of children from parents who were judged unfit or abusive. By mid-century, the New York judiciary had firmly established the principle that parents had a legal obligation to support their children, a principle that overturned the previous conception of a nonenforceable moral duty. Parents who failed in this basic obligation risked the removal of their children. In France, the first piece of social legislation that was passed in the nineteenth century stemmed from this new concern with the protection of children: the law of 1841 limiting the duration of child factory labor. Under a law passed in 1851, private societies were invited to assume responsibility for abandoned or delinquent children; representatives of such societies were allowed to directly enter households to ascertain the condition of children thought to be at risk of abuse, even though the impact of this measure was limited by the fact that families could simply refuse them entry.

In practice, the state did not make any large-scale effort to monitor family life until the last decades of the century. In 1873, the first society dedicated to the prevention of cruelty to children was formed in New York, and the subsequent creation of similar organizations throughout the nation led to a raft of legislative measures designed to protect children. In France, a law passed in 1898 eventually gave judges the legal right to remove a child from parental control and assign guardianship to a state-run or charitable institution. However, while not yet finding substantial practical application, the argument that such measures were necessary in the interests of the nation was becoming pervasive at mid-century. The Larousse encyclopedia was very clear on this point:

> By leaving the domestic household, children will one day enter into this grand *family* which is called the fatherland and, in its name, society has the right to demand that it is supplied with men and not with brutes. Parents can thus be obliged...to give their children a certain degree of basic education which is indispensable to all citizens.[30]

This increasing acceptance of the state as a regulator of family life soon entered the Mortara controversy. Defenders of the Vatican cleverly exploited the tension between the ideal of the family as a private sphere whose boundaries could not be infringed, and the increasing readiness of the state to intervene in its workings. An argument repeatedly put forward by the Catholic press was that the rights of parents were not, in fact, inviolable, and that the state routinely interceded to ensure the welfare of children. According to the Catholic intellectual Orestes Brownson, "The natural rights of parents to the guardianship of their children are not so absolute that they can retain it, if they be incompetent or unfit to educate them, whether from moral or physical causes."[31] In France, the most determined of the church's defenders, Louis Veuillot, made a similar point: "As for the right of the father...this right has limits. In every country in the world, it happens that public authorities take the child from the father...in order to guarantee the life or morality of the child."[32]

Of course, as opponents of the Vatican argued, there was a vast difference between the state's intervening to protect a child from violent or neglectful parents, and the papal government's removing a boy on the grounds that, as a baptized Catholic, his soul was at risk from the influence of his Jewish family. At times, this argument that the Mortaras were unfit parents also seemed to stem from a deplorable anti-Semitism: both the *Univers* and *Brownson's Review* repeated the allegation that the boy was at risk of being murdered by his own parents if he were returned to them. The broader point, however—that the family unit was neither wholly self-governing nor immune to outside regulation—was increasingly finding concrete application in judicial ruling and government policy in both nations.

* * *

Another great issue that soon entered the debate over the future of Edgardo Mortara was slavery. It is perhaps not surprising that, in antebellum America, slavery would feature in the Mortara controversy. Opposition to slavery and opposition to Catholicism were, as scholars of nativism have long remarked, entirely compatible.[33] The ability to combine anti-Catholic and antislavery principles hinged on a number of factors. To begin with, the church in America was involved in the institution of slavery. The majority of Catholic newspapers in the North and South supported slavery, and some Catholic religious orders bought, sold, and traded slaves. The church in America gave very little support to abolitionism. From the 1850s, national pastoral councils stayed aloof from the issue for fear of attracting political controversy. Even the small number of Catholics who opposed slavery, such as Mathew Carey of Philadelphia, largely rejected an abolitionist movement which they identified with anti-Catholic bigotry. In the nineteenth century, Irish-Catholic immigrants were renowned for their hostility to abolitionism. Scholars in the field of "whiteness studies" have argued that an adherence to white racial supremacy was a strategy that allowed the Irish to gain acceptance in mainstream American society.[34] For contemporaries, however, the deep hostility to abolitionism evinced by Irish-Catholic immigrants was less a strategic choice than an expression of a fundamental affinity between Catholicism and slavery. In attacking abolitionism, the church in America was, in this argument, coming to the aid of a slave-owning class whose principles and beliefs it shared. The tripartite alliance between the church, the Democratic Party, and the South was thus understood by its opponents as a formidable grouping intent on extending slavery, whether in physical, intellectual, or moral terms, as far and as wide as possible.

Slavery, too, was seen to be as much a metaphor as a terrible reality. As Eric Foner has convincingly argued, a range of groups, from temperance and women's rights advocates to labor leaders, employed the language of slavery as a "master metaphor" for any subordinate, unequal position in society.[35] As a metaphor, slavery was particularly useful for opponents of Catholicism since it dramatized not only the sad state of the Catholic, but also their own awful fate if the church's suspected assault on the Republic were to succeed. Anti-Catholic literature often described the hierarchical relationships within the church—the priest over his flock, the Mother Superior over the nun, the Jesuit General over his novices—as directly akin to the dictatorial, ruthless authority enjoyed by the slave-owner over the slave. Like the slave, the Catholic was held in a state of utter mental and moral subjection. The preoccupation with the alleged sexual exploitation of Catholic nuns and the sexual crimes within convents was yet another indication of the imagined affinity between the church and slavery; abolitionists, too, often depicted the slaveholding South as a vast arena of unrestrained sexual debauchery.

The identification of slavery with Catholicism was apparent in other ways also. Above all, anti-Catholics argued that slavery and Catholicism shared the goal of expanding their reach, and thereby enslaving otherwise free Americans. The church, in this view, would always come to the aid of similarly ambitious Southern slave-owners. But the church's strategy was even more devious. By corrupting the fundamental institutions of American freedom, the ballot box and the public schools system, the church, according to its opponents, hoped to weaken any resistance to its power. The result would be nothing less than the enslavement of the Republic. As one nativist declared, "Fellow Citizens, there are two dangers which threaten our noble Republic. Between these two co-operating foes, the Papacy and Slavery, stands Young America sorely beset."[36]

To what extent, however, did slavery function as a metaphor for oppression and dependence in France? For Foner, the rhetorical use of slavery derived much of its power from the existence of chattel slavery in the Southern states; for this reason, he argues, whilst the metaphor of slavery was found in other countries in this period, it was only in the United States that it appeared particularly persuasive. In relation to the concept of "wage slavery," for example, Foner argues that "this vocabulary took on a special power in the United States. Because slavery was an immediate reality, not a distant symbol…the idea that the wage earner, because of economic dependence, was less than fully free retained considerable power as a criticism of the emerging order."[37]

For French anticlericals, however, this rhetoric of enslavement was extremely powerful. Like American anti-Catholics, French opponents of the church often employed this language to describe the extremes of unfettered authority and passive obedience which they identified with the Catholic Church. What, after all, was a slave? For Eugène Pelletan, a slave was "a man doomed from father to son to think with the brains and will through the volition of another; a man divested of the first sacred right of man, to wit, individuality…in a word, an artificial monster, a moral eunuch." A slave was, in Pelletan's terms, an "automaton."[38] Such a description perfectly matched the state of subservience which, French opponents of the church alleged, was imposed on Catholics by their hierarchy. In a rare expression of sympathy for priests, Jules Michelet pitied their "slavery" at the hands of the church.[39] The nun, too, was often termed a slave. Reflecting on the abuse and suffering she had endured as a nun in Naples, Enrichetta Caracciolo described Catholicism itself as "a machine of ignorance and of slavery."[40] Prey to sexual abuse, physical torture, and bound in a state of utter subjection to an often despotic Mother Superior, the position of the nun and the slave were clearly seen to be analogous. Describing the pitiful obedience of Carmelite nuns to their Superior, the heroine of *La religieuse*, the scandalous novel published by Jean-Hippolyte Michon in 1864, lamented that they "serve her like slaves."[41]

Like their American counterparts, French opponents of Catholicism also identified a more concrete social and political alliance between the church and slaveholders. The *Siècle* accused the church of propping up slave-owning elites throughout the New World. "It is sad," the paper declared, "to observe that the institution of slavery is held in honor above all amongst the Catholic nations of the new world." The paper went on to conclude that "the papacy indirectly encourages the owners of slaves to hold this human property."[42] In a preface to Oscar Comettant's account of his travels in the United States, Louis Jourdain, a fellow journalist at the *Siècle*, expressed his indignation at a Catholic clergy that lived "peacefully side by side with the slave."[43] Only a priesthood thoroughly imbued with the spirit of slave-owners, Jourdain suggested, could display such equanimity before the sight of human bondage.

Slavery, then, was as much a "master metaphor" for French opponents of Catholicism as for their American counterparts. It is worth considering the factors that maintained the vitality of this language of slavery in the French context. France, of course, had its own history of slavery in its colonies. The use of slavery as a metaphor for disempowerment and dependence was common during the French Revolution, a period that had witnessed fierce debates over abolition. By the time of the Mortara Affair, the final abolition of slavery, decreed a decade earlier in 1848, was a still recent reform. Yet this recourse to the language of slavery by French opponents of the Catholic Church can be largely explained not by the history of French slavery, but the continued and active French interest in the institution of chattel slavery in the American South. Amidst the broader fascination with the United States amongst French liberals and republicans in the period leading up to the Civil War, the question of slavery occupied a special place. Throughout this period, French commentators, including many leading opponents of Catholicism, had described, reflected upon, and condemned the institution of slavery. For this reason, French opponents of the church had access to a vital and widely understood language of enslavement and liberation in their campaign against Catholicism.

The most famous portrayal of Southern slavery to appear in France was, of course, Harriet Beecher Stowe's *Uncle Tom's Cabin*, which ran through eleven French editions within a year of its publication in 1852.[44] Though by far the most popular, *Uncle Tom's Cabin* was one of many denunciations of chattel slavery in the American South that captivated French readers. Another fictional account of American slavery, *The White Slave* by the historian and journalist Richard Hildreth, was published in six separate editions in the year after its appearance in France in 1853, often in a single volume with *Uncle Tom's Cabin*. The vogue amongst certain French liberals and republicans for the doctrines of William Ellery Channing extended to his antislavery writings; in 1855, Édouard Laboulaye translated Channing's *On Slavery*. The writings of other American abolitionists such as Theodore Parker and Frederick Douglass were regularly reviewed in journals such as *La Revue Des Deux Mondes*.

Of course, this fascination with slavery in the United States was not confined to opponents of Catholicism. Yet for French republicans and liberals who looked to the United States as a model of political and social advancement, the continued existence of slavery was a particular concern. Some French republicans, notably Victor Schoelcher, the leader of the campaign to abolish slavery in the French colonies, and the geographer Élisée Reclus, who toured Louisiana and Mississippi in 1854–1855, visited the American South. However, other leading republicans who had never experienced American slavery firsthand, such as Victor Hugo, threw their support behind the cause of abolition. It is hardly coincidental, then, that many of the key American antislavery texts were translated by republicans who were also deeply hostile to Catholicism. Among the many translators of both *Uncle Tom's Cabin* and *The White Slave* was Jean-Mamert Cayla, who would go on to write a series of pamphlets denouncing the sexual crimes which, he alleged, were rampant in Catholic convents and monasteries. Another was Emile de la Bédollière, a journalist for the *Siècle*, who often denounced the policies of the Vatican.

Given this shared propensity on both sides of the Atlantic to associate Catholicism with slavery, the issue inevitably intruded into the controversy over the fate of Edgardo Mortara. Defenders of the Mortara family in the United States attributed the neutral position of the Buchanan administration to a sinister political coalition between the slaveholding South and a Democratic Party reliant on the votes of Irish Catholics. For the Chicago *Daily Democrat*, the unwillingness of the administration to launch a diplomatic protest against the Vatican's actions was a natural consequence of its pro-slavery principles:

> An Administration which defended slavery; not only defended and apologized for it, but glorified it as a moral and religious institution, could not protest against the gross injustice of tearing a child from its parents. Does not slavery daily tear children from their parents and parents from their children?... How could a pro-slavery Administration, then... denounce the sins of others when their own are as scarlet as the driven snow [sic].[45]

A resolution passed by the Pennsylvania antislavery convention in December 1858 made a similar point. Having praised the campaign to have Edgardo Mortara returned to his family, the convention lamented that the American government "dare not intervene even by word against this outrage, lest it should bring upon itself the jeers and derision of the whole civilized world."[46]

For American opponents of slavery, the Mortara Affair was thus an extremely useful tool for denouncing the tripartite alliance between the Catholic Church, the Democratic Party, and pro-slavery forces. The fact that the press commentary on the case reached a peak during congressional elections in some states only magnified the appeal of such a tactic. In Illinois, the Republican press repeatedly called on Jewish voters to express their hostility to the union of Catholic and pro-slavery forces by abandoning the Democratic Party. On the day of the election, the *Chicago Tribune* recounted the facts of the Mortara case to remind voters of the alliance between Catholicism and the defenders of Southern slavery. The election, the paper declared, would decide "the strength of the Catholicism and Slavery when united for an unholy purpose, and when opposed by the combination of all that is tolerant in religion, liberal in politics and progressive in society." By voting for the Republican Party, Jews would express their support for "the preservation of the tolerance and equality which are the basis of our institutions, and which are now threatened by the cooperation of the two elements of Despotism."[47]

In France, defenders of the Mortara family invoked slavery just as often. In an editorial in the *Journal des Débats,* Louis Alloury specifically compared the position of Jews in the Papal States to that of Africans at the time of the slave trade. In particular, Alloury expressed his hope that "the trade in Jews will be condemned, proscribed and abolished in the civilized world in the same way as the negro trade has been."[48] Writing in the *Siècle*, Léon Plee also depicted the removal of Edgardo Mortara as a crime that recalled the evils of the Atlantic slave trade: "While slavery is gradually abolished and the slave trade is prosecuted as a crime by all nations, do not authorize paternal expropriation, the kidnapping of children from their fathers."[49]

Slavery was also invoked to discredit the arguments advanced by defenders of the Vatican, notably that Edgardo was happier in the House of Catechumens than he had been in his home. In a long editorial, Louis Alloury compared the Vatican's insistence that Edgardo Mortara was treated better in his new position to the claims of American slaveholders to be acting in the best interests of their slaves. Both claims, Alloury argued, were specious:

> The great argument put forth by the partisans of slavery in the United States is that black slaves enjoy an incomparable well-being and happiness in the home of their masters. In the same way, those who wish to justify the kidnapping of the young Israelite have tried to tell us that they understand "what happiness it is for him to be Christian, and that he blesses the servant who baptized him." Whether applied to negro slaves or to the child at Bologna, this argument has the same effect for us. Slavery, kidnapping and violence cannot be either justified or excused.[50]

Defenders of the Mortara family did not, however, enjoy a monopoly over the use of slavery as a political metaphor. In both the United States and France, pro-Catholic advocates also referred to slavery in an effort to undermine the arguments of their opponents. In an article that was subsequently translated and published in the American press, *L'Univers* noted that those Americans calling for their government to lodge a protest with the papal government would hardly tolerate a similar action from European states on Southern slavery: "No one ever heard that the Christian and philanthropic governments of Europe made representations to the Government of the United States, with a view that the negroes of the slave states should in future be treated like Christians and human beings, and that at any rate when a family was sold it should be sold to one master."[51] American Catholics soon followed the French paper's lead. Orestes Brownson referred to Americans who urged their government to intervene on behalf of the Mortara family as hypocrites. In a coded reference to slavery, Brownson wrote: "Our own 'domestic institutions' are quite as unintelligible to those of other countries, and far more liable to become the matter of censure: but whatever individuals may opine in regard to them, we know of no instance in which men in authority denounce them."[52]

Northern abolitionists with little sympathy for the Catholic Church in turn accused defenders of the Mortara family of hypocrisy for remaining silent while slave families were routinely split apart at auction. The *Independent*, a paper that had strongly criticized the Vatican in relation to the Mortara case, conceded that there were "multitudes of cases worse than that much nearer to our own doors."[53] In a subsequent edition, the paper reported just such a case—that of a free black man in Washington D.C. who had been tried and convicted for harboring his son, a runaway slave—that starkly demonstrated the contempt for the family at the heart of slavery.[54] Even a vehemently anti-Catholic journal such as the *Zion's Herald and Wesleyan Journal* was forced to acknowledge that the Catholic allusions to the double standard adopted by the Vatican's opponents were "apt."[55]

* * *

For years after the events of 1858, the name Mortara served as a byword for Catholic intolerance and cruelty. Subsequent cases involving the removal of children from their families were compared to the great scandal of 1858. In 1864, for example, the dramatist and historian Prosper Mérimée, in a letter to his friend Antonio Panizzi, described a case in Rome of a Jewish boy called Cohen who had also been surreptitiously baptized. The case, he wrote, was a "new edition of the Mortara Affair."[56] Memories of the Affair remained equally fresh in the United States. Just as they had done in the midst of the scandal, the pro-Republican press continued to invoke the name Mortara to rally Jewish voters. In the presidential election of 1876, *Harper's Weekly* demanded, "What Hebrew can give his support to those savage Churchmen who tore the Mortara child from his parents?"[57]

By then, the fate of Edgardo Mortara was no longer in doubt. To the satisfaction of the Vatican's defenders, he had embraced the Catholic Church. In 1873, he was ordained as a priest, and five years later, in his first meeting with his mother since 1858, he tried to convert her to Catholicism. On March 11, 1940, Edgardo Mortara died at the abbey of the Canons Regular in Bouhay, Belgium.

Within both France and the United States, the Mortara Affair significantly intensified opposition to the Vatican. Scholars of anti-Catholicism in the United States, bound by their preoccupation with the effects of Catholic immigration, have overlooked the scandal. Yet it is clear that no account of hostility to Catholicism in either France or the United States can be written without reference to the controversy over Edgardo Mortara. This was not the only controversy surrounding the Vatican in this period. From the Dogma of the Immaculate Conception to the convocation of the Ecumenical Council, there was a series of Vatican initiatives around which international opposition could coalesce. Yet the Mortara Affair was special because it struck a very personal note. In the wake of the removal of Edgardo Mortara, many mothers and fathers in France and the United States imagined the Catholic Church targeting their own families. Whether through the wiles of the confessor, the luring of a daughter into a convent, or simply, as it was understood by the defenders of the Mortaras, a kidnapping, the church appeared a threat not just to Jewish families, but to all families. The Mortara Affair resonated with many people because, like so much of the campaign against the Catholic Church, it concerned individual happiness as well as national stability. By undermining the family, the very bedrock of society, the Vatican appeared intent on fomenting social disorder. However, as the sad fate of Momolo and Marianna Mortara so vividly demonstrated, the church was just as capable of reducing men and women to utter misery.

For its opponents, the church was guilty of inflicting such anguish even on its own members. In particular, the celibate priest and nun struggling to subdue their sexual instincts became a compelling image of the inhumanity at the heart of Catholicism. The corrosive effects of ecclesiastical celibacy provided some of the most persuasive points of evidence in the Transatlantic case against Catholicism.

3
Natural or Unnatural? Doctors and the Vow of Celibacy

Throughout the middle decades of the nineteenth century, few elements of Catholic rite attracted as much condemnation as ecclesiastical celibacy. Opponents of Catholic celibacy began with the blunt assertion that the sexual instinct was a legitimate and powerful element within the human constitution which could never entirely be contained. Speaking in 1856 to the Pennsylvania Assembly, the future Republican congressman and Minister Resident to Turkey, E. Joy Morris, declared in a speech opposing the establishment of monastic orders on American soil that "the natural passions are not to be suppressed by mere vows and the formal restraint of rules and regulations."[1] Worse than futile, the attempt to remain celibate was held to intensify sexual desire, leading to a desperate battle between body and mind with only two possible outcomes. The victim might suffer a mental breakdown. But in what seemed to many a more likely outcome, enforced celibacy would create a build-up of desire which could only be alleviated through a sudden erotic frenzy. This vision of the celibate Catholic as either deranged or lustful was contained in a pamphlet published by the Presbyterian Board of Publications. The author claimed to have been acquainted with many Catholic priests whose desire "long resisted, seized them at length, like madness. Two I knew who died insane: hundreds might be found who avoid that fate by a life of settled systematic vice."[2]

In France, opposition to the vow of celibacy was framed in identical terms. The figure of the male priest wrestling with sexual desire had become almost a cliché in French literature by mid-century. Frollo, the cleric tormented by his lust for Esmeralda in Victor Hugo's *Nôtre Dame de Paris*, was one of the most famous literary depictions, but a range of writers took on the theme. In a review of one such novel, Alfred Assollant's *La confession de l'abbé Passereau*, the anticlerical *Opinion Nationale* described the central message of the story in the following terms: "M. Assollant has been struck by this truth which appears, to us, elementary, but which the Church has obstinately denied for centuries: the priest is a man."[3] Such was the popularity of this subject in French literature that Emile Zola was greatly troubled by the difficulty of devising an original angle for *La faute de l'abbé Mouret*, his story of illicit passion between a priest and a young woman; as he complained, "The priest in love with another being, wrestling with the hot fever of passion, feeling his heart swell and explode the vows which bind him, is a hero whose poignant, profoundly human struggles have tempted a great many contemporary novelists."[4]

While the celibate Catholic could sometimes attract sympathy as the victim of an inhuman institution, the priest in particular was more often cast as a figure of menace. In their effort to discredit the church-run education system, anticlericals cited judicial statistics on the sexual crimes committed by teaching brothers, crimes which they often attributed to the celibate vows.[5] Driven mad by the constant battle against his desire, the celibate priest appeared capable, in the eyes of opponents of the church, of nothing less than murder. For French anticlericals, the crimes committed by the infamous *curé* Mingrat stood as a constant reminder of the social toll exacted by the vow of celibacy. In 1822 Mingrat, the *curé* of Saint-Quentin, was found guilty of the brutal murder of one of his mistresses, for whom he had acted as confessor. In a judgment that later generations would continue to cite, the literary critic and leading liberal of the Restoration period, Antoine Jay, concluded that the case of Mingrat proved "to what excess of barbarism men can reach when the most energetic urge of nature is blocked."[6] In France, the figure of Mingrat was still being invoked by opponents of celibacy thirty years after his crimes. Hugo denounced Mingrat in *Les Châtiments*, one of his most vitriolic attacks on the Catholic Church. In its entry on the sinister priest, the Larousse encyclopedia suggested that the vow of celibacy was largely responsible for turning Mingrat into a murderous sexual predator. Mingrat's infamy even reached the United States, where a lengthy account of his crimes appeared in nativist works such as *Pope or President?*[7]

Such attacks on Catholic celibacy were not new. Martin Luther had made his marriage to Catherine von Bora one of the starkest demonstrations of his rejection of the Vatican, and ribald descriptions of convent life had long been based on the presumption that the vow of celibacy was an unnatural brake on human desire. What was novel to the nineteenth century was the manner in which medical writers threw their considerable weight into this discussion. For although politicians, theologians, and pamphleteers might blithely assert that ecclesiastical celibacy was an impossible and destructive imposition on the mind and body, doctors armed with the tools of science and rational inquiry set out to prove or disprove the point. On both sides of the Atlantic, medical writers thus assumed a leading role in the debate over Catholic celibacy.

These medical writers were diverse in training and in orientation. Some were the elite of the emerging medical profession, men whose work was intended largely for their peers, and who were keen to denounce as quacks and charlatans those physicians aiming at a more popular audience. But many others, such as Auguste Debay in France or Frederick Hollick in America, were proud popularizers intent on satisfying the great public thirst for accessible guides to health and healing. These physicians offered their readers prescriptions for healthy living which covered an enormous range of topics, from clothing to diet to the design of houses, and they were not afraid to deal with the sensitive issues of sex and reproduction. Particularly in America, many popular medical writers were avowed opponents of allopathic medical practice and espoused alternative theories such as hydrotherapy, homeopathy or phrenology. Some courted controversy by advocating contraception; in this area in particular, some merely adopted medical pseudonyms to bolster the credibility of their works. The term "medical writers", as I use it in this chapter, encompasses a broad range of practitioners, from the elite to the authors of popular health manuals which proliferated throughout the nineteenth century.

Recognizing the central role played by medical writers in the debate over Catholic celibacy offers a new understanding of the medicalization of sexuality in the nineteenth century. In Michel Foucault's famous argument, a fundamental shift in authority occurred in post-Enlightenment societies as the priest was displaced by the doctor as the authority on questions of sexual morality.[8] By the end of the century, a new alliance of medical men and state institutions had come to dominate the regulation of sexual practice, a transfer of power that occurred at the expense of, among other institutions, the church. Yet a reading of the medical discourse on celibacy also suggests that we should not exaggerate the extent to which medicine usurped religion. The two forces, religious and medical, remained interlinked. In part, this was a question of personnel. In France, where female Catholic religious comprised a large percentage of the hospital staff, the presence of Catholicism at the heart of the medical establishment was difficult to ignore. Far from simply ceding their traditional authority to doctors, these Catholic nurses continued to wield great influence within medical institutions.[9]

The intermeshing of religion and science went even further as doctors invoked the tools of modern science both to attack and to defend the Catholic Church. A number of scholars have noted the prominence of French physicians in the anticlerical movement.[10] Yet many doctors also rallied to the church, particularly in the middle decades of the century. For them, there seemed to be no contradiction between the claims of religion and of science. As Dr. Théodore Perrin declared in a report to the Medical Society of Lyon, physicians could still effect "a treaty of alliance between theology and medicine, a reconciliation between science and religion."[11] For these doctors, the relationship between Catholicism and medical science was one of cooperation rather than antagonism. Whether cast in a positive or negative light, the Catholic priest and nun assumed a key place within medical discourses. Some medical writers tried to discredit the vows of celibacy as contrary to the laws of science; others refuted such claims, and offered the church a physiological defense of celibacy. Very few doctors, however, chose to ignore Catholicism. Rather than a simple transition of authority from priest to doctor, Catholicism remained at the heart of debates about sexuality in the nineteenth century.

This medical debate about Catholic celibacy is another example of the movement of books and ideas across the Atlantic. Like the broader flow of works which were hostile to Catholicism, the vast bulk of this medical literature went from France to the United States. This was a reflection of the great prestige enjoyed by French medicine in the nineteenth century. French doctors exercised a crucial influence over their American counterparts in the middle decades of the century. Attracted by a range of factors—a reputation for excellence, the absence of tuition fees and the availability of cadavers for dissection—American doctors flocked to Paris to complete their training.[12] At the same time, monographs by French physicians on a range of illnesses and treatments were translated into English and published in the United States, often in multiple editions. In making the case against ecclesiastical celibacy, then, American physicians drew heavily on the work of their French colleagues.

* * *

The medical case against celibacy began with the assertion that the sexual instinct was a normal and healthy component of the human body which, if expressed in a manner deemed to be "reasonable" or "moderate," provided a range of physical and mental benefits. In France, a range of physicians declared that physical desire, like the appetite for food and drink, was a powerful and legitimate need whose attempted suppression entailed an enormous mental and physical cost. The celebrated physician Claude-François Lallemand bluntly stated that "the vow of chastity does not suit even the coldest of temperaments: absolute continence...is sooner or later fatal to individuals."[13] In 1858 Dr. Menville de Ponsan affirmed, in his *Histoire philosophique et médicale de la femme*, that "wherever a being breathes, he is under pressure to obey the most imperious of instincts"; de Ponsan went on to specify that the instinct to which he referred was that "which brings him to reproduce."[14] For Dr. Louis Seraine, the writings of the Classical era retained their authority on this subject. Citing Plutarch, Seraine argued that the power of the sexual drive was divinely sanctioned: "Sexual love must have its role in the life of man, and the Creator has clearly shown his will in this regard by making this instinct an almost irresistible force."[15]

Those Americans who were convinced that French society was morally corrupt would not have found such declarations surprising. However, American medical writers were just as willing to acknowledge the commanding role played by the erotic drive. In his *Ladies' Medical Guide*, Dr. Seth Pancoast, who lectured at the Pennsylvania Medical University before devoting himself to his expanding private practice, declared that the "passion of sexual love" was akin to the "the appetite for food" in its claims for satisfaction.[16] The English physician Robert James Culverwell, whose books circulated widely in the United States, described at some length the force and function of sexual desire. In *The Institutes of Marriage*, Culverwell affirmed that "we have the most powerful of all human desires planted within us, and that is the sexual desire." Such desire, he argued, had not been created merely to ensure the reproduction of the species, but as a means of creating pleasure and maintaining the proper functioning of the body. At times, Culverwell even suggested that sex, rather than an expression of love, might play the primordial role in shaping sentimental relations. "Love," he wrote, "is not the parent of sexual desire—it is the offspring."[17] A similar emphasis on the positive power of sex was contained in the later writings of the phrenologist Orson Squires Fowler. Love, he argued in his magisterial *Creative and Sexual Science*, "comes from the sexual organs in action;" Fowler then cited the familiar metaphor of appetite and food. The relationship between love and the reproductive organs, Fowler continued, was "precisely what appetite and the digestive organs are to each other."[18]

Admittedly, for many doctors this sexual need appeared less pressing for women than for men. Many of the physicians who confidently proclaimed sexual desire an irresistible element in human physiology balanced such views with the qualification that women, in the words of the French doctor Léopold Deslandes, "participate in this act more than they initiate it." Deslandes went on to affirm that "it is therefore an incontestable fact that generally women are less sensual than men."[19] However, this assumption did not lead doctors to conclude that women were entirely oblivious to sexual desire. In much of this medical literature, the belief that the sexual instinct was an irresistible element in the human constitution was applied both to men and women, though with greater insistence in the case of the former.

One of the most common places in which this argument was found was the literature justifying the use of contraception. For proponents of contraception, the famous argument put by Malthus that sexual abstinence was the best means of limiting population growth was founded on an unrealistic assessment of human nature. An honest approach to human sexuality would conclude, in this view, that abstinence was impractical and that family size could be limited only through contraception. Charles Knowlton's *Fruits of Philosophy*, perhaps the most notorious guide to contraception in nineteenth-century America, made this point clear by referring to Catholic figures: "Malthus, an English writer on the subject of population, gives us none but celibacy to a late age. But how foolish it is to suppose that men and women will become as monks and nuns during the very holiday of their existence."[20] The central message of such works, some of which were bestsellers, was that the demands of the sexual drive could not simply be ignored.[21] In his *Science of Reproduction and Reproductive Control*, the purported New York physician Dr. J. Soule dismissed the arguments in favor of sexual abstinence as a means of limiting family size. As he wrote, "*absolute* continence is *absolutely* impracticable."[22]

French doctors were a key source of information for American advocates of contraception. Most of these guides cite France as the country in which the art of limiting family size had been most successfully developed, and American authors of works on contraception often assumed a French identity to bolster their credibility. In 1842 the first American edition of a work entitled *The Physiologist, or Sexual Physiology Revealed* appeared. The book's author, Dr. Eugene Becklard, who was described as "one of the most distinguished physicians of France," argued that since adult men and women could no more suppress their sexual appetites than their desire for food or drink, contraception was the only satisfactory method of controlling family size. Dr. Becklard, however, did not exist; the entire work was, in the words of the *Philadelphia Medical Examiner*, nothing but a "trumpery and indecent production."[23] Despite such condemnation on the part of the medical establishment, the public seemed not to detect the fraud, or perhaps not to care: the book was published twice in New York, three times in Boston, and once in Philadelphia.

Public declarations of the central place of sexual desire also came from more reputable figures. In France, leading members of the medical establishment argued not only that sexual desire was natural, but also that abstinence, far from being commendable, was a direct path to physical decline and moral degradation. Medical dictionaries were very clear on this point. The *Dictionaire des sciences médicales*, which remained a key reference work well after its initial publication in 1813, offered this harrowing description of the effects of sexual abstinence: "It is not rare to see, amongst people of both sexes, an abstinence which is too prolonged lead to hideous pustules covering the surface of the body, and especially the forehead."[24] Such grim warnings of the physical deformities wrought by sexual abstinence were also made by American medical writers, and notably one of the most successful authors and lecturers of the era, Dr Frederick Hollick. The author of eleven books, Hollick also became a successful, if controversial lecturer on medical topics; in 1846 he was put on trial for obscene libel, a charge of which he was acquitted. In *The Marriage Guide*, a work which first appeared in 1850 and was published in scores of editions, Hollick argued that sexual excitement played an important role in maintaining physical vitality. "It is very seldom the case," according to Hollick, "that there is perfect health without it, and scarcely ever is there an exemption from severe nervous affections."[25] As proof, Hollick cited the cases of eunuchs who, denied the regenerative power of the sexual organs, become "stunted or deformed in body, imbecile in mind, and perverse in disposition."[26] But while the eunuch had been deprived of his sexual organs, the case of those living in celibacy was just as dire. Total sexual abstinence, Hollick argued, led to physical diseases for both men and women, while inducing "the most singular and distressing vagaries of mind and thought."[27]

Physicians offered a variety of explanations for the manner in which celibacy "destroyed" men and women. One of the most common was that shunning sexual relations would only encourage that practice which, perhaps more than any other in the nineteenth century, was feared for its baleful effects on the human constitution, masturbation. The range of evils attributed to masturbation was virtually endless, ranging from hair loss to cancer to insanity. Among the many habits and customs which encouraged the practice, physicians included the effort to refrain from sexual relations. In his *De l'Onanisme et des autres abus vénériens*, a work which was published in the United States in three separate editions between 1838 and 1841, Léopold Deslandes cited celibacy as "the only cause of onanism."[28]

For men, sexual abstinence was thought to induce another feared sexual disorder, *spermatorrhea*, or the involuntary loss of seminal fluid. Untreated, *spermatorrhea* was said to progressively weaken the sufferer's body and mind. Following the first symptoms of listlessness and fatigue, the patient would begin to feel a dull pain in his groin; as the emissions continued, constipation, watery eyes and memory loss would set in. At length, the condition would lead to epilepsy or some other nervous disorder, and a premature death. The acknowledged expert on *spermatorrhea* was the French physician Claude-François Lallemand, whose three-volume study *Des pertes séminales involontaires* was translated and published, in both abridged and complete forms, in seven separate American editions from 1839 to 1866. For Lallemand, one of the main causes of the disease was the attempt to live in a state of perfect sexual continence. For men with healthy sexual organs, celibacy created, Lallemand wrote, "a kind of torture which may induce the most serious abuses," among which were "abundant and frequent nocturnal pollutions."[29]

In the case of women, the most common disorder associated with an absence of sexual relations was hysteria. Physicians from antiquity had attributed the onset of hysteria to the accumulation of female sperm in the uterus, a condition which could only be relieved through sexual intercourse. By the mid-nineteenth century this explanation for hysteria had been refuted, but theorists of the disease continued to cite a lack of sexual intercourse as a key causal factor. In France, one of the leading theorists of hysteria at mid-century, Dr. Hector Landouzy, adjunct professor at the Reims School of Medicine, argued that the "genital influence" remained predominant in the development of the disease.[30] For Landouzy, the classical identification between the uterus and hysteria remained fundamentally valid; while the precise mechanism by which hysteria occurred remained unclear, Landouzy identified the "viciation" of bodily organs as a key contributing factor. This "viciation" occurred when, as he wrote, "an organ is deprived of the function for which it has been created."[31] In adopting the state of celibacy, a woman was guilty of not employing her reproductive organs, thereby inviting the "viciation" which led to hysteria. The cure for hysteria was therefore obvious. Though careful to emphasize that sexual union would not cure forms of hysteria which had been brought on by, for example, a hereditary predisposition to the disease, Landouzy considered sexual intercourse to be an otherwise effective treatment. In comparison to epilepsy, where it was most often harmful, sexual union in cases of hysteria was, he argued, most often effective as a cure.

Landouzy's work had a wide influence in the United States. The New York obstetrician Gunning S. Bedford praised Landouzy as the leading authority on the causes of hysteria. Bedford enjoyed both a large public readership and an impeccable professional reputation. Founder of the University Medical Clinic in New York, his *The Diseases of Women and Children* went through five editions within two years of its publication, and was one of the few mid-century American medical works to be translated and published in France. In another work, *Clinical Lectures on the Diseases of Women and Children*, Bedford referred specifically to Landouzy in support of his assertion that the major cause of hysteria was what he termed "the irritation of the sexual organs." To prove the link between disorders of the reproductive organs and hysteria, Bedford reproduced Landouzy's statistical tables and agreed with his conclusion that the majority of hysterical cases occurred between the ages of fifteen and thirty-five, a period when the influence of the genitals on the rest of the body was thought to be greatest. Though such disturbances in the reproductive organs could be attributed to a range of factors, one of the chief culprits, for Bedford as for Landouzy, was an absence of sexual relations.[32]

More broadly, many doctors condemned celibacy as a fatal disruption of the body's inherent equilibrium. Just as men and women were thought to possess complementary physical and intellectual attributes which kept the relations between the sexes in harmony, the proper functioning of the body was held to be dependent on a regular usage of all its component parts. If any one element was neglected or over-used, the vitality of the whole would be lost. The celibate, then, by leaving his or her reproductive organs idle, upset this delicate balance, and with disastrous consequences. Perhaps the most influential proponent of this view was a former army surgeon who would become the most successful popularizer of medical theories in nineteenth-century France, Auguste Debay. First published in 1848, Debay's *Hygiène et physiologie du mariage* had reached its 172nd edition by 1883. Like so many opponents of celibacy, Debay began by arguing that the attempted suppression of the sexual instinct would only inflame it. But in a key passage of the book, Debay came to the fundamental problem with celibacy. Sex, he argued, was essential for both men and women to maintain their inner harmony:

> The general law of harmony requires a moderate exercise of all the organs in our physical structures. If one of the organs is condemned to absolute repose, the other organs soon suffer, and since the perfect equilibrium of all functions has been destroyed, health is affected and illnesses follow. The genital act is, therefore, a necessity for man and for woman; its absolute privation can only be harmful to the physical and moral health of the individual.[33]

For opponents of Catholic celibacy, these declarations of the ghastly effects of sexual abstinence by popular and respected physicians supported their case that the imposition of such a vow was both cruel and futile. The implications of these medical theories for the wider debate on Catholic celibacy thus seemed clear. But in a far more direct intervention in the argument over ecclesiastical celibacy, medical writers specifically cited the ruined health and deranged mind of the priest and nun to prove their contentions. The Catholic clergy were prey, these doctors alleged, to a range of physical and nervous disorders whose chief cause was an unnatural state of sexual abstinence. In the haggard expression of a priest wrestling with his desires, or the shrunken body of the childless nun, the physician's eye could immediately discern the withering touch of celibacy.

In France, medical dictionaries were replete with references to the celibate Catholic. In his entry on celibacy in the *Dictionaire des sciences médicales*, Dr. Charles-Chrétien Marc, a founder of the *Annales d'Hygiène Publique et de Medicine Légale* and personal physician to King Louis Philippe, concluded with a long reflection on the state of nuns and priests. For Marc, the majority took their vows before their sexual faculties were fully developed; some years later, by now caught in a terrible struggle with their desires, the folly of what he called their "crazy vow" became only too apparent: "the darkest sadness takes hold of them, illness overwhelms them, and from the good spouses they would have been, they become bad priests."[34] In order to prevent such cases, Marc argued that the state should mandate a minimum age for the taking of religious vows. For women, Marc suggested, the minimum age should be thirty-two, while for men it should be forty!

Statistical surveys of life expectancy rates among the clergy compared to those among the laity were invoked as proof of the harmful effects of the celibacy vow. In an editorial, the *Nation* cited the results of a survey conducted by the French physician Dr. Alexandre Mayer. For both the male and female clergy between the ages of sixteen and twenty-five, the mortality rate was 2.68. The rate among the laity in the same age group, however, was 1.48. Between the ages of thirty-one and forty, the respective mortality rates were 4.4 and 2.74. Mayer, as we shall see, considered such results to be misleading, and went on to argue that celibacy was not in fact physically damaging. But for the editors of the *Nation*, the bare evidence of Mayer's figures showed that celibacy was injurious to health and morals, particularly as his figures closely matched those obtained in 1743 by the French statistician Antoine Deparcieux. The effects of celibacy, the journal noted, were clearly "more prejudicial than advantageous."[35]

For nineteenth-century French physicians, the work of one of the most celebrated naturalists of the Enlightenment, George-Louis Leclerc, comte de Buffon, provided incontrovertible proof of the mental and physical disorders suffered by the celibate priest. In his *Histoire naturelle de l'homme*, Buffon included a letter which had been addressed to him by a priest who became known as the *curé* of Réole. In this letter, the priest vividly described his battle to suppress his sexual desires, as well as the psychological disorders, ranging from periods of delirium to ongoing hallucinations and furious acts of violence, with which he had been afflicted.[36] Leading physicians of the early nineteenth century such as Cabanis and Esquirol cited the case of the *curé* of Réole to prove that sexual continence could provoke episodes of mental illness, and Buffon's account had lost little of its persuasive power by the mid-nineteenth century. In his influential study of the causes of sterility and impotence, Dr. Félix Roubaud warned of the damaging effects brought on by any attempt to suppress the sexual instinct. For proof of what he referred to as the "infinite evils" which any attempt to maintain a strict chastity would inflict, Roubaud referred to the most famous example of a person he termed a "victim of chastity," the *curé* of Réole.[37] Michel Lèvy, author of *Traité d'hygiène publique et privée*, noted that Buffon's *curé* had only recovered his reason following "abundant pollutions."[38] (Such "pollutions," of course, ran the risk of inducing the dreaded disease *spermatorrhea*.) In his *Traité des maladies mentales*, Benedict-Auguste Morel acknowledged the authority of Buffon's account in demonstrating the link between mental illness and celibacy: "All the authors who have dealt with this matter relate the description left to us by Buffon of the nervous accidents due to this cause."[39] So regular were the references to the *curé* of Réole in medical literature that one Catholic doctor was led to make the following complaint: "it's an observation that everyone cites, everyone repeats endlessly, to such a degree that one can believe oneself permitted to think that it is about the only case of this type."[40]

Perhaps in response to such criticisms, nineteenth-century physicians found their own sickly and suffering priests. In support of his treatise on the causes of "nocturnal pollutions," Dr. Lallemand cited correspondence from "many respectable priests" which demonstrated the importance of sexual abstinence as a causal factor. In the case of a forty-year-old priest suffering from stomach pain, fatigue and a loss of memory, Lallemand concluded that "the absolute continence in which this priest has lived must have helped to maintain this disposition."[41] In fact, Lallemand suggested, the debilitating effects of *spermatorrhea* appeared to be rampant in seminaries whose novices were "pale, thin, exhausted, less by diet, inactivity or bad habits, than by nocturnal pollutions."[42] For Dr. Deslandes, the debilitating effects of "onanism" were everywhere visible in the Catholic orders; as he wrote, the revolting habit "fastens itself to monastic orders as a consequence and punishment for vows that are contrary to the laws of the human body."[43] The sexual disorders wrought by the vow of celibacy seemed, to Deslandes, pervasive: "Satyriasis, nymphomania, hysteria, convulsions and other illnesses, have often had no other source than a struggle of religious faith against the senses."[44] Dr. Louis Seraine agreed that hallucinations and hysteria were pervasive in monasteries and convents. Both priests and nuns, he wrote, were prey to passions which "wear out...the animal economy and accelerate the illnesses of a hasty ageing."[45]

American physicians made less reference to the Catholic clergy than their French colleagues. However, many of the bestselling contraceptive guides written under medical pseudonyms chose the priest as an exemplary lesson in the dangers of a strict adherence to the rule of celibacy. In his guide to contraception, the fictitious Dr. Soule cited the case of a priest bound by a vow of celibacy who, like Buffon's *curé*, was prone to delusions and bouts of hysteria. "At this period," Soule reported, "he fixed his eyes on two women, who made such an impression on him, that they appeared to be illuminated, and to glitter with an electric fire, so that he retired, thinking it was an illusion of the devil."[46] The anonymous author posing as the esteemed Dr. Eugene Becklard also cited cases involving priests tormented by their vow of celibacy, including one in Bordeaux who, unable to "starve out his desires" had tried to expel them by putting a bullet into his heart.[47]

The fate of the celibate nun received specific attention. In his entry in the *Dictionaire des sciences médicales,* Dr. Marc claimed that all the serious disorders to which celibate women were subject—irregularities in menstrual flow, paleness, dull pains, mental instability—could be observed "among the inhabitants of cloisters."[48] In his bestselling treatises, Auguste Debay referred extensively to priests and nuns. As he proudly affirmed, physiologists were no longer "fooled" by the vows of perpetual celibacy taken by monks and nuns; modern medical science had proven that only those whose anatomy was deformed or incomplete through, for example, the absence of genital organs, could possibly resist the longings of their sexual instinct. Debay then related the sad case of a young woman who, having been forced into a convent by her family, had experienced a swift decline in health. First, Debay recorded, she "slipped into a deep state of exhaustion, then passed through all the stages of hysteria, erotomania and nymphomania."[49] Fortunately, the cure was at hand—a prompt marriage. Today, Debay reported, the woman was a wife and mother, and "remarkable for her sweetness of character."[50] Debay's message was clear: the imposition of the vow of celibacy was such an affront to human nature that it could only lead to insanity, death or, in the case of the hypocritical, utter vice, and this was proven by the pitiful state of Catholic nuns. Referring to two of the ailments most commonly associated with women, Debay concluded that "the convent and the confessional are the cradle of hysteria and nymphomania."[51]

Such French descriptions of sickly nuns were often reprinted by American doctors. Both James Ashton, the author of a popular guide to contraception, and Dr. Frederick Hollick, author of *The Marriage Guide*, cited the work of the leading French physician Hermann Pidoux to prove that nuns were prone to a range of genital disorders.[52] Hollick borrowed from other French authors as well. In a work entitled *Facts for the Feeble*, Hollick argued that women who for religious reasons repressed their sexual desires were vulnerable to what he termed an "uncontrollable erotic furor." For this reason, Hollick continued in terms that echoed those of Debay, "in France, it is a common proverb that the Convent and the Confessional are the Parents of Hysteria and Nymphomania!"[53] Even without reference to their French colleagues, many American physicians appeared convinced that the celibate nun was certain to be afflicted with a variety of illnesses. Dr. George Henry Napheys, author of *The Physical Life of Woman*, a work which sold fifty thousand copies in its first year of publication, argued strongly that married women enjoyed better health than single women, and looked to female religious communities for proof of this contention. "Too often the history of those sisterhoods who assume vows of singleness in the interest of religion," Napheys concluded, "presents to the physician the sad spectacle of prolonged nervous maladies."[54]

A lengthier account of the poor health of Catholic nuns was found in Dr. Seth Pancoast's *The Ladies' Medical Guide*. Having expressed his belief that the sexual drive could no more be suppressed than the desire for food, Pancoast described the religious vow of chastity as essentially futile. For Pancoast, "men and women who, from religious zeal, devote themselves to an eternal chastity, often contract an obligation which is above human power to fulfill." Even worse, the struggle to maintain this impossible vow would, according to Pancoast, incite a range of sexual disorders with disastrous moral results. Absolute continence, he wrote, would cause "sexual frenzy in males" and in women "the use of horrible means of sexual gratification."[55] For proof, Pancoast referred explicitly to renowned episodes of madness and hysteria among communities of nuns. In one such case, Pancoast reported to his readers, the nuns, driven mad by what he termed "erotomania," had begun to bite each other.[56]

Another popular medical author, Edward Bliss Foote, cited the example of nuns to prove a different malady caused by celibacy. Foote was a pioneering advocate of birth control and the author of two of the most popular medical guides of the nineteenth century, *Medical Common Sense* and *Plain Home Talk*. In the former, he extolled the energizing benefits of what he labeled "sexual magnetism" on the entire human constitution. For Foote, the problem of sexual abstinence was not that it induced a state of erotic frenzy, but that it robbed the sufferer of the electric vitality provided by the sexual drive. The fact that nuns were denied the radiating power of this force explained, for Foote, their sickly, wan appearance, and their frail physical condition: "Nuns are seldom if ever vigorous looking. Even if they are apparently healthy, there is a paleness about them which indicates a deficiency of that magnetic vitality...They may protest they are healthy, but their countenances tell a different story, especially to the practised eye of a medical man."[57]

* * *

For medical men, the priest stricken with seminal emissions, or the nun prey to hysteric fits, served to underline the perverse nature of Catholicism. Yet the energy with which physicians pursued their case against Catholic celibacy suggests not only a concern to discredit the church, but also a wider set of anxieties related to nothing less than the future health and stability of the nation itself. The broken health of the celibate Catholic stood as warning to the wider community that all forms of life which entailed total sexual abstinence, whether involving bachelors, spinsters, widows or widowers, carried an enormous toll not just for the individual sufferer, but for society as a whole.

The debate about celibate vows derived much of its intensity from a wider anxiety that celibacy, defined as a state of non-marriage, was becoming the norm for larger and larger sections of society. In both countries, newspaper editorialists regularly commented with dismay on the apparent rise in the number of bachelors and spinsters. Armed with a battery of statistical surveys, advocates of marriage set out to prove that single men and women, in comparison with the married, suffered from lower life expectancy, higher rates of mental illness and suicide, and a greater propensity to commit crime. In a study that attracted much commentary in both France and the United States, the Scottish physician, Dr. James Stark, argued that life expectancy rates were far higher for married men than single. In Scotland in 1863, according to Stark, out of a sample of 10,000 unmarried men between the ages of twenty and twenty-five, 1,174 had died. The equivalent figure for married men was only 597.[58]

In the case of female life expectancy rates, other surveys reached identical conclusions. The pioneer of demography in France, Dr. Jacques

Bertillon, cited surveys conducted in France, Belgium and Holland to prove that married women enjoyed better health and lived far longer than unmarried women. This difference occurred despite the dangers of childbirth which, Bertillon assumed, married women were more likely to face. "Love and maternity," he wrote, "in the salutary conditions of marriage, far from wearing out health, in fact conserve it, protect it in the present and in the future."[59] On the question of insanity, American doctors referred to research conducted by the French statistician Alfred Legoyt which demonstrated a higher incidence of mental illness among the unmarried.[60]

The medical debate on sexual abstinence thus formed part of a wider campaign against the perceived growth in the numbers of the unmarried. As marriage was understood to be the only framework within which sex could legitimately occur, the effort to prove that an absence of intercourse engendered a range of disorders became, in effect, an injunction to marry. Of course, as those who commented on surveys such as Dr. James Stark's conceded, sex was not the only reason that married men and women tended to outlive the single. In its analysis of Stark's findings, the *Nation* speculated that the responsibilities associated with marriage led men to moderate their behavior in a range of activities, from drinking to smoking and gambling. Conversely, for single men, as the journal reported, "the opportunities for dissipation and immorality of all kinds are at their maximum."[61] Furthermore, it is important to remember that celibacy was often defined simply as non-marriage. To be celibate, then, was not necessarily to be chaste. In fact, the opposite was occasionally true—both prostitutes as well as sexually active bachelors came under the banner of the celibate in the nineteenth century. Nevertheless, these were considered to be extreme cases. In all of these surveys, celibacy was more commonly understood to entail chastity. The majority of those adults who remained unmarried were thus assumed to be vulnerable to the physical and mental risks associated with sexual abstinence.

But celibacy, of course, was about much more than the individual. The crux of the celibacy question was less the well-being of men and women than the nature of responsible citizenship. As Isabel V. Hull has argued in relation to attitudes toward sexuality in the German-speaking states, individual sexual maturity was understood to be a crucial determinant of social stability; only an individual possessed of a mature sexual drive could display the qualities of intellectual balance and sound judgment which were the mark of a good citizen. The energy conferred by the sexual drive was, Hull concludes, "the very motor of productivity and of public life."[62] The democratic order was thus built, to a large degree, on a sexual foundation. Hostility to the bachelor was in fact a hallmark of classical Republican thought in both France and America. In the United States, as Mark E. Kann has argued, the Founding Fathers stigmatized the bachelor as belonging to a class of "disorderly men." By refusing to assume family obligations, the bachelor lacked the manly independence that marked a true citizen; even worse, in his apparent shiftlessness and selfishness, he posed a threat to the new democratic order based on virtue and a commitment to the public good. Hostility to bachelors was also a feature of French Revolutionary thought.[63] The suspicion of bachelors and spinsters as agents of political turmoil and social decline endured into the nineteenth century. By denying society the benefits conferred by sexual energy, the celibate was guilty of a grave social fault.

By choosing the path of sexual abstinence, the celibate was also guilty of offending the ideal of moderation in all things, the notion of the *juste milieu*. As Robert A. Nye has outlined, the bourgeois moral code stressed balance as the foundation of sexual virtue as well as of political stability. In individual behavior as much as political action, extremes were to be avoided at all costs; a responsible citizen displayed above all the quality of restraint. Republican school primers of the Third Republic, for example, stressed "moderation" in their effort to mould future citizens.[64] The celibate, however, bore the stigma of the fanatic. Whether successful in the effort to blanket the sexual instinct, or lost to an unbridled indulgence of the erotic drive, the celibate was far from reasonable or pragmatic. A commitment to sexual abstinence was not, in this view, commendable, but a mark of excess. And again, the sin was not merely individual, but social.

A concrete sign of the celibate's failure to fulfill his or her obligations to society concerned the duty to reproduce. Demography was a particularly urgent question in France and the United States. In comparison with all other Western nations, these two nations showed the most dramatic decline in birth-rates. In the United States, the fertility rate of white American woman fell from 7.04 to 3.54 over the course of the nineteenth century; in France, where the decline had begun even earlier, French couples were producing 4.3 legitimate children in the period 1800–1805, 3.1 between 1851 and 1855, and fewer than 3 in the late 1880s.[65] A near panic over such declining birth-rates would ensue in the last decades of the century. In the United States, social commentators looked with alarm at the high birth rates among recent immigrants compared with the native-born, and warned of an impending "race suicide." In France, a parliamentary commission was established in 1902 to study the problem of depopulation. But the attack on ecclesiastical celibacy suggests that such fears of national decline through falling birth-rates were already strong at mid-century. By the 1850s, French social commentators were beginning to warn that a decline in fertility was endangering the nation.

In 1854 and 1855, deaths exceeded births in France, and by 1867 the Emperor himself was expressing alarm that the supply of army recruits was beginning to taper off.[66] The problem was not simply a failure to marry, but an unhealthy reluctance to do so at a young age. In his *Traité d'hygiène publique et privée*, Michel Lèvy cited recent research which attributed the growing infertility of marriages to the unwillingness of men and women to enter marriage until their thirties, a tendency which, in his view, had contributed to the declining birth-rate.[67]

Although scholars have analyzed this fear of depopulation, and in some cases studied the hostility to bachelors and spinsters that stemmed from such anxieties, the manner in which Catholic celibacy was held responsible for the trend has not been fully appreciated. Yet in many of these warnings about the national decline brought about by falling marriage and birth rates, the Catholic clergy were branded the instigators of the trend. The pioneering demographer Dr. Jacques Bertillon pointed to France's great rival, the German confederation, for proof of the connection between Catholicism and falling marriage rates. The German-speaking states with the lowest rates of marriage, Bertillon alleged, were those where Catholics formed a majority of the population.[68]

The New York physician Dr. Edward M. Dixon came to a similar conclusion. For Dixon, celibacy was both an individual and a social scourge. The man or woman who chose not to marry, Dixon declared, was "committing a sin against nature and society."[69] Among those he accused of propagating this ideal of celibacy, or what he termed "arid selfishness," was the Catholic priest; for Dixon, all the arguments against marriage emanated from "the casuistry of a designing priesthood and other selfish men."[70] In a similar vein, the *New York Times* denounced the growing numbers of monks, whom it termed "inactive drones." In a society in which the female population outnumbered the male, the paper charged, the expansion of Catholic monasteries created "much social degradation" and robbed women of potential husbands.[71] A similar point was made by Catharine Beecher and Harriet Beecher Stowe in their bestselling domestic advice manual, *The American Woman's Home*. They attacked the Catholic Church for fostering a wider hostility toward home and family. The church, they lamented, "had made celibacy a prime virtue, and given its highest honors to those who forsake the family state." As a result, they concluded, the domestic ideal had been degraded.[72]

Even when not held directly responsible, the celibate Catholic was criticized as the most conspicuous manifestation of this alarming tendency for men and women to avoid the duties and responsibilities of marriage, a tendency which, if continued, would end in economic stagnation, declining population and political disorder. For Dr. de Ponsan, one of the clearest signs that a society had slipped into a state of decline and decadence was the spread of monasteries. "Despotic states," he wrote, "are filled with monasteries, beggars, solitary monks." The shift from an active and committed citizenry to a passive and selfish population was both signified and accelerated by a disenchantment with marriage. "At the same time as a nation marches towards decadence," de Ponsan warned, "the number of marriages decreases, and the quantity of single men and women increases."[73]

* * *

In the middle decades of the century, then, doctors on both sides of the Atlantic appeared to have constructed an impregnable case that Catholic celibacy was both fatal to individuals, and responsible for a range of social ills. Yet such views did not go unchallenged. Another group of doctors soon began to argue that sexual abstinence was an attainable goal which did not impair either the health or well-being of men and women. Countering the argument that celibacy led inevitably to disease and madness, these physicians insisted instead on the debilitating physical and mental effects of sexual over-indulgence. In making this case, these physicians drew, like their adversaries, on the physical and mental condition of the Catholic clergy.

What factors led certain physicians to argue that ecclesiastical celibacy was harmful and others to maintain that it was benign? Some of these doctors, such as the Frenchman Francis Devay, were doubtless motivated by their Catholic faith to offer a physiological defense of ecclesiastical celibacy. For others, such as the Boston physician Horatio Robinson Storer, who converted to Catholicism at the age of forty-six, or Dr Nicholas Cooke, also a convert to the Catholic faith, a defense of ecclesiastical celibacy may have been an expression of a budding affinity toward the church. The career of Thomas Low Nichols provides a remarkable example of a medical reformer whose views shifted dramatically with a conversion to Catholicism. Nichols was a leading advocate of hydrotherapy, otherwise known as the water-cure, a system of treatment which extolled the benefits of pure, cold water, and which encompassed a range of issues, from diet to work patterns to sexual activity. In 1853 Nichols published a medical textbook entitled *Esoteric Anthropology*, a work which sold in the thousands and which won Nichols a reputation as a provocative, even scandalous reformer. Most controversial were Nichols' views on sexual ethics which he expounded in one section of the book, artfully entitled *Miscellaneous*. The aim of sexual union, he argued, was not only reproduction, but pleasure for both men and women. Only the "full, varied and complete gratification" of the sexual instinct could ensure health and happiness, Nichols argued, a position which led him to denounce the indissolubility of marriage and even to defend polygamy. Sexual abstinence, Nichols continued, was unnatural, and in men and women endowed with normal levels of desire, a "terrible discordance".[74] In a later work written with his wife, Mary Gove Nichols, he tacitly referred to Catholic orders to denounce the philosophy of sexual repression and denial: "The morality which teaches men that it is their duty to be miserable, has existed long enough. It is the moralism of penance and torture; hair shirts, filth, poverty and fasting; of perpetual celibacy, self-denial, and self-abasement."[75]

Thomas Low Nichols converted to Catholicism in 1857, and subsequent editions of *Esoteric Anthropology* show a remarkable shift in his attitude to sexual relations. Refraining from sex, Nichols now argued, was the best means of avoiding conception, and, as the example of Catholic priests and nuns showed, was "easily done by most women, and by many men."[76] In another work, *Human Physiology*, Nichols reversed his earlier claim that pleasure was a legitimate object of sexual relations, and was adamant that reproduction alone justified the sexual act. Furthermore, sexual abstinence, far from a threat to health and happiness, had become a formula for physical and mental strength: "Every one knows that men can live in perfect continence for years, and all their lives, in full bodily and mental vigour, all the more strong and vigorous for the disuse of the amative function."[77] Not surprisingly, Nichols pointed to monks and nuns as models of such a virtuous celibate life. Admittedly, elements of Nichols' previous attitudes endured after his conversion to Catholicism. In particular, he continued to condemn the double standard by which women were expected to be virgins at marriage while men were tacitly encouraged to gain sexual experience. Furthermore, as Stephen Nissenbaum has argued, even in his radical phase Nichols was a proponent of sexual moderation as the key to health and happiness.[78] Yet concerning sexual abstinence and its effects, his embrace of Catholicism was clearly associated with a transformation in his views.

But for the majority of physicians, the interests of the Catholic Church were at best peripheral, and some even expressed trepidation that their work might be cited in defense of ecclesiastical vows. The American physician Augustus K. Gardner, one of the leading proponents of the theory that the sexual drive could successfully be subdued, left a damning portrait of Catholicism in his account of his days as a medical student in Paris. Commenting on a display of relics at Nôtre Dame, Gardner ridiculed Catholicism as a form of superstition rather than religious faith, and praised Jules Michelet's attacks on the confessional and the Jesuits as works of genius.[79] Yet as we shall see, Gardner's views on sexual abstinence tacitly supported ecclesiastical celibacy.

In countering the medical case against Catholic celibacy, these physicians began with the assertion that the sexual instinct could be successfully mastered with little or no cost to health and mind. In *Les passions dans leurs rapports avec la santé et les maladies*, a work which was translated and published in the United States in 1873, Dr. Xavier Bourgeois stated that "it is possible for a man to be continent for a certain time, even for all of his life." Furthermore, he added, "continence does not, in general, harm the health."[80] The Boston physician William Alcott agreed, citing the example of Sir Isaac Newton, a man free "from every degree and form of sexual indulgence," as compelling proof that a "pure and virtuous" celibacy might be as beneficial as the married state.[81] Alcott went on to praise an earlier associate, Sylvester Graham, with whom he had founded the American Physiological Society, and who had argued that the frequency of sexual relations over the course of one year should be limited to the number of lunar months. Though attracting ridicule during his lifetime, Graham's views, Alcott reported, had now won widespread approval.[82] As in the writings of their opponents, doctors such as Bourgeois and Alcott considered such sexual restraint to be far easier for women than for men. Nevertheless, even men were now seen as capable of mastering their sexual desires and abstaining from intercourse with few or no ill effects.

In making this argument, none of these authors advocated complete celibacy as a fitting life for men and women. Furthermore, all argued that the act of reproduction was a sacred task, and that the state of marriage was generally most conducive to human happiness. Alcott, for example, followed his reflection on the case of Isaac Newton by assuring his readers that he had no intention of dissuading men and women from marrying. Nevertheless, these authors did explicitly refute the assertion that absolute sexual abstinence amounted to a death sentence. As Dr. Nicholas Cooke, the author of *Satan in Society*, asserted, "let no one contend that continence is incompatible with health or longevity."[83] In France, Dr. Alfred Becquerel, the author of *Traité élémentaire d'hygiène privée*, a work published in seven editions between 1851 and 1883, likewise argued that for individuals endowed with a constitution that was "strong" and "robust," the absence of intercourse carried no physical cost. In Becquerel's opinion, any accumulation of seminal material in the reproductive organs as a result of extended periods of chastity would be compensated, for men at least, by the nocturnal emission of semen, a condition which Becquerel did not, unlike Lallemand, consider dangerous. Women, whom Becquerel described as wholly passive in the domain of sexual desire, presumably did not require any form of compensatory mechanism.[84]

Concerning the sexual disorders to which women were thought peculiarly vulnerable, other physicians opposed the argument that sexual abstinence was a key causal factor. On the question of hysteria, for example, a group of physicians on both sides of the Atlantic began to challenge the consensus, which had prevailed since the Classical era, that sexual abstinence provoked attacks of the disease. The work of one French physician, Dr. Pierre Briquet, proved particularly influential. In a monograph entitled *Un traité clinique et thérapeutique de l'hystérie*, Briquet persuasively argued that the ancient conception of a causal relationship between abstinence and hysteria, which had recently been reformulated by Dr. Landouzy, was based on little more than supposition and prejudice. Applying what he declared to be a rigorous and objective scientific method to the problem, Briquet came to the conclusion that a lack of sexual relations played little or no role in stimulating episodes of hysteria. Hysteria commonly occurred, Briquet noted, in girls who had not yet reached the age of puberty. The statistical incidence of hysteria among widows appeared even more persuasive. Of the 430 patients he had diagnosed as suffering from hysteria, Briquet revealed, only fourteen were widows (who, he assumed, were sexually inactive).[85]

The opinions of such influential French physicians soon appeared in America. One of the most active reporters of French medical theories to an American audience was Dr. Augustus K. Gardner. In 1870 Gardner published *Conjugal Sins against the Laws of Life and Health*, a book which would become a bestseller. Based on his knowledge of French medical theory, and particularly the writings of Dr. Alexandre Mayer, Gardner strove to convince Americans that sexual abstinence was entirely compatible with good health. As Gardner informed his readers, Dr. Mayer, author of *Des rapports conjugaux considérés sous le triple point de vue, de la population, de la santé et de la morale publique*, claimed that "no peculiar disease, nor any abridgement of the duration of life, can be ascribed to such continence, and in fact the statistics testify to the contrary."[86] Gardner also referred to the French physician and Trappist monk Pierre Debreyne in support of his contention that the true cause of diseases such as *spermatorrhea* was not sexual abstinence, but rather mental and physical idleness. Debreyne, Gardner reported to his readers, recommended "manual labor, corporeal exercise, an incessant material or mechanical occupation" as the best measures to prevent such disorders.[87]

What, then, was to blame for the sexual diseases that seemed so prevalent in society? For men like Gardner, the true culprits were those physicians who, by arguing that the sexual drive could never be entirely suppressed, had inadvertently encouraged dangerous practices. Dr. Nicholas Cooke denied that the sexual instinct was akin to the desire for food. This was, he claimed, "the argument of libertines, of those who seek a pretext for excesses of every sort."[88] Such excesses included masturbation. Whereas Léopold Deslandes attributed the spread of masturbation to the unwise attempt to suppress the sexual drive, doctors such as Gardner and Cooke argued that an easy acceptance of the irrepressible nature of sexual desire was at fault. The message that any attempt to lead a chaste life was futile had, in this view, only encouraged men and women to indulge in masturbation. Another dangerous sexual practice which this message was held to have fostered was contraception. Rather than a prudent measure to ensure individual health and happiness, contraception was portrayed by many medical writers as a deadly threat to the health of parents and child. The French physician Louis-François-Étienne Bergeret, whose book, *Des fraudes dans l'accomplissement des fonctions génératrices*, was translated and published in the United States in 1870, was one of the leading opponents of contraception. Bergeret ascribed many physical and mental illnesses, from uterine cancer to sterility to insanity, to the various "frauds" committed by men and women in order to avoid pregnancy.[89]

What is interesting is that on many points, the protagonists in this debate shared similar assumptions. All were in agreement that women were less sensual than men, that masturbation was a great social scourge, and that the health of future generations, and by extension society, was at stake. All were engaged, too, in the effort to define what exactly constituted a "reasonable" amount of sexual intercourse. But in the writings of men like Alcott, Gardner and Bourgeois, the definition of "reasonable" had clearly narrowed. For Auguste Debay, ten to twelve times a month constituted a normal and reasonable amount of intercourse for married couples. But for Alcott, once a month was more than sufficient. More fundamentally, while not necessarily advocating sexual abstinence, these physicians argued that such physical restraint was both attainable and benign for men and women. In making this case, they turned, like their opponents, to the Catholic Church.

In France, a number of Catholic physicians defended ecclesiastical celibacy on medical grounds. In a lengthy treatise, Jean-Ennemond Dufieux set out to offer, as he wrote, "a physiological argument to the clergy in favor of continence."[90] Dufieux conceded that the sexual instinct was found in humans, but argued that the presence of such an instinct did not thereby render the act of intercourse a necessity. The sexual instincts, he argued, are subject to willpower, and could therefore be controlled. Furthermore, Dufieux argued, none of the sexual disorders which abstinence was said to induce were found among priests or nuns. Nymphomania, for example, was not found among nuns devoted to God, but single women amidst secular society. The true cause of such disorders as nymphomania, Dufieux speculated, was the unrestrained sexual behavior which seemed to characterize modern society. Medical criticisms of ecclesiastical celibacy, he concluded, "seem to be born from prejudice rather than a serious and profound study of the question."[91]

Doctors such as Dufieux also seized on the belief that semen possessed replenishing powers. The notion that semen was a vital fluid which could be reabsorbed by the body dated back to the Classical era, and continued to appear in medical writings in the nineteenth century. The American physician Dio Lewis, who had completed his medical training in Paris, quoted Dr. Xavier Bourgeois' contention that sperm was "the prolific fluid destined to communicate the spark of life." Its loss was therefore debilitating to the physical organism.[92] For the priest, the medical implications were clear: by guarding this vital fluid within his body, he was not only spared the physical and mental exhaustion to which ejaculation gave rise, but was also able to benefit from semen's rejuvenating power. The Catholic physician Francis Devay, for example, argued that ecclesiastical celibacy, rather than afflicting the priest with physical and mental troubles, allowed him to conserve his "vital energy," an energy he was then able to "turn to the benefit of humanity."[93]

Far from being a pitiful creature prone to sexual vices and wracked by disease, many physicians described nuns and priests as vigorous and healthy. Dr. Bergeret, for example, noted that "Having been physician for a long number of years to several religious institutions, I have never seen there any serious disorders of the organs of generation."[94] Doctors such as Briquet and Gardner, who dismissed any notion of a link between hysteria and continence, referred as much to the nun as to the priest. Briquet, for instance, concluded that "hysteria is extremely rare amongst nuns."[95] The *American Journal of the Medical Sciences* also affirmed that "Hysteria has been said to be...common among nuns...But in point of fact it is rare in convents."[96] Furthermore, the health of the celibate clergy was sometimes said to be superior to that of the general population. In an appendix to his work *La médicine des passions*, J.B.F. Descuret provided statistics to support this argument. Of the 302 Carmelite monks who had died in the convent in the Rue d'Enfer during the time when he was the attending physician, Descuret reported, sixty-nine were older than sixty, fifty-nine older than seventy, and twenty-three older than eighty, a rate of life expectancy higher than that found in secular society.[97]

The argument that sexual excess rather than abstinence was the root of the myriad disorders afflicting society equally found support in the institutions of the church. Xavier Bourgeois noted a higher prevalence of hysteria and madness in brothels than in convents.[98] Seminaries and convents, Bourgeois argued, provided compelling proof that the sexual instinct could be mastered with little or no difficulty. The evidence of such institutions, Bourgeois wrote, was that "venereal needs arise slowly, are moderate, and soon die out, when they are neither satisfied nor irritated."[99] For the physician Alfred Becquerel, author of *Traité élémentaire d'hygiène privée*, the abstention from all sexual relations was in fact far easier for priests and nuns than for members of secular society. The rigorous training experienced in the seminary had prepared the priest, Becquerel wrote, for the harsh struggle to subdue the sexual elements of his own nature. Furthermore, the life of the monastery, with its fasting and physical mortification, simple diet and, above all, lack of temptation and excitement which the proximity of women might otherwise have created, made the observation of the vow of chastity far easier. "We must consider," Becquerel concluded, "continence as possible, and even easy, amongst ecclesiastics."[100]

Far from being responsible for the spread of harmful notions of sexual abstinence, as many of its opponents suggested, the church won praise in these works as a resolute defender of salubrious sexual practices. Some physicians praised the Catholic Church for its determined stand against abortion and contraception. In his prize-winning essay on the evils of abortion, the Boston physician Horatio Robinson Storer charged that this practice was more frequent among Protestant than Catholic women. For Storer, who would later convert to Roman Catholicism, this difference was due to the "Romish ordinance, flanked on the one hand by the confessional, and by denouncement and excommunication on the other." This religious arsenal, he argued, "has saved to the world thousands of infant lives."[101] The French opponent of contraception, Dr. Bergeret, agreed. In the conclusion to his monograph on the diseases caused by contraceptive measures, Bergeret praised the Catholic Church's unflinching opposition to such practices.[102]

Opponents of ecclesiastical celibacy soon responded to these arguments. The case in favor of celibacy by Dr. Dufieux came under attack in a treatise by Dr. Paul Diday. The reproductive instinct, Diday asserted, had been given to humans by their Creator in order to encourage the formation of family groups. How could the celibate's struggle to restrain this instinct, then, be considered part of God's plan for His creation?[103] Dr. Becquerel's view that continence was "easy" for priests and nuns was dismissed as "greatly naive" by the physician Jules

Arnould, a contributor to the *Dictionnaire encyclopédique des sciences médicales*. According to Arnould, Becquerel was blind to the temptations offered by the intimacy of the confessional box. In such dark and enclosed spaces, Arnould argued, the celibate vow was virtually meaningless.[104] In the United States, many commentators attacked the notion that Catholicism promoted salubrious sexual practices by pointing to the example of France. On the issue of abortion, for example, some writers cited France as proof that Catholicism was no barrier to the practice. Abortion, as one reviewer in the *Medical and Surgical Reporter* argued, was rife in Catholic France.[105]

Furthermore, some physicians betrayed a suspicion of the Catholic Church even as they offered a physiological defense of one of its key practices. Such an equivocal stance was evident in the work of Dr. Alexandre Mayer. As we have seen, Mayer's own statistical survey had found mortality rates to be far higher among the clergy than the laity. Yet Mayer argued that sexual abstinence was not harmful to the health. How, then, could he reconcile this argument with the evidence of his own survey? The solution was to cast doubt on the faithfulness of the Catholic clergy to the rule of celibacy. For Mayer, the argument of certain physicians that sexual abstinence among the clergy led to higher mortality rates was based on a false assumption; namely, that the clergy in fact upheld their vows. As Mayer wrote, "to announce that continence causes a greater mortality, based upon the statistics of religious corporations, it should be assumed that the rules of chastity are not infringed upon, which we dare not guarantee."[106] Priests and nuns, Mayer alleged, were not in fact celibate, and their value as test-cases for the effects of sexual abstinence was thus limited. In the United States, the phrenologist O.S. Fowler made a similar point. Phrenologists labeled the part of the cerebellum which governed attraction between the sexes as "amativeness" and held its proper expression to be of great benefit. While amativeness could be trained, Fowler, as we have seen, celebrated the power of sex and its role in fostering human happiness. As for the Catholic clergy, Fowler cast doubt on its value for those studying the effects of sexual abstinence. "Are you **quite** sure," he wrote in response to writers who based the case for celibacy on priests and nuns, "the Catholic clergy either **have** no Amativeness, or else exercise none in any way?"[107] The possibility that their arguments legitimating sexual abstinence might be exploited by defenders of Catholicism also appeared to trouble many of these physicians, particularly in the United States. This fear of inadvertently bolstering the Catholic Church was evident in the writings of Dio Lewis. Though he argued that sexual abstinence was a feasible condition which was entirely consistent with good health, Lewis took pains to stress that his model of celibacy was based on voluntary assent rather than the sort of forced vows that many American Protestants associated with convents and monasteries:

> It is said that 'celibacy profanes and debases women, making her the plaything of the passions.' As a historical fact, such has been the effect of *systematized* celibacy. But many and many a one has walked in celibate chastity all through life, increasing in purity and loveliness of heart to the end.[108]

By contrasting the effects of systematized celibacy, surely a coded reference to convents and monasteries, with celibacy as an individual choice, Lewis was doubtless trying to rebut the accusation that he was defending Catholicism. Nevertheless, his efforts to avoid even a tacit endorsement of Catholic celibacy is revealing of the way this medical discourse threatened to have precisely this effect.

* * *

In a suggestive metaphor, Dr. Augustus K. Gardner compared the workings of human physiology to the operation of the undersea cable linking Europe and the United States: "The relation of one part of the body to the other was seen to be established through the nervous system, as the two hemispheres of the world are connected by the Atlantic cable."[109] Just as the completion of the cable led people like Gardiner to ruminate on the interconnected nature of the world, Americans in the middle decades of the nineteenth century willingly looked beyond their national borders in their effort to combat the evils of ecclesiastical celibacy. In particular, American physicians turned to France which, in the middle decades of the century, was famed for the quality of its medical research and training.

The prominence of the Catholic priest and nun in a specifically medical discourse offers some revision to our understanding of the influence of doctors in the nineteenth century. In particular, it suggests that the standard account of physicians displacing priests as the custodians of sexual ethics is far too simplistic. Many physicians, particularly in the middle decades of the century, strove to reconcile the demands of medicine and religion. Furthermore, even those physicians who were hostile to Catholicism placed the priest and nun at the centre of their analyses. The medical argument over the feasibility of maintaining celibate vows thus demonstrates the extent to which religion continued to intrude into the realm of medical science.

The medical debate about ecclesiastical celibacy also offers striking proof that opposition to Catholicism was embedded in a wider series of discourses. Far from being isolated from broader social questions, the case against the Catholic Church was at their heart. In the case of Catholic celibacy, these questions concerned not only the sexual nature of men and women, but also the future health of the state. Social commentators in both France and the United States discerned a creeping selfishness at work in their societies. More and more men and women appeared to be turning away from the duty to marry and raise children; falling birth-rates, particularly when compared with those of other Western nations, seemed to signal long-term national decline. Celibacy was not just a recipe for individual misery, but also for social catastrophe. It was this prospect which drove much of the hostility to the celibate priest and nun. As the most visible representatives of what was construed as a disastrous tendency, the priest and nun were at the centre of a far wider polemic about the relationship between sexuality and social progress.

Both the celibate priest and nun were accused of betraying a fundamental duty of their sex: the duty to reproduce. Ecclesiastical celibacy, however, was understood to be only a part of Catholicism's assault on the tenets of true manhood and womanhood. The next two chapters take up the theme of Catholicism's alleged violation of conventional ideals of masculinity and femininity. In the first case, by far the most troubling figure was the Jesuit, a figure whose masculinity was shrouded in ambiguity.

4
Neither Male nor Female—The Jesuit as Androgyne

In the nineteenth century's cast of villains, the Jesuit was an unrivalled figure of menace. As countless authors warned, the Jesuit would resort to any means in order to impose papal rule throughout the world. Construed as the ultimate hypocrite, the Jesuit had, through years of rigorous training, perfected the skill of concealing his evil intentions beneath a mask of piety and good intentions. The unwary allowed the Jesuit access to the most sensitive and influential domains of society—not only the halls of government but the innermost sanctuaries of the family. Faced with such a slippery opponent, the anti-Jesuit had always to be on guard; as the American historian Francis Parkman warned, in terms identical to those of French anticlericals, "The Jesuit was, and is, everywhere."[1]

As a number of scholars have argued, this anti-Jesuit discourse bears many of the features of a conspiracy theory, particularly its ascription of immense powers to a numerically small enemy, and its assumption that the course of history was set by covert and hidden forces.[2] Prior to the work of the scholar of German anti-Jesuitism, Róisín Healy, historians had been slower to appreciate the manner in which this discourse was gendered. Healy argues that, in the German-speaking states, the Jesuit was consistently portrayed as an androgyne, a figure uniting characteristics of both sexes. The figure of the Jesuit appeared to muddy the carefully constructed divisions between men and women. On the one hand, the unfettered authority enjoyed by the Jesuit gave him an aura of potent manliness. At the same time the Jesuit displayed a passivity and subservience in relation to his own superiors that mirrored the subordinate status of women. As Healy writes, "the Jesuits' domination of the Catholic population made them the most masculine of men; their submission to another man made them the most feminine of men."[3] The Jesuits, Healy suggests, "challenged the assumption that people were either masculine or feminine...The Jesuits were both at the one time."[4]

Healy's argument that opposition to the Jesuits was framed in terms of androgyny can be applied to both France and the United States. In both nations, the Jesuit stood accused of upsetting the delicate balance between male and female on which social stability was held to rest. Healy's analysis, however, can be extended further into the domains of class and race. As an effeminate creature, the purportedly male Jesuit was associated not only with women, but also with two other groups which were equally understood to be feminine in nature and which also figured as enemies lurking on the fringes of civilized society: the working-classes and savages. The portrayal of the Jesuit as an androgyne thus extended beyond the immediate task of distilling his essential perversity to encompass a more fundamental understanding of the masculine nature of the liberal citizen.

* * *

As a figure uniting the characteristics of men and women in one person, the androgyne stood out as an aberration in an age dedicated to the belief that the sexes were radically different. In what Thomas Laqueur has labeled the "two-sex model," the sexes were assigned distinct and complementary physical and intellectual characteristics. Men were deemed to be active, rational and independent; women passive, emotional, and submissive.[5] Both science and religion were invoked to justify this gender bifurcation. Physicians traced the divergent capacities for thought and feeling that men and women displayed to the fundamental difference in their reproductive organs. For the French physician Léopold Deslandes, "It is also to the influence exercised by the genital organs on other parts that the sexes owe their peculiar differences. Their organization, influenced by a different genital apparatus, presents a different mode of existence, action and sensation."[6] Religion was employed to make the same case. According to Sarah Josepha Hale, an influential writer and editor of the popular *Godey's Lady Book*, gender difference derived from the manner in which God had created Adam and Eve: "He was formed of the earth, and had in the greatest development those powers of mind that are directed toward object of sense; she, formed from his flesh and bones, had in greatest development those powers of mind which seek the affections."[7]

For proof of this divergence between the sexes, contemporaries looked to virtually every facet of human behavior. Jules Michelet returned again and again to the theme of gender difference. In *L'Amour*,

Michelet described a gulf between the sexes. "She does nothing as we do," he wrote. "She thinks, speaks, and acts differently. Her tastes are different from our tastes. Her blood does not even flow in her veins as ours does."[8] Women, Michelet went on to argue, breathed differently, digested food differently, and even spoke a different language. As we have seen, Michelet's views on women were often criticized as extreme in France and abroad. But his underlying argument—that the sexes were essentially different—was supported by writers whose conception of the sexual divide was far less stringent. The French reformer Ernest Legouvé won applause from American feminists for his advocacy of divorce and a comprehensive system of female education. Yet Legouvé summed up his theory of relations between the sexes as "equality in difference."[9] Such extensive classifications of sexual difference were also common in the United States. For the phrenologist O.S. Fowler, the number of human traits that could be classed either male or female was almost endless: physical form and intellectual aptitude, of course, but equally manners, gait, and handwriting. "Even," Fowler concluded, "the very rap at the door has gender."[10]

This bifurcated model of sexual relations provided the conceptual framework against which androgyny was defined. The androgyne was depicted as a confusing amalgam of male and female qualities, a figure straddling the dividing line between the sexes. In part, this confusion was anatomical. Major dictionaries on both sides of the Atlantic defined *androgynous* as a synonym of *hermaphroditic*; both terms denoted a single being endowed with the genitalia of the male and female sexes. But androgyny entailed much more than genital duplication. In both France and the United States, the androgyne was understood as a being who displayed a range of physical, intellectual, and moral traits that more properly belonged to the opposite sex. Medical texts looked beyond anatomy in their assessments of female and male identity. As Alice Dreger has argued, there was no easy medical consensus over the precise structure and form of the male and female genitalia, and cases of apparently mixed genitalia often gave rise to heated debates between doctors as to the gender of the patient.[11] One of the means by which physicians attempted to identify sexual identity in such cases was through behavior. A taste for domestic work, for example, was considered a sign that the patient was a woman. In its entry on hermaphroditism, the *Dictionnaire des sciences médicales* reported the case of Marie Marguerite, born in 1792 near the town of Dreux, who had been raised as a girl. At the age of nineteen Marie began to act in ways that appeared distinctly masculine. According to a Dr. Worbe, dresses no longer fitted her, her tastes became more capricious, and, perhaps most significantly, she began to display masculine work habits. As Worbe declared, Marie showed more interest in sowing seed and driving a harrow than doing housework. It was this behavior, more than the precise configuration of Marie's genitalia, which led Dr. Worbe to officially pronounce Marie to be a man.[12]

This sense of androgyny—encompassing a set of moral and social traits ascribed to the opposite sex—appears often in the literature of the period. It was employed, for example, by one writer in *Godey's Lady's Book* who, in an article criticizing mothers for pampering their sons, lamented the resulting number of "androgynous boys" with "long curled scented hair...and a girlish horror of rough sports."[13] This was also the androgyne who appeared so regularly in novels, particularly in France. While the most famous literary androgyne was Henri de Latouche's *Fragoletta*, it was another writer whom Latouche had encouraged and supported in her youth, George Sand, who provided perhaps the most revealing literary depiction of the androgyne in her play *Gabriel*. Sand's Gabriel is anatomically a girl but, having received a boy's education, embodies key male traits: she is a free-thinker who shuns Catholic confessors, engages in duels, and exasperates her male lover with her tendency to philosophize. Gabriel/Gabrielle is thus a balance of the two sexes, a girl with, as her lover describes her, a female heart but a male head.[14]

In the eyes of his French and American opponents, the Jesuit was an equally ambiguous figure. In the case of the Jesuit, the key issue was authority. According to the conventions of nineteenth-century society, authority and submission were sex-specific. Men, by virtue of their superior reasoning and judgment, were understood to be the only dependable carriers of authority; women, in contrast, with their propensity for sentimental excess and their reliance on instinct, were duty-bound to submit. Although women might properly exert a moral influence over their immediate circle of family and friends, and even act as models of virtue for the wider society, the wielding of bare power was understood to be a masculine privilege. The Transatlantic consensus on this issue can be seen in the works of one of the leading American theorists of domesticity, Catharine Beecher. For Beecher, public authority ultimately rested with men. To demonstrate the manner in which American society had embraced this enlightened principle, Beecher cited Alexis de Tocqueville. The Frenchman, Beecher explained to her readers, had praised the gendered division of authority which he had encountered during his stay in the United States. American men held the ultimate authority in society, while women, as Beecher quoted from de Tocqueville's work, "attach a sort of pride to the voluntary surrender of their own will."[15] The happy result of this female abstention from public authority, as both de Tocqueville and Beecher concluded, was that American women retained the manners and the appearance fitting to their sex.

As this last statement implies, the association between authority and masculinity was so deeply embedded that women who acquired or even aspired to such overt power were held to be masculinized. Feminists who defied the boundaries of private and public were commonly derided as "Amazons," manly creatures devoid of the delicate and nurturing qualities associated with femininity. In a stinging denunciation of the attempts by the feminist Lucy Stone and others to ensure Antoinette Brown a place on the public platform of a temperance convention in 1853, for example, the *New York Times* derided these feminists as "she-males." An article in *Putnam's* magazine expressed this association between feminists and masculinity even more aggressively. We advise, the author wrote, "our mannish women of the Woman's Rights Convention to transplant the hair from their heads to their chins, and with bold fronts and strong beards, make good their claims to man's privileges."[16] Feminists did not fare any better in France. Even a female reformer such as Madame Romieu, who criticized many of the legal disadvantages imposed on women by the Napoleonic Code, rejected feminism on the grounds that it transformed women into what she termed "viragos."[17]

For proof of the way in which the acquisition of public authority turned women into men, defenders of the separate spheres model often looked to Catholic figures, and in particular the Mother Superior. In the convent atrocity literature, the Superior invariably assumes the role of merciless tyrant who revels in the misery and pain which she inflicts on the nuns. Sadism, however, is not the only trait of the Superior. In a fundamental challenge to gender conventions, the Superior's thirst for authority is sometimes depicted as extending beyond the walls of the convent, and even to encompass men. The runaway nun Rebecca Reed, whose account of her alleged suffering in the Ursuline convent at Charlestown, Massachusetts, was published just months prior to its destruction in 1834, describes her Superior reprimanding male servants and porters.[18] The terrifying Carmelite Superior depicted by the priest Jean-Hippolyte Michon in his bestselling work *La religieuse* manages to intimidate the local village *curé* to such an extent that he bows unquestioningly to her imperious demands. Lacking any of the sentimental qualities that were said to form the core of female nature, and brazenly exerting an undisguised dominance over men, the Superior in such literature takes on a masculine aura. In the words of the narrator of the most famous American convent atrocity story, the *Awful Disclosures of Maria Monk*, the Superior was "bold, and masculine."[19]

Men, in turn, who showed signs of submission rather than authority were routinely dismissed as effeminate. For many Americans in the middle decades of the nineteenth century, the sorry state of French manhood provided a telling lesson in the perils of submission. In scores of travel accounts and newspaper articles, Americans ridiculed the Frenchman who, having failed to resist (yet again) political dictatorship as well as the yoke of a despotic church, lacked the manly and democratic qualities of independence and fortitude. A long description of French society in the *Atlantic Monthly* was typical of a broader American attitude: Frenchmen are described as childish, fickle, and devoted to the superficial arts of conversation and fashion. French society, in this depiction, is dominated by women. Obsessed with mere amusement, Frenchmen, the author writes, "make no such demands upon reality as full-grown men and educated citizens instinctively crave."[20] In his account of his travels in France, newspaper editor Horace Greeley found some admirable traits in Parisians, notably their intelligence and generosity. But, in terms which were identical to those used to describe the negative aspects of femininity, he also found them "impulsive, fickle, sensual and irreverent."[21] Androgyny thus appeared to many American observers to be a hallmark of French society. Mark Twain, for example, poked fun at what he called "a thing that is neither male nor female, neither fish, flesh, nor fowl—a poor, miserable, hermaphrodite Frenchman!"[22]

This perception that Frenchmen were effeminate did not, however, impede the flow of French anti-Jesuit works into the United States. As was so often true of the Transatlantic case against Catholicism, national stereotypes which emphasized difference co-existed with a sentiment of acting as allies against a shared enemy. French and American opponents were united in their belief that the Jesuit embodied a disturbing androgyny, and in their view this androgyny began with one of the fundamental principles of the Society of Jesus, submission.

* * *

In the United States and France, opponents of the Society routinely alleged that it reduced its members to a state of utter and unquestioning subservience to the General. As countless books claimed, the despotic authority of the General had been established by none other than the founder of the Jesuits, Ignatius Loyola, when he laid down this fundamental rule on his deathbed: "Every member of the Order must obey as if he was a cadaver or a walking stick in the hands of an old man." Even if compelled to engage in illegal or immoral behavior, the Jesuit, in this view, had no choice but to obey. In an article warning Americans of a secret Jesuit plan to seize control of the Western territories, Harriet Beecher Stowe provided her readers with apparently compelling proof that Jesuit obedience knew no legal or ethical bounds. In a conversation with "one of the chief Jesuits of the West," Stowe reported, one of her friends had put the following question: "Suppose your Superior directed you to perform an act which you considered morally wrong; what should you do?" His reply, as Stowe informed her readers, was chilling: "*I should unhesitatingly obey.*"[23] French critics of the Jesuits were equally convinced that the principle of blind obedience had displaced individual judgment as the basis of their action. The Larousse *Grand dictionnaire universel* declared the Jesuit's sole duty to be "the execution of the order given by the superior. From that point on," the entry concluded, "no more personal responsibility, no more morality."[24]

Such a state of complete servility was only reached, as anti-Jesuit writers affirmed, after years of rigorous and pitiless training. Jesuit seminaries, in this view, employed a number of sophisticated techniques which aimed to strip the novice of any trace of intellectual or spiritual independence. First, the novice's capacity for physical resistance was broken by severe fasting and self-flagellation. Having subdued the body, the Jesuits then turned to putting the mind, as one account of the process from the *Ladies' Repository* described, "into the crucible."[25] All contact with family or friends was forbidden; left in a state of sentimental isolation, the Jesuit was less likely to resist this reshaping of his character at the hands of his superiors. The novice's intellectual faculties were then systematically degraded by a skilful manipulation of his senses and emotions, a process allegedly set out in the Jesuits' own *Spiritual Exercises*. In his analysis of this work, the republican Charles Sauvestre deplored the manner in which the Jesuit novice was encouraged to imagine the smell of Christ's body, the sound of divine voices, the touch of the clothes of Christ and the saints. The objective of these exercises in emotional exaltation, argued Sauvestre, was simply "the annihilation of reason."[26] First-hand accounts by survivors of this process provided a similarly disturbing picture. One of the most sensational came from a writer known as the Abbate Leone. In a work which appeared with an introduction by the leading *Fouriériste* Victor Considérant, and which was subsequently translated into English, Leone described his own (purported) experience of Jesuit training. As a novice, Leone alleged, he was urged to exalt in the power of relics and the elation felt by witnesses of miracles. The aim of such exercises was sinister. Through such means his Jesuit teachers aimed, Leone declared, "to obscure and mutilate my understanding, so that they might at length become its absolute masters."[27]

The images employed to characterize the individual Jesuit all served to heighten this impression of unnatural and inhuman docility. In an age of industrial expansion, anti-Jesuit writers everywhere turned naturally to mechanical science to convey the nature of Jesuitism. In one of his lectures entitled "machinisme moderne," Jules Michelet accused the Jesuit of being "a machine, a simple instrument of action."[28] His colleague at the *Collège de France*, Edgar Quinet, similarly described Loyola's maxims as designed to produce "the Christian automaton."[29] In a series of articles from its French correspondent, the *New York Observer* denounced the mechanical stamp which Jesuitism had apparently imposed on spiritual inquiry. The *Spiritual Exercises* were, according to the paper's correspondent, little better than the religious equivalent of a factory timetable: "the man who prays is but a machine to groan, weep, cry out, stop at moments marked out beforehand according to Loyola's ritual!"[30] The Jesuit had lost his conscience and his soul, becoming an amoral creature capable of unquestioningly carrying out the monstrous schemes of his superiors.

These descriptions of the Jesuit as an automaton, a helpless tool of an astute and ruthless General, undoubtedly made him appear more sinister and threatening. But independence was not the only quality forfeited by the slave-like Jesuit. The submissive Jesuit had also been stripped of his masculinity. Freedom, after all, was a defining virtue of manhood; one could not, in the view of much of nineteenth-century society, be both a slave and a man. In the eyes of many French anticlericals, the Jesuit, having relinquished his independence of thought and will to the crushing authority of the General, had thereby been emasculated. The Larousse dictionary, for example, cited the following quotation from the essayist and novelist Pierre-Simon Ballanche: "The Jesuits profess passive obedience which is the abolition of man."[31]

In the United States, such descriptions of the Jesuit losing his manhood were even more common than in France. In an American review of a purported theological debate between an English pastor, Reverend Seymour, and a series of Jesuits in Rome, the ease with which the Protestant defeats his opponents is attributed to "the leaden pressure of authority, the early submission to that mockery of reason" which had, in the reviewer's opinion, "*emasculated* their intellects."[32] For the historian Francis Parkman, the Jesuit missionaries of the early American frontier, despite their boldness and courage, remained almost tragic lessons in the emasculating spirit of the Society. In reference to the missionary Brébeuf, Parkman wrote that "nature had given him all the passions of a vigorous manhood, and religion had crushed them, crushed them, or tamed them to do her work."³³ The figure of the emasculated Jesuit was equally common in popular fiction. In Helen Dhu's bestseller *Stanhope Burleigh: The Jesuits in our Homes*, the Jesuit Jaudan, like all other Jesuits, is forced to acquiesce to the radical submission demanded by his superiors. The cost of this submission, however, is high. As Dhu writes, "The Jesuit conquered the man."³⁴ For American readers, then, there could be little doubt as to the price to be paid for embracing the Society of Jesus. As the Italian ex-priest Alessandro Gavazzi declared in one of his controversial lectures in New York in 1853, "The Jesuit...is a good Jesuit when he is no more a man: when he is a man he is no more a Jesuit."³⁵

In some accounts, it was not even necessary to be a member of the Society to undergo this loss of masculinity. The budding masculinity of adolescent boys in Jesuit schools was thought to be stunted by the influence of their teachers. In one of his letters on the Jesuits, the Belgian jurist and philosopher François Laurent described the state of students who had been educated in Jesuit-run schools. Most, he wrote, lacked initiative or sincerity, and were equipped with little more than a superficial knowledge of science and mathematics. The products of such schools were, Laurent alleged, almost exact matches of the Jesuits themselves. To conclude this damning portrait, Laurent posed this question: "Are they men?"³⁶ The claim that Jesuit schools robbed students of their masculinity was also made in the United States. Noah Porter, professor of moral philosophy at Yale University, warned Protestant fathers that the manliness of their sons would not survive a Jesuit education. If a father, Porter pronounced, "desired to send him where he would be trained to think and feel like a man, he would not expose him to the influence of those whose ideal of manhood is realized in the sophist, the diplomatist, the driveller, and the devotee."³⁷

The thoroughness of this emasculation was thrown into stark relief by the virility of the General, the one Jesuit whose independence, and therefore manliness, remained intact. Of course, the Jesuit General was in turn subordinate to his ultimate master, the pope, though some anti-Jesuit writers suggested that even the papacy had come under Jesuit control. In relation to other Jesuits, however, the General was held to enjoy a despotic power which made him not only the undisputed leader of the Society, but its only man. "Amongst the Jesuits," as one anti-Jesuit work declared, "there is only ever one man, the general."³⁸ The General's status as the only masculine Jesuit was confirmed for American readers by Jean-Claude Pitrat, a purported French ex-Jesuit and author of *Americans Warned of Jesuitism, or, the Jesuits Unveiled*. Pitrat's book was widely reviewed in America, and accepted as an authentic, insider's account of Jesuit training. Having outlined the General's unremitting hold over all other Jesuits, Pitrat concluded that, within the Society, he was "a single man."[39]

Not only had the Jesuit forfeited his masculinity, but he had also taken on an aura of femininity. The attribution of qualities and traits normally associated with the feminine sex to the purportedly male Jesuit could be seen on a number of levels. To begin with, the Jesuits were portrayed as masters of seduction. Both in gaining recruits and winning over members of the laity, the Jesuit allegedly relied on flattery and personal charm rather than reasoned argument. In Pitrat's account, the Jesuit mode of recruiting novices was to "attract with caresses, flatteries, with every kind of seducing means."[40] The charge of recruiting through seduction rather than persuasion was also made by the Abbate Leone. The secret of the Jesuits, Leone alleged, "consists in subduing, either by *caresses* or by the weariness of useless resistance when caresses have failed, the more enlightened of the middle classes."[41] This emphasis on seduction is significant because, in the nineteenth century, it was not a technique of persuasion associated with men. The masculine strategy was understood to be far more direct, relying on the weight of evidence and appealing to the reasoned judgment of the other party. Seduction was thought a favorite weapon of women, particularly women whose virtue was deemed suspect. The Jesuit's use of such a weapon thus immediately hinted at femininity.

The manner in which the Jesuit took on a series of feminine traits was further demonstrated in the alleged hold of *imagination* over his mind. Men, of course, also possessed imaginations. But according to conventional descriptions of the sexes, the function and power of the imaginative faculty was essentially different for men and women. The male imagination was above all creative, while the female imagination was essentially imitative. This difference was used to explain the apparent imbalance in the number of men and women who could be classed as "geniuses." At the same time, women, like children, were held to be far more susceptible than men to appeals to their imagination, particularly those that were couched in sensory form. In its article on imagination, the *Dictionaire des sciences médicales* argued that women "remain subjugated to the tricks and to the empire of this faculty"; their subjection to the pull of imagination, in turn, explained why women "can be more easily seduced and enchanted by shows, vivid impressions."[42]

In both France and the United States, this purported female vulnerability to sensory manipulation was cited as a major factor in the growth of female Catholic orders. In this view, the theatrical appeal of Catholic ritual—the incense, music, and skilful staging of the Mass—overwhelmed the judgment of otherwise sensible young women, and lured them, even in the face of parental opposition, into the embrace of the church. Such accusations were fueled by changes in Catholic religious worship and prayer, notably the rise of devotional piety. By the mid-nineteenth century, the number of devotional guides had increased dramatically, and prayer books were filled with rituals such as devotions to the passion and death of Jesus, the Sacred Heart, the Blessed Sacrament, Mary and popular saints.[43] Runaway nuns often admitted their vulnerability to this flourishing devotional sensibility. One famous escaped nun, Josephine Bunkley, conceded that she had not been forced to convert to Catholicism, but had chosen the life of the nun, a decision due to her vulnerability to spectacle and ritual, or as she put it, to her exposure to the "seductive allurements of a sensual system" which had left "marked and permanent effects."[44] In France, a striking fictional account of the peculiar susceptibility of young girls to the sensuousness of the church is contained in Gustave Flaubert's *Madame Bovary*. Having been put into a convent at the age of thirteen, Bovary is entranced by the romantic interior of the convent chapel. The process is gradual, but eventually the young Emma succumbs to "the mystic languor exhaled by the perfumes of the altar, the coolness of the holy-water fonts and the radiance of the tapers."[45] In Emma Bovary's case, the enchantment was short-lived. But as scores of hostile accounts of convent life warned, for many girls the decision to adopt the life of a nun was not so easily reversed.

The Jesuit novice too is portrayed as drawn into the Society by a skilful manipulation of his imagination and senses. For Edgar Quinet, the Jesuits were masters of manipulating the sentimental weaknesses of their novices. Rather than a coherent theology or an appeal to spirituality, the Jesuit relied on a "preoccupation with arrangements and theatrical tricks."[46] Jean-Claude Pitrat, the purported French ex-Jesuit, warned American readers that the Jesuits attracted novices by "flattering their senses"; the goal of Jesuit training, Pitrat concluded, was to "fire their young, ardent and impulsive imaginations."[47] The Jesuit novice thus displayed a sentimental vulnerability that was normally attributed to young women. Men, after all, were thought to possess the intellectual faculties which could provide a sufficient defense against such strategies. If the Jesuit succumbed and became a willing tool in the hands of his General, there could only be one reason: like a girl, he lacked that eminently masculine attribute, intellectual independence, which would enable him to resist.

This association between Jesuitism and effeteness was clearly on display in fictional representations of the Jesuit. The Jesuit's body is lithe: his face beardless; his features delicate; his fingers long and thin. At times, this impression of effeminacy is made even more explicit. In a work dedicated to Michelet, the future Communard

Casimir Bouis described the "effeminate pride" of the Jesuit which was only partly hidden by his severe features. Within each Jesuit, Bouis alleged, were the "coquetteries of women."[48] In Helen Dhu's *Stanhope Burleigh*, the evil Jesuit Jaudan actually begins to take on the appearance of a woman. If it suited his sinister purposes, the author claimed, his eyes "melted to the liquid softness of a woman's." His hands, too, are those of a woman: "Small, white, and soft,—indeed, almost too feminine."[49]

The Jesuit's distinctly feminine appearance explains another curious feature of much of this literature. In some cases, young women easily manage to disguise themselves as Jesuits. In Dhu's book, for instance, one of Jaudan's accomplices is a young boy named Carlo. But in the world of the Jesuits, masculine identity was never certain. As part of his plan to lure the beautiful Genevra into a convent, and thereby acquire her immense inheritance, Jaudan orders Carlo to insinuate himself into her household. To accomplish this task, Carlo becomes Inez, a young maid. Finally, at the end of the story, Inez once again becomes the male Carlo, displaying a dexterity with gender-crossing that would have appalled, but perhaps not surprised, the opponents of the Society.

The Jesuit's feminine nature was most powerfully on display in one of the strangest figures in the anti-Jesuit arsenal, the *Jésuitesse*. In the minds of anti-Jesuits, there appeared to be two types of *Jésuitesse*. The first was a member of a female religious house which had once been affiliated with the Society of Jesus. Although some authors assumed that such female affiliates had been abolished, others continued to speculate about their ongoing existence. Michelet, for example, declared that the order of Sacré-Cœur was not only led by the Jesuits, but also was governed by the same constitution.[50] The *Jésuitesse*, however, was more often defined as any woman who acted, whether consciously or not, at the behest of the Jesuits. The Larousse encyclopedia, for example, defined the *Jésuitesse* as a "woman who shares the doctrines, the morality of the Jesuits."[51] For many anti-Jesuits, such women numbered in the millions and, as an amalgam of the seductive charms of womanhood with the moral corruption of the Jesuit, often evoked even more fear than the Jesuits themselves. Popular works of fiction on both sides of the Atlantic were replete with such female accomplices of the Jesuits. In Eugène Sue's *Le juif errant*, the sinister Jesuit Rodin is matched in guile and treachery by Madame de Saint-Dizier, who schemes against her own niece, the heroine of the novel, Adrienne de Cardoville. Such women, Sue claimed, were the most dangerous foes of all.

The fear of the female Jesuit was equally strong in the United States. Here the female Jesuit was often imagined to be a maid or nanny insinuating herself into Protestant families in order to serve the Society's nefarious plans. For proof of this practice, anti-Jesuits pointed to the notorious *Monita Secreta*, or *Secret Instructions*, the alleged constitution of the Society. According to the *Secret Instructions*, the use of such spies was a legitimate means of obtaining family secrets.[52] Protestant pastors regularly put their flocks on guard against such wily creatures. In a letter published in the *New York Observer*, one reader recounted his own chilling encounter with just such a female Jesuit. A Catholic servant in the reader's household had been caught indoctrinating a young niece of the family in elements of Catholic belief such as the Immaculate Conception and transubstantiation. "Never," the reader warned, "could the most wily Jesuit have shown more skill and cunning."[53] Popular works contained equally sinister depictions of the female Jesuit. Two books by the English author Jemima Luke, the *Female Jesuit* and its sequel, provoked a great deal of discussion about the presence of feminine Jesuits in Protestant households. Allegedly based on real events, the two books contain the disturbing figure of Marie, a young woman who falsely claims to be a runaway nun in order to slip beneath the defenses of a series of Protestant families. Though the truthfulness of the story was not universally accepted, many American reviewers praised the works for alerting Americans to the dangers posed by the *Jésuitesse*.[54]

What does the specter of the *Jésuitesse* reveal about the androgynous nature of the Jesuit? The female Jesuit was clearly a woman, even if, in some circumstances, she was imagined disguising herself as a man. But the *Jésuitesse* was plausible only because the Jesuit was understood to embody many of the characteristics of the female sex. The similarity in their natures led the submissive Jesuit to turn to women as a natural ally in the task of undermining family and nation. But aside from dictating the choice of women as his preferred tool of subversion, the Jesuit was able to attain such an influence over women through his peculiarly insightful understanding of female nature. The alleged weak points of female nature, such as vanity and a love of luxury, were, in the eyes of anti-Jesuits, mercilessly exploited by the Society. The Jesuit, in this view, cynically encouraged such traits in women in order both to weaken their moral resoluteness and to win their loyalty.[55] Because he was himself feminine in nature, the Jesuit was particularly well-equipped to identify the sentimental weaknesses of women, and turn them to his ends. In his denunciation of the Catholic confessor, Michelet accused him of being "willing to make himself weak, to resemble woman."[56] It was precisely this capacity to make himself weak, which is to say, unmanly, that made the Jesuit such an effective recruiter of women, the sex with whom he shared so many qualities.

Hostility to the Jesuits was, of course, nothing new; the Society had been expelled from a range of countries, including France, in the eighteenth century. Elements of the nineteenth-century attack on the Jesuits were simply a repetition of earlier themes and images. But what was novel to the nineteenth century was this association between Jesuitism and androgyny, an association which made the Jesuit loom as a particularly terrifying figure. Several scholars have argued that the androgyne only became a monster in the nineteenth century. In his introduction to the memoirs of a famous French hermaphrodite, Herculine Barbin, Michel Foucault argues that attitudes to such cases had shifted markedly with the Enlightenment. During the Middle Ages, there was little doubt that it was possible for a human being to possess the sexual organs of both sexes. By the nineteenth century, however, such sexual and gendered confusion had become intolerable.[57] The cultural imperative to assign a complementary identity to the two sexes led to an abhorrence for any being which threw such a division into question. Physicians, for example, now labeled hermaphroditism a physiological impossibility in complex organisms like human beings, and strove to assign one sex in all apparently doubtful cases, even if their choice was contrary to the opinion of the patient.[58] The mere idea of male and female residing in one body had become, it seems, unbearable.

This was not true, it must be admitted, for all sections of society. In the hands of some feminists and social theorists, androgyny became a far more positive symbol of harmony and equality. Feminists such as Jeanne Deroin and Margaret Fuller invoked the androgyne's potential to overcome the rigid bifurcation at the heart of gender codes, and thereby inaugurate a society based on male and female equality.[59] At the same time, the power of the androgyne to overturn social distinctions extended beyond gender to class. For French social reformers such as Auguste Comte or Pierre-Simon Ballanche, the androgyne, a figure able to bring about a union of male and female traits, stood as a potent symbol of class as well as gender harmony.[60] But these more positive conceptions of androgyny do not alter this fundamental point: the androgyne, whether cast in a positive or negative light, subverted conventional gender and social norms. Critics of these norms appealed to the figure of the androgyne for precisely this reason; although in their minds androgyny may have inspired hope rather than fear, its potential to reshape society was still very clear. As Jean Molino has written, whether inspiring veneration or horror, androgynes "put in peril the order of the world by violating that organizing principle which situates and classifies all things in one of the fundamental bipolar categories."[61]

On both sides of the Atlantic, the prospect of any weakening of such bipolar categories was deeply unsettling. Social commentators often warned of the disastrous consequences which would ensue if the boundaries between the sexes were to tumble. One of the first casualties would be love itself. In *La femme au XIXe siècle*, Eugène Pelletan reflected at length on the dire results if the division between male and female were to be removed:

> Woman must remain woman, as man for his part must remain man...if the dream of Plato, who wished to assimilate man and woman under the name of Androgyne, could have been realized, there would only be friendship in the world...there would no longer be love.[62]

American social commentators were just as insistent that love depended on a steadfast commitment to gender difference. In an appraisal of *Aurora Leigh*, the influential poem by Elisabeth Barrett Browning, the *North American Review* reflected on the relationship between gender difference and love. The moral difference between the sexes, according to the *Review*, was "necessary, radical, and most unchangeable. It consists in opposite and complementary qualities. If it were otherwise, the sexes could never meet, much less unite."[63]

More than individual happiness was stake. Social order itself was deemed to rest on the maintenance of these gender dichotomies. For Jules Michelet, one of the lessons of French history was that whenever women abandoned the home for the public sphere, political and social chaos ensued. In his 1854 work *Les femmes de la Révolution*, he identified the political influence of ambitious women—the women of the counter-revolutionary Vendée, for example, with their devotion to priest and confessor, or the fashionable women of the Salons, whose charm and sophistication had so enthralled the Girondins—as one of the major factors preventing the installation of a durable Revolutionary regime.[64] American defenders of gender conventions agreed with Michelet that femininity was a destabilizing and destructive intrusion into the public domain. An article entitled "The Social Condition of Women" which appeared in the *North American Review* expressed this fear of publicly assertive womanhood through that stock figure of corrupted femininity, the Amazon. Whether, the author asserted,

> the story of the Amazons be authentic history, or only a cunningly devised fable, it presents at all events a poor picture of what society would become, if our councils were filled and

our armies *manned* with women, and they rather than men, or equally with men, discharged the external and political duties of society.⁶⁵

Yet more than gender was in question here, for the threat to social order posed by the Jesuit also encompassed class. Just as the Jesuit was imagined to possess a peculiar affinity with the female sex, he was also supposed to have mastered the secrets of manipulating another group which was understood to be feminine in nature, the mob. As several scholars have argued, the nineteenth-century middle classes understood the masses and mass culture to be feminine in nature.⁶⁶ Social psychologists such as Hippolyte Taine, Gabriel Tarde, and in particular Gustave le Bon, whose popular work *La Foule* was published in English as *The Crowd*, argued explicitly that the mob shared many distinctive traits with women. Like women, the mob was dangerously impulsive, impervious to rational argument, impressed by theatrical displays, highly impressionable and profoundly conservative. Even when composed exclusively of men, crowds, as Le Bon wrote, are "everywhere distinguished by feminine characteristics."⁶⁷ As in the case of the Jesuit, the association between femininity and the mob served to underscore its menace. As a number of scholars have argued, post-Enlightenment societies defined the body politic as masculine. Dorinda Outram, for example, contends that the French Revolution enshrined the bourgeois, masculine individual as the only legitimate bearer of civic rights; the figure of *homo clausus*, in turn, symbolized the exclusion both of women and the working-classes from the post-revolutionary political order.⁶⁸ In such a masculinized polity, the threat embodied in a mob shrouded with feminine characteristics became even more disturbing.

Though the bulk of these sociological analyses of the feminine mob emerged in the final decades of the century, the evidence of anti-Jesuit literature suggests that this association was present much earlier. If the mob was feminine in nature, then the androgynous Jesuit, as in the case of the *Jésuitesse*, possessed all the tools to bring it under his command. Since the mob and women were understood to possess similar natures, the same Jesuit tricks—music, theatrical ceremonies, appeals to the senses—would work on both. In 1843, the *New York Observer's* correspondent in France outlined this process. The Jesuits, he wrote, "flatter...the radical passions, in order to obtain the support of the lower classes." The Society, he went on, attracts the working classes by giving them lessons in music and dazzling them with "theatrical pomps."⁶⁹ The susceptibility of the crowd to such strategies was, of course, a sign of its feminine nature. But it was also an expression of the Jesuit's peculiar insight into the workings of that nature; through his own androgyny, the Jesuit was able to detect and cleverly manipulate the key points of influence in the mob, just as he could in women.

At the same time, the Jesuit's affinity with women and the mob invited comparison with another figure hovering menacingly at the borders of civilized society, the savage. As Le Bon argued, many of the features of the mob, such as its incapacity for reflection and its instinctive recourse to violence, were also apparent in "inferior forms of evolution"; for Le Bon, such forms included both women and what he described as "wild savages." In many hostile accounts, the spirit of Catholicism as well as Jesuitism is explicitly described as savage and uncivilized. In 1851, for example, Horace Greeley described a Mass he had witnessed at the Madeleine church in Paris. Like so many Americans, he emphasized the theatricality of the Mass; the "bowings and genuflexions, the swinging of censers and ringing of bells," Greeley wrote, were "inexplicable dumb show" to him. But Greeley also saw a trace of savagery. The "gorgeously dressed priests," he wrote, were "bearing what looked like spears."[70] In just one article, the French correspondent of the *New York Observer* compared the Jesuit emphasis on sensualism to the "fetishism of savages," the countless regulations governing the Society to those "imposed on the Brahmins of Hindostan," and the suppression of spiritual inquiry to the "method of the Chinese."[71]

The ascription to the Jesuits of savage values was equally employed to undercut the Jesuits' renowned effectiveness as missionaries. Many American Protestants alleged that the Jesuits' own semi-civilized state gave them an unfair advantage over other missionaries. Far from converting savage tribes to enlightened religious belief, the Jesuits, in this view, merely offered one set of superstitions in exchange for another. This was made clear in reviews of Francis Parkman's history of the Jesuit missionaries in North America. As one reviewer noted of the Jesuits' practice of baptizing Indians, there was a discernible "relation between their superstitious belief that every wild Indian so signed with the cross was safe, and the superstitions and necromancy they denounced."[72]

Perhaps the most forceful affirmation of the savage nature of Jesuitism was contained in Eugène Sue's *Le juif errant*. Rodin, the archetype of the sinister and evil Jesuit, takes on many of the traits of savagery. To cite just one example, having engineered the death of his rival, d'Aigrigny, he is pictured in "all the *savage* majesty of his infernal triumph."[73] Sue's novel also contains a striking example of the common femininity between the androgynous Jesuit, the savage and the mob. The scene occurs when the factory of Mr. Hardy, a member of the Rennepont family which Rodin has sworn to destroy, comes under attack from a mob called the "Wolves." Though not present, Rodin conspires to whip up the mob violence through one of his underlings, Morok, a tamer of wild beasts described as a "Siberian savage." In their destruction of the factory, the Wolves display the traits both of savagery, mob violence and corrupted femininity. Though mostly composed of men, they are led by a creature described as a "hag," Ciboule, who hurls stones with her "steady, masculine" hand; her exhortations to the men around her to destroy the factory are greeted with "savage cries" and "savage cheers" of approval.[74] In the minds of anti-Jesuits, then, androgyny, savagery and the fear of the lower orders all combined to cast the Jesuit from the bounds of civilized society.

* * *

One of the characteristics which the Jesuit was deemed to share with women was his tendency to oscillate between the most extreme forms of identity and behavior. Just as women were held to incarnate, in the words of Pierre Larousse, "that which is the best, and also that which is the worst in the world," the Jesuit was understood to embody a radical dualism.[75] In a long review of the history of the Society of Jesus, the *Southern Quarterly Review* noted this tendency for the Jesuit to be understood as a creature of extremes: "Seldom have they been viewed except as angels or devils...we are apt to form no calm and healthy judgments respecting these celebrated men. We love them, or we hate them, cordially and decidedly."[76] In France, the Larousse *Grand dictionnaire* cited Denis Diderot as its authority on the dichotomous nature of Jesuitism. Each individual Jesuit, according to Diderot, embodied "reason next to fanaticism, virtue next to vice, religion next to impiety...all the contrasts brought together."[77] Like the celibate priest and nun, the Jesuit defied the cultural imperative to show moderation in all things. He veered instead from one unreasonable extreme to another.

This imagined dualism allowed anti-Jesuits to portray their opponent as simultaneously a figure of pathetic submission and daunting authority. As we have seen, the Jesuit was understood to be held in a state of complete subservience to his General. But in relation to other members of the church, the Jesuit himself was alleged to enjoy a despotic power. In the United States, anti-Jesuit writers routinely claimed that the church hierarchy had fallen under the Society's control; the Society, according to one of the characters in Helen Dhu's *Stanhope Burleigh*, "controls absolutely, the Catholic Church in the United States."[78] Many French anti-Jesuits also pictured the Jesuits as masters of all Catholic orders. Michelet, for example, claimed that the Jesuits were virtual tyrants in many religious establishments: "How many convents have opened the door to them. Deceived by their sweet voice; and now they speak firmly there, and everyone is afraid, everyone smiles while trembling, and everyone does what they say."[79]

In the United States, the ability of the Society of Jesus to gain control over the church was understood to be an extension of its peculiar hold over female nature. Like women and the working classes, Catholicism itself was conceived as essentially feminine in nature. Dominated by a rigid hierarchy, denied the right to independently interpret Scripture, and held entranced by the superficial ritual of the Mass, the individual Catholic was often described in many of the same terms—passive, emotional and dependent—as women. As Thomas Whitney, the leader of the nativist *Order of United Americans* affirmed, the individual Catholic could never "lay claim to the prerogatives of perfect manliness."[80] American Republicanism, in contrast, with its belief in independent judgment, "puts in every bosom the heart and impulses of a *man*."[81] If further proof of Catholicism's effeteness were needed, many Americans looked to France, where religious observance seemed to be a purely feminine concern. Visitors to France often noted the large proportion of women among churchgoers, a phenomenon which was attributed to the inherent aversion felt by men for the Catholic religion. As the author of one Protestant tract observed, the absence of male parishioners was a result of "a distaste for the priestly character, and for some parts of the Romish ceremonial" among Frenchmen.[82]

There was a factual basis to the observation that Catholic devotion was increasingly taking on a feminine cast. Though all orders were growing in the nineteenth century, the greatest expansion was occurring in those composed of female religious. Among parishioners, it is also true that women were far more numerous than men.[83] The shift in theology to a more loving and compassionate God, and the rise of Marian devotion, were also considered signs of a more female-oriented religious practice. Indeed, the *Catholic World* itself recognized this, in its view, regrettable trend. "Though France is a Catholic country," it declared in 1869, "the humiliating fact that a considerable portion of its male population manifests a certain religious apathy, cannot be disguised."[84] What American critics of a female-dominated Catholicism in France ignored, however, was that a similar process of the feminization of religion was occurring in the United States.[85] For those American Protestants uncomfortable with this tendency, attacks on Catholic effeminacy may well have served to deflect attention from what was happening in their own churches. In any case, from the perspective of many Americans, not even the avoidance of Mass could save Catholic men from the emasculating effects of their religion.

Much of this emasculation was said to occur at the hands of the authoritarian Jesuit. Eclipsed by the Jesuit's authority, the clergy had lost all the markers of manhood. Michelet, for example, drew a clear contrast between the humble, timid parish priest, and the bold, confident Jesuit. Imagine, Michelet told the reader, the priest and the Jesuit walking in the street. The former, oppressed by his subordinate status, "walks sadly, looking shy and more than modest, gladly taking the edge of the path!" The Jesuit, on the other hand, exuded a manly authority and confidence: "Do you want to see a man? Watch the Jesuit pass by...The voice is soft, but the step is firm."[86] The Catholic laity fared little better. In *Stanhope Burleigh*, the dominance of the Jesuit Jaudan is so complete that the heroine's father, Vincenzi, rejects the pleas of his devoted daughter and insists on sending her to a convent, an act of cruelty which stems from the controlling hand of the Jesuits. Having been "under the all-powerful pressure of the hand of Jesuitism" for many years, the mind of Vincenzi "grown feeble... could no longer assert its independence."[87]

This authority over the laity was most clearly seen in the figure of the secular ally of the Jesuit, commonly referred to as the *Jésuite de robe courte*. In both the United States and France, the Jesuits were believed to control many of the most influential members of secular society, from politicians to doctors to newspaper editors. The relationship between the Society and its secular affiliates was set out in *Le jésuite*, another novel by the priest Jean-Hippolyte Michon, author of *Le maudit* and *La religieuse*:

> Those affiliated to the Order take an oath to support the order and to offer it all the assistance in their power; to the general, they take a simple vow of obedience. For its part, the order commits to protecting them, and to helping them in all the circumstances where they, and all who[m] they control, could require such assistance.[88]

The belief that many of the leaders of secular society had traded their independence for the inducements offered by the Jesuits was equally pervasive in the United States. Nativist novels commonly depict politicians agreeing to support Jesuit goals in exchange for Catholic votes, or newspaper editors suppressing damaging information on the Society in return for money.

In part, the Jesuits had managed to acquire this influence through the confessional box. By offering sinful men and women an easy forgiveness, the Jesuit director managed, in this view, to win them to his cause. But the key tool which had enabled the Jesuits to create this lay army was the education system. For their opponents, the Jesuits were at the heart of the vast expansion in Catholic educational establishments that was occurring in the middle decades of the nineteenth century. The Larousse Encyclopaedia noted this alarming expansion:

> Under the Second Empire...they have made enormous progress in our country, and have particularly sought to take control of the education of our youth, in order to destroy the principles which our society is built on and to mould the new generations in the ideas of clericalism.[89]

While the Jesuit take-over of the educational system appeared less complete in the United States, many Americans worried about Jesuit ambition in his area, particularly in the territories of the West. Noah Porter was only one respected authority to raise the alarm. "If Western society is left destitute of seminaries of a decidedly Protestant character," he warned, "the Jesuits will occupy the field."[90] Such Jesuit schools were designed, according to their critics, to produce the lay equivalent of the passive, pliable Jesuit himself. As the *Southern Quarterly Review* declared, "had it not been for their perseverance and activity in their schools, they could never have controlled so effectually, men and women."[91]

But authority was not the only manly virtue that the Jesuit displayed. The Jesuit was said to possess an extraordinary degree of willpower and resolution. In his quest to usurp temporal government and install the rule of the papacy, the single-minded Jesuit would brave all obstacles and face all dangers. As numerous histories attested, the Jesuits had managed to survive countless setbacks and expulsions throughout their history. Rodin in *Le juif errant* is just one of many portrayals of this unbending Jesuit resolve: though desperately ill with cholera, and while subjected to the excruciating pain of surgery, he continues to orchestrate his schemes against the Rennepont family. As many accounts emphasize, the precedent for such resolve and willpower had been established by the Society's founder, Ignatius Loyola. Loyola had, in this view, never deviated from his objective of elevating the status of his Society; as the French correspondent of the *New York Observer and Chronicle* was forced to admit, men with Loyola's unbending determination "are so rare in the world that this quality alone will enable them to effect great things."[92]

The Jesuit also possessed exemplary courage. The narrator of Michon's *Le jésuite* described the insistence in Jesuit seminaries on daring and audacity as the necessary qualities for any member: "Through weakness, we can lose everything. A good Jesuit pushes courage to the point of heroism."[93] The Jesuit was also ambitious. His goal was nothing less than world domination, an ambition vividly displayed in the image of d'Aigrigny in *The Wandering Jew*, running his hands over a globe covered in red crosses, his expression that of an "infernal genius of insatiable domination."[94] Finally, the Jesuit was active. On this point, the Jesuits, as numerous authors attested, were different to other religious orders. While monks were thought to devote themselves to little more than an otherworldly contemplation, the Jesuits were energetically striving to enact their worldly ambitions. The historian Francis Parkman described the Jesuit as "emphatically a man of action."[95] In an otherwise hostile entry, the *Encyclopaedia Americana* conceded that in relation to the Jesuits, "Nobody could accuse them of idle brooding in prayer and psalm-singing."[96] In Michon's fictional account, the General himself describes the unique nature of the Jesuits in an interview with the young Father de Sainte-Maure. "The others," the General boasts, "are only invalids from the world, sheltered in their cells; we are soldiers, prepared to go into combat in the world itself."[97]

In these descriptions of the Jesuit's power, independence and fortitude, it is difficult not to detect a note of admiration, and even envy. An avowed opponent of the Jesuits like Edgar Quinet, when contemplating the scale of Jesuit ambition, was forced to concede that "in this audacity there is something which attracts and pleases me." Furthermore, Quinet praised the Society's endless capacity to renew itself after being expelled from a variety of countries.[98] In his preface to the memoirs of the purported ex-Jesuit Abbate Leone, Victor Considérant described the Jesuits as a "great human force" which encapsulated the following qualities: "Boundless ambition, a mighty organization, indomitable perseverance, and absolute devotedness, all directed to the attainment of an impossible object."[99] Francis Parkman also acknowledged the positive elements in an otherwise deplorable system. "No religious Order," Parkman wrote, "has ever united in itself so much to be admired and so much to be detested."[100] As all of these grudging concessions to Jesuit bravery and resolution imply, if only the goal to which he adhered were not so monstrous, the Jesuit might figure as a model for other men to follow.

The fascination with the authoritarian Jesuit points to an underlying anxiety about masculinity in the middle decades of the century. Masculinity in France and the United States was certainly understood in different ways. In France, as Robert A. Nye and William Reddy have argued, honor and shame functioned as key concepts in the construction of a male bourgeois code of behavior.[101] This preoccupation with honor was most starkly manifested in the practice of dueling, which achieved its greatest popularity in the nineteenth century.

The persistence of the aristocratic concept of honor did not work in the same way in the intensely democratic United States. In his analysis of codes of manliness, E. Anthony Rotundo identifies the dominant model at mid-century as what he terms "self-made manhood." Masculine identity, according to Rotundo, was grounded in professional achievement and financial independence. The self-made man was committed above all to personal advancement, and exhibited all the qualities—hard work, independence, an absence of sentiment—upon which such success hinged.[102]

Whether identified with honor or with self-advancement, masculinity rested on unstable foundations. Though most scholars identify a "crisis of masculinity" toward the end of the century, there is much evidence to suggest that many of these tensions around masculine identity were present much earlier.[103] In the case of post-Revolutionary France, William Reddy has argued that the ability of more and more men to attain honor was accompanied by a nagging fear that it might be lost, creating, as he writes, "a powerful dilemma for the nineteenth-century male."[104] Similarly, Robert A. Nye has suggested that among bourgeois men, sexual potency became an important marker of honor, provoking a new set of anxieties around impotence and sexual performance.[105] Making masculinity contingent on material success, as the model of the self-made manhood implied, was hardly more reassuring; personal fortunes, after all, could be lost as well as won.

How could a man prove his manliness? One means may have been to engage in battle with a fearsome enemy like the Jesuits. Anti-Jesuit literature is replete with martial imagery, a call for, in the words of the radical newspaper editor and subsequent Communard Benjamin Gastineau, "men of heart" to throw off the "odious yoke" that the Jesuits had thrown over the nation.[106] Defeat at the hands of the Jesuits, in turn, is frequently equated with military capitulation. In an analogy repeated by other anticlericals, Edgar Quinet warned that conceding defeat to the Jesuits would be a repetition of the terrible retreat from Moscow endured by the *Grande Armée* in 1812.[107] Such analogies served, of course, to brand the Jesuits as a foreign invader intent on subjugating the French nation. But underlying such martial imagery, it is difficult not to detect a belief that fighting against Jesuit invasion was a means not merely of defending the nation, but also of asserting one's manliness.

Reasserting one's masculinity through a crusade against the Jesuits also seemed to motivate many American nativists. As Susan Griffin has argued, many nativist men appeared to be driven by a need to escape the long shadow cast by the Founding Fathers. In the popular nativist novels of the early 1850s, worthy and noble young republican men set out to save their beautiful lovers from wily and scheming Jesuits. At stake in this battle was not just the purity of the American maiden but, as Griffin writes, "the republican rights that the new generation of American males have failed to inherit."[108] Defending the legacy of the Founding Fathers against Jesuit subversion gave nativist men the chance to prove not only their claim to be worthy successors to the glorious Revolutionary generation, but in so doing, their manhood as well.

If engaging in an anti-Jesuit crusade gave many men the chance to reaffirm their masculinity, however, there was no guarantee of success. The authoritarian Jesuit threatened to beat men at their own game. Courageous, disciplined, hard-working and ambitious, the Jesuit had the potential to eclipse the majority of middle-class men. In many ways, he was even understood as having an advantage. Free from the demands of family or the rules of moral propriety, the Jesuit was not subject to the constraints imposed on respectable men. Striving toward a clear objective, and armed with the weapon of moral expediency, the Jesuit represented a fearsome competitor in the race to get ahead. At the same time, the submissive, emasculated Jesuit loomed as a state which might conceivably afflict any man. The Jesuit, in both his authoritarian and submissive guises, thus served as the locus for a host of anxieties about the stability of masculine privilege and identity in the middle decades of the century.

* * *

In the eyes of his opponents, the Jesuit was a multi-faceted and baffling figure. Particularly disturbing was his disregard for boundaries. National borders were thought to be no obstacle for the Jesuit. The sinister Rodin might appear in Paris or in New York; the Jesuit's ambition was, after all, to reign over every nation. At times, anti-Jesuits might claim that their nation was a privileged target of the Society. American writers sometimes warned that their nation's democratic institutions made it particularly vulnerable to Jesuit subversion. French writers suggested that the Jesuits were determined to reign in France, the leading nation (in their view) of Europe. But all agreed that the Jesuit could not be quarantined in any one nation, and that Jesuitism would, if left unchecked, spread across the world.

The crusade against the Society of Jesus thus exemplifies a fundamental reason for the construction of a Transatlantic case against the church: combating an enemy understood to be international in spirit and ambition required a similarly international response. Opponents of the Jesuits followed the progress of the Society in other nations, and looked abroad for guidance on the best means of combating their enemy. The understanding of Jesuitism as a global menace dictated an international consciousness among its opponents, thereby feeding the cross-border trade in literary attacks on the Society.

A thorough account of anti-Jesuit sentiment must therefore adopt an international approach. But it must also incorporate theoretical advances made in other national fields. In this case, Róisín Healy's discovery of the role of androgyny in motivating anti-Jesuit sentiment in the German-speaking states has revealed a hitherto unexplored aspect of the discourse in France and the United States. Like the German anti-Jesuits studied by Healy, French and American opponents of the Society imagined their enemy as a confusing and subversive mix of gender traits. In his passive, unflinching obedience to his General, the Jesuit seemed to occupy the submissive position assigned to women. His adroitness in the art of seduction, and his apparent empathy with his female collaborators, the *Jésuitesses*, reinforced this impression of femininity. But viewed from another perspective, the Jesuit exuded an irresistible masculinity. Commanding the obedience of other Catholics as well as influential members of secular society, and exemplifying the supposedly male qualities of courage, ambition and willpower, the Jesuit seemed to overshadow his secular opponents to the point that their own masculinity appeared under threat.

The defense of masculinity was not the only concern for the opponent of Catholicism. The case against the Catholic Church also revolved around a certain conception of true femininity. In this area, one Catholic institution in particular, the convent, became the focus of suspicion and hostility on both sides of the Atlantic. It is to this facet of the case against Catholicism that we now turn.

5
The Captivity of Sister Barbara Ubryk

In July 1869, an investigating judge in the city of Cracow, at that time part of the Austrian province of Galicia, made a shocking discovery that would lead to an international scandal. Having received an anonymous letter informing him that a Catholic nun was being held against her will in the city's Carmelite convent, the judge had demanded the right to search within its walls. The international press provided breathless accounts of what apparently occurred next. Brushing aside the protests of the Mother Superior, confessor and other nuns, the judge, along with several other officers and, by some accounts, the local bishop, forced his way into the convent and rushed toward a row of cells. Opening the first door, the investigators recoiled in horror. A figure later described as half-beast, half-human lay before them, naked, shivering, and covered with mud and excrement. Cowering at the sight of her liberators, the "creature," in the terms of the press, begged them for mercy.[1] Shocked and angered by their discovery, the officers led away the nun, by now identified as Barbara Ubryk. When news of the scandal reached the town's citizens, mobs gathered outside the convent and were only prevented from attacking the building by the presence of armed soldiers.[2] It was later alleged that Ubryk had been held captive in her miserable cell for twenty-one years.

News of the alleged captivity of Barbara Ubryk provoked two distinct reactions. On the one hand, certain details of the Ubryk case shocked many commentators in France and the United States. In particular, the pitiful physical state in which Ubryk was discovered, as well as the incredible length of her confinement, made the Ubryk case particularly notorious. At the same time, though exceptional in its severity, the case was seen as only one in a series of scandals involving nuns held against their will and subjected to psychological and physical abuse in the shadowy depths of the convent. Over the three decades prior to the discovery of Ubryk, the belief that nuns were incarcerated and ill-treated had become an article of faith for opponents of the convent in the United States and France. The Ubryk story was thus the culmination of a growing Transatlantic body of literature that branded the convent a site of imprisonment, misery and death.

In the United States, the discovery of Barbara Ubryk hit front pages in August 1869. Not content with reproducing the shocking details, editorialists added their own commentaries. The *New York Times* denounced the "horrible cruelties practiced upon the unfortunate Carmelite nun at Cracow." The *New York Weekly Herald* described the tale as "a melancholy story, a rather revolting narrative" and declared that the case would "command universal attention."[3] In France, interest in the case was just as strong. Throughout late July and early August, major French newspapers joined in condemning what the *Journal des Débats* described as "the odious imprisonment of the Cracow nun." The republican *Siècle* concluded that the suffering endured by Ubryk demonstrated the urgency of abolishing "practices which claim to be ascetic but which are simply barbarous."[4] In both countries, book-length accounts were published in the aftermath of the scandal to profit from public indignation.[5]

Yet what exactly had happened to Barbara Ubryk? Although the mainstream press displayed some discretion on the reasons for her incarceration, a number of clues left readers with little doubt as to the true cause. All of the press accounts include the telling admission, made by Ubryk herself at the moment of her liberation, that she had broken the vow of chastity. In a sign of the sexual corruption which apparently reigned in the convent, Ubryk was recorded as immediately turning toward the other nuns present and shrieking, "But these, too, are not angels." The key to the story, then, was sexual vice, and the two chief villains the Mother Superior and the Confessor of the convent. Again, though no direct accusation was contained in these initial reports, enough information was given to identify the culprits. In a clear sign of her guilt, the Superior, as all the press articles note, had initially tried to bar the investigating judge from entering the convent. As for the Confessor, his guilt was even more obvious; upon catching sight of him as she was being escorted from the convent, Ubryk was said to have cried out, "You beast!" If any doubt were left as to their complicity in the crime, both the Confessor and the Superior were subsequently reported to have been arrested. The book-length accounts of Ubryk's captivity which appeared in the United States and France confirmed these tacit accusations. According to these narratives, Ubryk had been raped by the Confessor soon after entering the convent. Upon discovering this crime, the Superior, far from responding with pity, had flown into a jealous rage, as she had once been the Confessor's sexual favorite. Together with the Confessor, the Superior had then, according to these narrative, locked Ubryk up in her subterranean cell.

One of the striking features of the reportage in both countries was the immediate acceptance that Ubryk's incarceration could only have been the result of the convent's regime of cruel punishment and sexual perversion. A more skeptical eye might have noticed the many inconsistencies in the reporting of the event. In an account published in the *Opinion Nationale*, for example, the cell is located at the end of a subterranean passage; in another in the same paper, on the upper levels of the convent. Some accounts refer to Barbara Abrick, or Ubrick. In many accounts, the Bishop of Cracow is present at the discovery of the nun; in others, such as the *Chicago Tribune* article of August 13, only the prelate sent by the bishop witnesses the scene. Such inconsistencies, however, were barely noticed by the mainstream press.

Alternative and credible explanations for Ubryk's presence in the cell were, however, available, and reported by the Catholic press. The *Univers* set out the defense. The Mother Superior of the convent, while admitting that Ubryk had indeed been physically isolated from the rest of the community, claimed that the nun's mental instability had left her with little choice. According to the Superior, Ubryk had been dumped in the convent by her own family, who were unable to cope with her mental illness. The family had not revealed Ubryk's mental condition to the convent authorities, and soon after her entry to the convent she had become such a disruptive presence that her separation from the other nuns had become unavoidable. Furthermore, the Superior claimed, the doctor of the convent had approved this course of action. The story of incarceration and abuse was nothing other than a conspiracy, the *Univers* claimed, led by freethinkers, Protestants and Jews, in order to justify legislative regulation of Catholic convents.[6]

Although not entirely mitigating the accusation of severity on the part of the Superior, this defense was immediately dismissed by the press. The *Philadelphia Public Ledger* sought to discredit the Superior's explanation by noting that "The present doctor, who has held the position seven years, stated that he had never even seen Barbara once."[7] The *Moniteur Universel* ridiculed the Superior's story in almost identical terms.[8] Furthermore, a number of commentators argued that, even if Ubryk were indeed mentally disturbed, this was the result rather than the cause of her terrible ordeal. Several newspapers noted that Ubryk had shown signs of derangement in the hours after her liberation, and had therefore been placed in an asylum. The temporary nature of this measure was clear, however, from reports that after being clothed and fed, Ubryk had immediately begun to show signs of regaining her senses. In the words of the *Moniteur Universel*, "she has come out of her mindlessness and of the savage state into which isolation and solitude had plunged her."[9] For much of the press, the only plausible explanation for Ubryk's confinement appeared to be the cruelty of the Confessor and Superior.

The widespread acceptance of the veracity of this story was no doubt due to its familiarity. In the United States, stories of captive nuns held against their will and subjected to a range of abuses were some of the bestselling works of the age. The most notorious, *The Awful Disclosures of Maria Monk*, had sold more than 300,000 copies by the Civil War. Fictional portrayals of the convent invariably included all the elements of a prison: high walls, bolted gates and barred windows. In the words of one pamphleteer, the very architecture of the convent was "the apparatus of confinement."[10] Some accounts went even further by describing the existence of subterranean cells in which recalcitrant nuns were left to languish. The narrative of Maria Monk described a row of such sinister cells. In Isaac Kelso's sensational novel *Danger in the Dark*, the heroine Isadora is locked in a tiny cell; in an even more direct parallel to the Ubryk case, she has been imprisoned on the pretext that she is insane, a pretext invented by the convent hierarchy. Nor was the Ubryk story the first convent captivity story to appear in the mainstream American press. Newspapers regularly reported cases of runaway nuns or young girls held against their will in convents. In 1855, for example, both the *New York Times* and *Chicago Tribune* published an account of a writ of *habeas corpus* served against the order of the Sisters of Mercy in Illinois. The writ alleged that a young woman called Mary E. Parker was being prevented from leaving the convent.[11] Just weeks before news of the Ubryk case appeared, *Harper's Weekly* recounted the story of a nun who had escaped her convent, before being hunted down and forcibly returned. The story contained no names or places. But the reader was left to imagine the punishment which awaited the captured nun: "Who shall say," the author conjectured, "what agonies of mind and body have been inflicted upon her?"[12]

This accusation that the convent was little more than a prison was also widespread in France. Just as in America, popular descriptions of the convent dwell on their fortified, impenetrable exterior.[13] Many of the hostile descriptions of the convent which appeared in France in the middle decades of the century also warned of a sinister cell known under a range of names: the *cachot*, the *in-pace* or the *oubliette*. Several fictional depictions of such cells foreshadowed key elements of the Ubryk story. In Alfred Villeneuve's *Les mystères du cloître*, the Abbaye-aux-Dames, with its reinforced walls and imposing gates, is akin to a house of detention. After experiencing both the spiritual cruelty and physical torture which, according to the author, formed part of the nun's life, the heroine Blanche is imprisoned by a vindictive Superior in a *cachot* filled with wet straw and rats.[14] In Jean-Hippolyte Michon's *La religieuse*, the young Mathilde de Tourabel witnesses the imprisonment of a nun in an *in-pace* on the grounds that she is insane. As in the Ubryk case, insanity is merely a ploy by a vindictive Superior eager to punish a recalcitrant nun.[15] Some commentators also explicitly linked the Ubryk case to perhaps the most famous French narrative of sexual disorder in convents, Denis Diderot's *La religieuse*. Diderot's tale, though periodically banned in nineteenth-century France, remained influential; its heroine, Suzanne, is also locked up in a subterranean cell and becomes near-insane as a result. "This poor woman," wrote F.X. Trébois in the *Tribune*, "reminds us of Diderot's nun... Like Diderot's heroine, Barbara suffers from hunger, thirst, and the most unspeakable humiliations."[16]

Anticlericals could also cite earlier cases involving accusations of imprisonment and torture, cases which in many instances mirrored the basic narrative of the Ubryk affair. In Jules Michelet's papers, there is a folder with handwritten copies of press extracts concerning one such case, that of Soeur Sainte-Marie de Colombes in the town of Bayeux in 1845. Like Ubryk, Soeur Sainte-Marie was forced into a *cachot* by a tyrannical Superior; after eight days she was transferred to the Bon-Sauveur religious house in Caens, where she was locked up for a further ten months in a cell filled with "folles furieuses." As in the case of Ubryk, this treatment was defended on the grounds of Sainte-Marie's mental instability; however, for her defenders, her mental illness was a result, rather than a cause, of her treatment at the hands of the convent authorities.[17] The rigorous regime of press censorship during the Second Empire precluded further reporting of such cases, but by the late 1860s they began to return to the pages of the French press. In his attack on the convent system, Charles Sauvestre reported the case of a nun confined in a cell by the Superior of a Belgian convent on the grounds of her insanity. The nun, known as demoiselle Baudry, was eventually liberated by a justice of the peace who concluded that she was of sound mind. This liberation had only occurred, Sauvestre reminded his readers, after ten years of imprisonment.[18] Just weeks before the apparent discovery of Ubryk, Sauvestre also reported to readers of the *Opinion Nationale* the case of a young girl in the town of Villeneuve-sur-Yonne who had been kidnapped and held in a convent "under the pretext of a religious vocation."[19]

The belief that the convent was a torture-house was also nourished, as in America, by first-hand accounts from escaped nuns. In the 1860s, more and more such works appeared. In one, an escaped nun identified only as *La Soeur X* described the misery she had endured in the convent. Eventually, the fear that she will be imprisoned in the *cachot* leads her to risk escape.[20] By 1869, when the story of Barbara Ubryk emerged, the accusation that imprisonment and torture were carried out in convents was almost commonplace in the anticlerical press. Here, for example, is a description of convents in the anticlerical *Opinion Nationale* which appeared in the wake of the Ubryk scandal:

> In these living tombs the unfortunate victims' shrieks of pain normally fade away without finding any echo outside. Occasionally, however, through a lucky chance or a charitable indiscretion, they breach the walls of the religious fortress, move the people, and give rise in their breast to a noble anger and a generous indignation.[21]

The *Siècle* reported the discovery of a subterranean passage lined with wine barrels connecting a convent and a monastery. In its commentary, the paper added a grim note to the otherwise ribald tone of the article: "Nuns, monks, wine...everything has not been found. Let us search, the cadavers can't be far away."[22]

In a further sign of the way in which the story of Barbara Ubryk was understood to be merely the most glaring manifestation of a far deeper pattern of abuse and mistreatment, a host of commentators used the case, just at the *Univers* had feared, to renew calls for the mandatory state supervision of convents. Such proposals were already, as several papers observed, on their way to becoming law in the Austrian Empire. But the fate of Barbara Ubryk prompted demands in France and the United States for swift legislative action to liberate the many captive nuns far closer to home. The *Journal des Débats* used the Ubryk case to insist that convents "be submitted to common law, and that supervision on the part of the authorities be exercised at any time in these mysterious retreats."[23] The republican Henri Allain-Targé applauded such proposals. It was good, he noted, "that Catholics learn that freedom is necessary to men."[24] For the

Albion [New York], the significance of the Ubryk story was equally clear: "The moral we draw from this horrible story is that monasteries and nunneries must be thrown open to the free inspection of the civil power."[25] Just as the state was increasingly taking responsibility for the protection of children, so it should also, these commentators implied, intervene to defend vulnerable young women within convents.

* * *

The convent atrocity story was far more than a tale of individual suffering. In both the United States and France, these stories of confined and ill-treated young women served a range of cultural and social purposes. To begin with, the captive nun embodied a striking political symbolism. For French republicans in particular, the body of the captive nun was undoubtedly a metaphor for their own political and civic confinement at the hands of a regime allied with the church. In this context, the year of Barbara Ubryk's imprisonment—1848—had an obvious significance.[26] Many press reports suggested that Ubryk had attempted to flee the convent in that year, and soon afterward had been placed in her terrible cell. In the same year, French republicans had passed from the euphoria of the February Revolution to the violence of the June days and the final disappointment of the election of Louis-Bonaparte in December. The sense that their own fate mirrored Ubryk's could only have been heightened by her apparent victimization at the hands of the Catholic Church, a church which had initially offered some support to the 1848 revolution before eventually lending its authority to the autocratic regime. The confinement of Ubryk, then, and the church's alignment with the regime of Napoléon III, could be understood as comparable manifestations of Catholicism's despotic spirit.

However, the crux of the Ubryk story, like all other convent atrocity stories, was the female heart. As we have seen in relation to anti-Jesuit literature, women and men were understood to possess a set of complementary physical and moral traits. In conventional understandings of this gender division, men were deemed superior in all that concerned the intellect, while women were said to reign supreme in the qualities of the heart. Women, as countless authors emphasized, were animated to a far greater degree than men by sentiment and feeling, and thus had a natural genius for the expression of love, sympathy and compassion. In his advice manual for young women, the popular author John Angell James declared that "an unfeeling woman is a contradiction of her sex." A woman who exhibited a stony heart, Angell warned, had forfeited her role as "the ministering angel of humanity."[27] Medical writers also paid tribute to the power of the female heart. For Dr. Louis Seraine, "the spirit of woman is in her heart, as that of the man is in his mind."[28] In relation to women there was a Transatlantic consensus that, in the words of the reformer Ernest Legouvé, "Especially does she represent that fundamental quality...the heart."[29]

For all its power, however, the heart was a frail organ, and ill-suited to the storms and stresses of business and politics. Governed by their delicate virtues, women were thus thought obliged to seek refuge in the tranquility of the domestic sphere. In both France and the United States, commentators on the proper relations of the sexes insisted that only in the home could women's sentimental qualities flourish. Science and religion spoke in unison on this point. In his bestselling advice manual, *The Young Woman's Friend*, Daniel C. Eddy attributed the feminized private sphere to Divine will: "Home is woman's throne...there she exhibits the excellences of character which God had in view of her creation, and there she fills the sphere to which divine providence has called her."[30] Though motivated by very different beliefs, the French sociologist Auguste Comte arrived at an identical conclusion. "The direction...of progress in the social condition of women," Comte proclaimed, "is this: to render her life more and more domestic."[31] In both countries, women were among the leading proponents of this domestic ideal. In the United States, Catharine Beecher wrote several bestselling treatises on domestic economy. In France, a writer such as Madame Romieu described the family as "the natural domain of women."[32] At the same time, industrialization, which at mid-century had advanced to a similar degree in both societies, was enabling more and more families to enact the separation of work and home which this cultural ideal of domesticity required.

No true female heart, however, could survive long in a convent. The convent atrocity story formed part of a body of sentimental literature that Joan Burbick has called "heart histories."[33] All the convent atrocity stories emphasize the manner in which the nun's sentimental qualities are systematically crushed, to the point where she barely resembles a woman. This process allegedly began with the nun's isolation from the outside world. Once a full-fledged member of the order, all contact with family or friends is censored or even cut. In the testimony of the runaway nun Josephine Bunkley, her letters to her father in which she complains of her treatment in the convent are intercepted by the Superior. Even worse, the Superior then forces her to rewrite them so as to give the false impression that she is happy in the convent.³⁴ The emphasis in this literature is on the radical disjunction between the convent and the outside world. In Victor Hugo's *Les misérables*, for instance, the nuns of the Petit-Picpus are so determined to resist the encroachments of secular society that they even resent the prospect of being buried in a cemetery located outside the convent grounds.³⁵ This separation served many purposes. On one level, it was presented as designed to forestall any possible rescue attempts. But isolation from the world was also seen as part of a deliberate strategy of destroying female nature. By banishing the comforts of domesticity from women whose very nature, according to the prevailing feminine ideal, dictated their dependence on the sentimental virtues of the home, the convent appeared to clash with one of the fundamental traits of femininity.

Within the convent itself, according to these narratives, sentimental attachments between the nuns are just as harshly proscribed. In yet another demonstration of Catholicism's cruelty, the captive nun is denied even the meager comfort afforded by a friendship with another member of the community. Nuns are presented as atomized individuals, walking past each other with faces turned down and hands clasped in front. The channel of feeling is blocked. "One sister," claimed Josephine Bunkley, "is not suffered to converse with another respecting her own private feelings."³⁶ A similar picture emerges in Michon's *La religieuse*, where Sister Thérèse soon discovers that "in the religious life, every outpouring of the heart is a serious fault." The narrator of *La Soeur X* claims that the rules of the convent specifically forbid any affection or friendship between the sisters.³⁷ Of course, friendships do occasionally flicker into life. In Barbara Ubryk's case, some accounts mention a fellow nun, Sister Mary, who had bravely informed the authorities of Ubryk's fate. But such attachments are held to be rare successes in overcoming the convent's rule of separation and isolation.

The accusation that the convent robbed women of their affective virtues was made in the aftermath of Barbara Ubryk's liberation. Commentators on the Ubryk case seized on what was, from their perspective, a particularly troubling aspect of the Affair: the failure of any of the other nuns to come to her aid. Newspaper accounts left a number of clues which suggested that much of the community had been aware of her imprisonment. The porteress, for example, was reported to have nearly fainted upon hearing the investigative judge's request to search for a nun called Barbara Ubryk. In some accounts, several nuns then tried to prevent the judge from opening the door which led to Ubryk's cell. Any doubt on this question would have been dispelled by the report of the bishop's furious admonition toward the nuns present at Ubryk's liberation: "You are furies, not women."[38]

As these words suggest, the indifference evinced by the nuns toward Ubryk was a clear demonstration that the convent had robbed them of one of their defining qualities as women, empathy. Much of the commentary on the case expressed amazement that the nurturing and sympathetic virtues of women had been so effectively crushed by the conventual system. The *New York Herald* described Ubryk in her cell, "unpitied by her sisters in religion."[39] The *New York Observer and Chronicle* similarly wrote of the nuns passing Ubryk's cell daily "without one look or word of love or pity."[40] In France, this lack of pity on the part of the nuns was equally the subject of much condemnation. As the *Temps* lamented, "the grey sisters passed every day before this cell and none of them had the thought to take pity on the poor victim."[41] There could be no better demonstration, these reports suggest, of the gulf between the heart of a true woman, and that of a nun.

All the tales of abuse in convents in France and the United States use the heart as a telling metaphor for the destruction of female nature carried out within their walls. The act of taking vows is described as a burying of the heart; once this step has been taken, the heart of the suffering nun is wounded, broken and crushed. As the nun Isadora Norwood laments in Isaac Kelso's *Danger in the Dark*, having entered the convent, "a frost, a killing frost, fell upon the garden of my heart."[42] A telling sign of this withering of the heart is a stock element in physical descriptions of the nun: her pale cheeks. In one American story set in a French convent, the Protestant Eliza Freeman declares to her friend, the novice Maria Gerard, that a woman's face was the surest indication of the state of her heart; as she writes, "you may judge from her countenance what passes in her heart, for they never could contradict each other."[43] If this were indeed true, the face of the nun was particularly revealing. Once her heart has been crushed, the nun's countenance loses any signs of vitality; in her cheerless resignation to her fate, she became, in the description of the popular novelist Jane Dunbar Chaplin, "an automaton in mourning."[44]

The result of this crushing of the heart was that nuns simply faded away. At its most provocative, the convent atrocity literature described the murder of nuns within the convent walls. But while such sensational claims attracted a great deal of attention, the most common cause of death was seen to be far more prosaic. Denied the animating spirit provided by the warm and effusive female heart, and barred from the solace of companionship, the nun was condemned, in the words of a member of the Pennsylvania assembly, "to languish and pine away in cheerless solitude, where no friendly word greets their ear and buoys up the sickening heart."[45] The final cause of death was often consumption, a disease which anti-convent writers alleged to be endemic among the nuns. But though consumption might deliver the final blow to the ailing nun, the true disease was the emotional malaise induced by the thwarting of female nature.

The convent atrocity literature was thus highly similar in the United States and France. In one important aspect, however, the convent atrocity story in France and the United States differed: the question of escape. Put simply, the captive nun was far more likely to become a runaway nun in the United States than in France. Of course, not all American captive nuns were depicted freeing themselves. In the nativist stories of the early 1850s, male heroes brave the high walls of the convent to liberate the helpless nun. Both rescue and escape from the convent appeared in French versions of the convent captivity tale. In Denis Diderot's *La religieuse*, Suzanne is hoisted over the wall of the convent with a rope. In Michon's *Le maudit*, the hero Julio snatches his sister Louise from the convent of Notre Dame de Forcassi. In an account which matched the initiative attributed to American runaway nuns, the anonymous *Soeur X* describes escaping through a window and across a river, where she takes refuge in a cottage. Nonetheless, the act of escape occurs far more frequently in American convent atrocity stories. This difference requires some explanation.

First, escape clearly made more sense in a majority-Protestant than in a majority-Catholic country. Where, after all, could an escaped nun find refuge in a Catholic society like France? In antebellum America, moreover, tales of captivity and escape were common. The nun was only one of a number of runaways; the narratives of escaped slaves, for example, were highly popular in the Northern states. More fundamentally, young women were perceived to enjoy more autonomy in the United States than in France. The independent young American woman was one of the great stereotypes of the nineteenth century. French observers of American society routinely expressed their amazement at the personal liberty granted to young women in the United States, a liberty which did not appear, to their even greater stupefaction, to lead to any loss of virtue on their part. The conclusions of the journalist Ernest Duvergier de Hauranne during his visit to the United States in 1864 were entirely typical of French perceptions in this regard. Young American women, he observed, enjoy a liberty which "can cause a foreigner to draw many false conclusions." Their propriety and virtue were, however, indisputable. "An unaccompanied woman," he noted, "enjoys perfect security. Public opinion, based on custom, punishes with certain ostracism anyone who dares to affront it."[46] Of course, the observations of visitors cannot be considered wholly reliable or accurate. But most historians agree that young French women of the *bourgeoisie* were subject to a degree of control and supervision far more stringent than in either Britain or the United States. In Protestant nations, as Gabrielle Houbre has argued, social custom permitted young women, for example, to flirt with their suitors. In France, on the other hand, where all contact with suitors could only occur in the presence of a chaperone, such behavior would invite condemnation and social marginalization.[47]

This difference underlay the greater proportion of runaway nuns in the convent atrocity literature in the United States. The depiction of the young woman who, through her own initiative and fortitude, manages to break through the physical and psychological barriers holding her in the convent undoubtedly appeared more plausible in the light of American social practice. The French nun, subject not only to the burdens imposed by the church but also to the circumscribed autonomy which was a feature of daily life for bourgeois girls, was considered far less likely to display the same independence and fearlessness.

* * *

In essence, the tale of Barbara Ubryk was a narrative of captivity. Though not identical to the Indian captivity genre which was so popular in the United States, the two forms shared many common features. Both involved the enforced separation of an innocent woman from the protective conventions of civilized society. In their more lurid versions, both contained scenes of sexual abuse and physical torture inflicted upon defenseless young women which appeared to serve a dual purpose: providing an efficient means of inciting hatred against the cruel captors, while offering a largely male readership a socially sanctioned outlet for voyeurism. The blurring between convent and Indian captivity forms even extended to the identity of the captors. In at least one American work, Isaac Kelso's *Danger in the Dark*, escape from the convent leads directly to recapture, this time at the hands of Native Americans on the frontier. At times, too, both captors are Catholic. This is the case in the popular novel for younger readers, *The Casco Captive*, where the Indians who kidnap the hero have been converted to Catholicism. More fundamentally, like Indians on the frontier, key Catholic figures were often described in terms of barbarity and savagery.[48] As we have seen, anti-Jesuit literature described members of the Society as savages. But the convent atrocity literature, too, reveals the extent to which gender codes allowed opponents of Catholicism to portray the church as beyond the boundaries of civilized society.

This identification of the convent as an unregulated domain peopled by savages can be seen in one of the most potent symbols of the assault on true femininity, the removal of the captive female's hair. In many convent atrocity stories, the most emotionally laden moment occurs during the ceremony of the taking of vows when the novice's hair, invariably described as long, thick and unbound, is cut away, and the tresses fall to the floor. In the Indian captivity tales, the loss of female hair occurs through a far bloodier act, scalping. But in both cases, the removal of female hair is filled with meaning. At one level, the loss of hair equates to a loss of feminine identity; by allowing her hair to be shorn, the nun is renouncing one of the most distinctive and prominent markers of her womanhood. No longer an individual, she will henceforth merge into the uniform ranks of the female religious. As the French account of Barbara Ubryk's captivity claimed, from the moment the nun's hair was shorn "she would no longer belong to herself. She would be a unit in this religious body."[49] The loss of hair also signified, as the scholar June Namias has argued in relation to scalping, sexual vulnerability.[50] Both the nun and the Indian captive, shorn of their hair and by extension their femininity, were prey to the worst, most "un-civilized" forms of sexual exploitation.

According to this literature, all nuns were thus vulnerable to incarceration and abuse. The lesson of the story of Barbara Ubryk, and the scores of other captive nuns, was that no woman would find refuge in a Catholic convent. Yet outside this narrow message, the convent atrocity story clearly served a wider cultural purpose. In both France and the United States, the convent atrocity literature helped to bolster the cult of female domesticity. The emphasis on the captive nun's vulnerability was a forceful argument in persuading women to rest within the confines of the home. As Jenny Franchot has observed, when set against the humiliations and deprivations experienced by the young woman in the convent, the middle-class home could be portrayed as a refuge rather than a prison, a site of female fulfillment rather than female oppression.[51] The convent atrocity story thus formed part of that prescriptive literature which aimed to persuade women that their exclusion from the public sphere was a blessing rather than a burden. What could be more effective in conveying the terrible price paid by those women who turned their backs on the family home than the horrible figure of the bald, emaciated and naked Ubryk? After all, the transformation in Ubryk appeared to be stunning. As many newspaper accounts emphasized, she had been a beautiful young woman before she entered the convent. The implication was clear—such an attractive young woman might have made a fine wife and mother. Instead, the convent had stripped away her youthfulness and beauty and produced the miserable creature discovered by the investigating magistrate. In an article which appeared just months before the Ubryk case, *Harper's Weekly* outlined the choice facing young women in the following poem:

> This sad, sordid prison, ladies,
> This mere death in life.
> Who would be a nun, ladies,
> That could be a wife?[52]

However, the message of the Ubryk story was far from straightforward. Though intended to serve as a lesson in the perils of straying from the home, such stories also exposed an anxiety that this cult of feminine domesticity was losing its persuasiveness. The eagerness with which opponents of convents seized on Barbara Ubryk's case suggests less a self-assured faith in the reign of domesticity than a fear that its appeal might be waning. Several forces had emerged to challenge the conventional view in favor of women's exclusion from the public sphere. The feminist movement provided one great challenge. But another came from mass reform campaigns and philanthropic movements which enrolled thousands of female activists in their cause. Female participation in such movements was, of course, justified in terms of conventional views of feminine virtue; women, in this view, had a duty to spread their redeeming moral qualities from the home to the public sphere. Whatever the justification, however, the result was that women were encouraged to step outside the boundaries of the home, and assume a more vocal and public role. A literature, such as the convent atrocity story, which emphasized the perils for women of venturing outside the home was thus timely. Yet was such a literature as necessary in France as it was in the United States? Many scholars have argued that both feminist and mass reform movements were far more advanced in Protestant nations such as America than in Catholic France.[53] Catholicism, in this view, acted as a brake on the development of such challenges to the public/private dichotomy. In recent years, however, scholars of France have begun to examine the many opportunities for Catholic lay women to participate in large-scale charitable and reform movements. In the same manner as their English or American counterparts, Frenchwomen flocked to join such organizations, thereby developing a visible and active public presence.[54] A story such as Barbara Ubryk's, then, may have appealed just as much to French as to American commentators keen to restore women to their rightful place in the home.

Feminist and mass reform movements were not the only rivals to the cult of domesticity. The story of Barbara Ubryk as well as those of other captive nuns points directly to yet another competitor for female allegiance, namely, the convent itself. The argument that the convent acted as a rival to the home has been put by several scholars of religion and gender in France. James F. McMillan argues that the growth in the number of nuns in nineteenth-century France was largely due to the fact that the convent offered women active, public careers.[55] This expansion of Catholic female religious orders was astounding. In 1808, there were approximately 13,900 nuns and novices in France; by 1850, this figure had increased to 66,000, and in 1878 stood at 127,000.[56] The vast majority belonged not to the contemplative orders, but the newer form of *congrégation*. Although both involved the taking of vows, the *congréganistes* were not confined to secluded communities, and dedicated themselves to working in the community as, among others, teachers and nurses. Indeed, in the absence of a comprehensive state welfare system, the Catholic *congrégations* performed a range of vital social services well into the period of the Third Republic.

The *congrégations* offered many French women a fulfilling and independent career that was not available in secular society. In her study of the diocese of Besançon, Hazel Mills cites the example of Jeanne-Antide Thouret, founder of an order dedicated to charitable works which, by 1847, numbered 106 houses. As Mills concludes, "The congregations of the nineteenth century...offered most of their thousands of members a very active, highly esteemed life."[57] Commentators from the period often came to similar conclusions. The reformer Ernest Legouvé lamented the widespread prejudice against convents. For Legouvé, "Convents have always been regarded as prisons for women, and no institutions have been accused of more unhappiness." The reality, according to Legouvé, was very different. Convents in fact appealed to women because "only there have they been free to show what they are capable of."[58] Indeed, at times the convent atrocity story offered a compelling lesson in the lack of well-paid and decent professions for single women. In comparison with American escaped nun tales, where the fate of the nun after her liberation is almost never discussed, some of the French convent atrocity stories suggest that the return to society was fraught with dangers for the ex-nun. In Diderot's *La religieuse*, Suzanne becomes a prostitute following her escape, while in the second volume of her purported memoir, the runaway *Soeur X* describes the pitifully low wages she earns as an unskilled worker.

From the perspective of French anticlericals, the expansion of female religious orders made the need to discredit the convent particularly pressing. French republicans were, after all, among the most committed defenders of the domestic ideal for women. The most popular school texts of the Third Republic continued to describe marriage and child-rearing as the proper social roles for women. For this reason, a highly significant aspect of the Barbara Ubryk story was that her ordeal had occurred in a Carmelite convent. Of all the religious orders, the Carmelites were most renowned for their radical rejection of the world and for their asceticism. Many literary attacks on convents target the Carmelite order. In George Sand's *Mademoiselle La Quintinie*, the heroine considers entering a Carmelite convent, but quickly changes her mind upon discovering the "asceticism without warmth" and the "savage contempt for humanity" which reigns there.[59] In Michon's *La religieuse*, Sœur Thérèse joins a Carmelite convent and is shocked by the profound cruelty and unremitting physical punishment and degradation she finds.[60] As we have seen, anticlericals argued that the Ubryk case was typical of a systemic regime of punishment and incarceration occurring in all convents. All Catholic convents were, in this view, akin to Ubryk's Carmelite. By grouping all convents under the banner of the Carmelites, French anticlericals were thus able to achieve two important goals. The first was to label every convent as other-worldly and essentially redundant in an age of social progress, thereby avoiding the fact that the great expansion in Catholic orders was occurring in the practically oriented *congrégations*. The second was to discredit the notion that the convent might actually liberate women from the restrictions imposed by secular society.

This fear of the convent as a serious rival to the home was also evident in the United States. Though a less visible presence than in France, Catholic female religious congregations were greatly expanding throughout the nineteenth century. According to one scholar, the number of nuns in America increased from 1,344 in 1850 to 40,340 in 1900.[61] Protestant organizations monitored this growth very closely. In an 1856 report reprinted in, among others, the *New York Times*, the American and Foreign Christian Union expressed alarm at the fact that 142 monasteries and convents existed in the United States. The paper also noted the proposals put forward by the authors of the report to prevent the forced imprisonment of monks and nuns, as well as the establishment of a minimum age of thirty.[62] As in France, the bulk of this expansion was occurring in orders devoted to practical work such as teaching and nursing. One order, the Sisters of Charity, staffed eighteen of the twenty-five Catholic hospitals opened between 1829 and 1860.[63] The prominence of nursing nuns was starkly demonstrated in the Civil War. Of the 3,200 nurses who tended to the injured on both sides, 640 were nuns.[64] Protestant sensitivity on the question of the philanthropic work undertaken by Catholic religious orders is clear in the determined effort to deride such activities as acts of self-enrichment or proselytism rather than charity. A scene which recurs in many anti-Catholic works is the discovery, usually by a young woman who has hitherto admired the charitable work undertaken by nuns, that the money collected is being wasted on items of luxury for the nuns themselves and their bishops. In Jane Dunbar Chaplin's *The Convent and the Manse*, the nuns are accused of spending the money they collect for charity on their own selfish pleasures. Like their French counterparts, American critics of convents also strove to label all such institutions as reflective, inward-looking and unconcerned for the ills of society. The nun, as the novelist Isaac Kelso alleged in *Danger in the Dark*, was far removed from "a sphere of usefulness."[65]

The increase in the number of nuns in the United States was partly, of course, a function of the growth in Catholic immigration. American Protestants, then, might have found some comfort in the idea that few Protestant women were being lured into such institutions. Yet the evidence of the convent atrocity story suggests otherwise. In both fictional attacks on the convent and the memoirs of runaway nuns, it is Protestant girls who fall under the spell of the Catholic convent. There appears to have been a real anxiety that the convent would find recruits in Protestant homes. Such an anxiety does have some basis in historical experience. One of the nineteenth century's most famous runaway nuns, Rebecca Reed, was raised as a Protestant, and chose to join the Ursuline convent in Charlestown. According to the historian Daniel A. Cohen, Reed was motivated by the desire to escape a life of poverty and menial labor.[66] Her attraction to the convent was due, in large part, to the financial security as well as the sense of comradeship offered by the vocation of the nun.

Leading Protestant women in America were also prepared to argue that the Catholic convent offered a degree of autonomy and responsibility that neither their own churches nor the wider American society could match. The first female doctors in the United States, Elizabeth and Emily Blackwell, attributed the growth in female Catholic orders to "the excellent opening afforded by them for all classes of women to a useful and respected social life." The active and useful life offered by such orders, the Blackwells concluded, would naturally attract many women.[67] Perhaps the most influential proponent of this argument was Catharine Beecher. In many speeches and articles, Beecher warned her fellow Protestants that Catholicism was gaining ground among young women. Reflecting her position as an educational reformer, Beecher was particularly impressed by the Catholic commitment to expanding its schools for girls. But Beecher went on to argue that Catholicism was attracting young women not merely through its growing educational network, but also the status it accorded its female members, a status higher than that offered by Protestantism. This was particularly true for unmarried women. As she argued in the revised edition of her manual on domestic economy, *The American Woman's Home*:

> In the Protestant churches, women are educated only to be married; and when not married, there is no position provided which is deemed as honorable as that of a wife. But in the Roman Catholic Church, the unmarried woman who devotes herself to works of Christian benevolence is the most highly honored, and has a place of comfort and respectability provided which is suited to her education and capacity. Thus come great nunneries, with lady superiors to control conscience and labor and wealth.[68]

Beecher is an interesting example because she just as often expressed her hostility to Catholicism. Her father, Lyman Beecher, was a fierce anti-Catholic, and much of his animosity seems to have passed to his daughter. But it was perhaps her own experience as an unmarried woman in a society governed by the cult of domesticity that led her to describe, in a spirit almost of envy, the alternative vocation that Catholicism offered single women. As she noted, "The clergy and leaders of the Catholic church understand the importance and efficiency of employing female talent and benevolence in promoting their aims, while the Protestant churches have yet to learn this path of wisdom."[69]

* * *

Presenting the convent as a site of despair and death rather than liberation thus offered adherents of the feminine domestic ideal a powerful means of discrediting one of its key rivals. However, the message embodied in the captive, whether in the convent or on the American frontier, was never quite so straightforward. Christopher Castiglia has argued that, far from simply upholding conventional views of gender and domesticity, the captive's narrative offered a radically different set of meanings. As Castiglia writes, captivity narratives "refuse to be static texts endorsing essential, unchanging identities and hence fixed social hierarchies of race and gender."[70] As a defense of female domesticity, Barbara Ubryk's story was in fact equivocal rather than convincing. In particular, a closer reading of her captivity cast doubt on the strength and effectiveness of the very domestic ideal her sufferings were supposed to legitimate.

Even if intended to reinforce the cult of female domesticity, the narrative of the captive nun contained a number of elements which undercut many its central assumptions. Convent captivity stories challenged the view that women were frail, delicate creatures who could only prosper in the haven of the home. Instead, women in these stories are often resourceful and robust, displaying a level of physical resilience that even men might envy. This is clearly evident in the story of Barbara Ubryk. One of the most astonishing aspects of the Ubryk case was the speed with which the liberated nun recovered from her ordeal. Just days after her emancipation, the *Moniteur Universel* reported that Ubryk's startling transformation from savage creature to comely woman was well underway. A simple dose of middle-class hygiene was sufficient; as the paper reported, "it is easy to see how clean linen and cleanliness make her happy."[71] American papers, too, noted the calming effects of being "properly washed and dressed" on Ubryk's demeanor. Even more remarkably, given her physical condition upon her discovery—emaciated, naked and shorn of her hair, to the point where she resembled a beast more than a woman—Ubryk's physical attractiveness quickly reappeared. This sort of recuperation, along with Ubryk's capacity to survive for twenty-one years in a dark cell on a diet of stale bread, moldy potatoes and dank water, suggested an incredible reserve of fortitude and strength.

The manner in which convent captivity narratives undermined conventional gender views is also clear in the circumstances around the young woman's entry to the order. The captive of Native-Americans on the frontier, in the same manner as the young Edgardo Mortara, was simply abducted. But kidnapping could not account for the large numbers of women entering convents. Why, then, did so many women become nuns? One answer might be, as we have seen, that convents offered women an autonomy as well as a vocation that compared favorably with that of wives and mothers. However, very few opponents of convents were prepared to concede this point; the overriding message of the convent atrocity literature was, after all, that any such promise of independence or satisfaction was little more than an elaborate ruse. How, then, to account for the growth in these institutions?

The answers provided by opponents of the church varied. In some accounts, the brittle judgment which bedeviled the female sex was at fault: the novice is depicted as filled with an irrational and unbending desire to enter the convent, a form of religious mysticism which no rational persuasion can deter.[72] Women, then, are the victims of their own sentimental natures. In other cases, the cruelty of men is ultimately the cause. The decision to enter the convent, in these stories, comes after a cynical or heartless suitor has broken off an engagement. Becoming a nun is thus a bitter and self-destructive protest against a disappointment in love. In much of this literature, however, the chief culprit is the home, and specifically parents who, through ambition, spite or callousness, force their daughter to join the convent. The taking of vows is thus presented as a direct consequence of parental failure. Despite confident depictions of the domestic setting as a haven for women, the convent atrocity story often provided a troubling lesson in just how fragile the home as a protective sphere could be.

In identifying which parent was at fault, narratives of the Ubryk story in the United States and France diverged. In France, Ubryk's father was held responsible; in the United States, it is Ubryk's mother who is at the heart of the drama. In the opening scene of *Les amoureuses cloîtrées*, the book-length account of Ubryk's story, the young Ubryk is pictured begging her stern father for permission to marry her lover Wladimir rather than the rich Count Sergy Radzwil. Ignoring her pleas, the father gives Ubryk an ultimatum: marry the Count or enter the Carmelite convent. The headstrong young woman chooses the latter rather than betraying her true love for a marriage of convenience. This explanation for Ubryk's plight tapped directly into a growing debate in France about the practice of arranged marriages. In contrast to the United States, where the practice had virtually disappeared, marriages based on calculation rather than attachment remained common among the French bourgeoisie. A number of social commentators and medical authorities criticized such unions as the cause not only of personal unhappiness, but also of the spread of socially corrosive practices such as infidelity. As Ubryk herself argues before her stern father, marriages based on financial incentive were "the first step towards adultery."[73] The fate of the captive nun was thus an indictment of fathers who ignored the romantic yearnings of their daughters, and elevated financial considerations over true love.

In the United States, however, this was not the preferred explanation for Ubryk's flight to the convent. In the version of her story which appeared there, Ubryk's fiancé had broken off their engagement upon discovering that she was not wealthy. The real villain, however, is not the callous suitor, but Ubryk's mother, who not only fails to offer any sympathy to her grieving daughter, but then immediately pressures her to find another potential husband. Eventually Ubryk is unable to bear this bullying any longer and, bitter at the lack of empathy shown by her mother, throws herself into the convent. The Ubryk story thus fits a pattern in American convent atrocity stories in which the mother is most often at fault in the young woman's decision to become a nun. In some cases, heartlessness on the part of the figure from whom empathy is most expected is the cause. In other cases, it is the mother's failure to inculcate sound religious principles in her daughter which is most blameworthy. In *The Awful Disclosures of Maria Monk*, for example, the narrator condemns her mother for neglecting her religious education, thereby leaving her vulnerable to the snares of the Catholic Church. Whether through insensitivity or neglect, the ultimate responsibility often lies, however, with the mother.

Admittedly, American convent atrocity stories also hold fathers responsible. This was particularly the case for the literature which accompanied the rise of the Know-Nothing movement. In these stories, fathers trade their daughters' lives for the immigrant votes promised them by the Catholic Church. In Charles Frothingham's *The Haunted Convent*, for example, the ambitious Mr. Abbot strikes a deal with the devious Jesuit McFaley: Abbot will send his daughter, Agnes, to a convent in exchange for the Catholic vote. Though troubled by his decision, Abbot's political ambition outweighs his paternal responsibility. "I love her dearly," Abbot admits, "but alas, I love fame more."[74] But many other convent atrocity stories followed the Ubryk tale in blaming the mother who, either through absence or callousness, failed to protect her daughter.

Both parents were at fault, however, in one of the crucial issues in the contest between church and state, education. The education issue was particularly sensitive in France, where, as we have seen, much of the schooling for girls was in the hands of women religious. The adoption of the Falloux Law in 1850 had precipitated a vast expansion in the number of schools run by female orders; in turn, the swelling demand for female education stimulated a huge increase in those female religious orders dedicated to teaching. Republican men such as Jules Ferry and Charles Sauvestre warned that by molding women in its own ideals, the church aimed at bringing the next generation under its control. To head off the nightmarish scenario of a generation of mothers inculcating the principles of Jesuitism in their children, it was imperative, French republicans argued, to establish a universal, state-run school system for girls. As we have seen, French republicans looked to the United States as a model here, yet also underestimated the extent to which Americans believed their public education system to be vulnerable to what they considered Catholic subversion. Indeed, a dispute over the use of the King James Bible in state-funded schools was raging in Cincinnati at exactly the moment that Barbara Ubryk was discovered.[75] The prominence of the education issue was reflected in the convent atrocity literature.

One of the primary goals of the convent atrocity story was to dissuade parents from sending their daughters to convent schools. By exposing the inhuman nature of the teaching nuns, this literature clearly sought to tarnish the reputation of their schools. As the purported runaway *Soeur X* observed, "is it not of any interest to know the spirit, the values, the practices of people to whom a large part of modern society entrust the education of the young?"[76] The educational worth of such schools is portrayed as minimal; the curriculum they offer is, according to this literature, essentially frivolous and superficial. In *Les misérables*, for example, Jean Valjean entrusts Cosette's education to the nuns of Petit-Picpus. The results, however, are pitiful:

> Her education was finished; that is to say, she had been taught religion, and even, or above all, devotion; then history, or that which bears its name in convents, geography, grammar, the participles, the kings of France, a bit of music, a little drawing etc.; but of all the rest she was entirely ignorant.[77]

Even if it were their intention, the nuns themselves as depicted are too ignorant to offer a more substantial education. The description of the Superior of the convent of San Gregorio given by Enrichetta Caracciolo, whose account of suffering in several Neapolitan convents was favorably received in France and the United States, is typical. Such is her ignorance that she has never heard the name of Napoléon Bonaparte.[78]

In any case the real goal of such schools is not the cultivation of intellect, but the induction of as many students as possible into the order. In American convent atrocity stories, young Protestant girls are described as prized targets of conversion by Catholic school authorities. These fears may not have been entirely groundless. In their study of the history of the Sisters of St Joseph of Carondolet, Carol K. Coburn and Martha Smith note several instances of Protestant girls who converted to Catholicism and joined the order as nuns after having attended convent schools.[79] In France, too, convent schools are seen to be expressly designed to lure girls into becoming full-fledged members of the religious community. Victor Hugo, for example, describes the manner in which Cosette and her fellow *pensionnaires* begin to imbibe the rituals and the mentality of the nuns who teach them. The young woman's descent into the miserable life of the nun begins, according to its opponents, in the convent-run school.

Parents who continued to send their daughters to such schools were thus guilty of the most blatant lack of care. The urgency of spreading this message was intensified by the continued growth in enrolments at such schools. The church's dominance of female education in France was undeniable. But to the dismay of American opponents of the church, a similar trend seemed to be occurring in the United States. The number of convent-run schools had increased from ten in 1820 to two hundred in 1860, an expansion aided by the fact that seven of the first eight orders of women religious in America established convent schools for girls.[80] Denied both the government funding and the donations provided by wealthy supporters that were available to their French counterparts, many American convents relied on the income provided by such schools. In certain regions, Catholic schools outnumbered Protestant institutions. In Kentucky, for example, Catholic female religious orders were running ten schools for girls as early as the mid-1830s. In contrast, there were only four Presbyterian schools, and most of these enrolled only boys. Nor was there a secular alternative; public education in Kentucky was not constitutionally mandated until 1849, and remained very limited until after the Civil War. As a result, many Protestant parents sent their children to convent-run schools, a pattern repeated across the nation.[81] One English visitor to Cincinnati, for example, observed that three-fourths of the boarders in convent schools were Protestant girls.[82] The fear expressed by opponents of convents that Protestant girls were being entrusted to the care of nuns was thus founded in actual practice.

Whether through driving their daughters into the convent or exposing them to the snares of the convent-run school, the resounding message of this literature was that girls were at the mercy of their parents' lack of judgment or compassion. Of course, such depictions of parental failure may ultimately have served to throw into relief the virtues of a kind and protective home. The implicit critique of domesticity contained in these stories may thus have been blunted by the more comforting moral that parents who remained vigilant could shield their daughters from the temptation of the convent. Nevertheless, even if intended to highlight the virtue of a true and benign family, the fate of the captive nun also suggested that the much-vaunted domestic sphere failed young women just as often as it protected them.

* * *

A constant message in the reaction to the Ubryk affair was that the captive nun, barred from any contact with the outside world, was hopelessly trapped in the oppressive spirit of the Dark Ages. The naked nun in her squalid cell so vividly described by the newspapers was a ghost from Europe's medieval past. Tellingly, the scene that awaited Ubryk's liberators as they swung open her cell door is described again and again as one "that even Dante...could not have portrayed."[83] A report in the *Siècle* expressed this sense of being removed to a sinister past. "You would think yourself," the paper declared in the wake of Ubryk's liberation, "taken back to the dark centuries of the Middle Ages."[84] This idea that Catholicism represented the darkness of the Middle Ages smuggled into the bright light of the nineteenth century was implicit in the location of the convent itself, neighboring the Botanical Gardens and the Observatory. Placed in proximity to these representative institutions of nineteenth-century municipal planning and science respectively, the convent, with its "sad walls," was a shadowy, cancerous presence. The Ubryk tale, then, like all the convent stories, carried the message that Catholicism was alien to the spirit of the age. As many of the reports in the press concluded, "And is this the nineteenth century?"

Proponents of the view that Catholicism was anchored in the Middle Ages took comfort from several acts of the Vatican itself, notably the notorious Syllabus of Errors of 1864. In that Syllabus, as we have seen, Pope Pius IX declared anathema many of the key developments of the modern age, from the separation of church and state to freedom of conscience and expression. Of the 80 propositions which the Syllabus condemned, the last was the most controversial: "That the Roman Pontiff can, and ought to, reconcile himself, and come to terms with progress, liberalism, and modern civilization." The response from large sections of American and French society was scathing. The *New York Times* labeled the Syllabus a "grand 'Declaration of War'...against the ideas of the Nineteenth Century."[85] In a letter to his father, the French republican Henri Allain-Targé declared that, following the publication of the Syllabus, "One is no longer allowed to be intelligent and catholic."[86] In both nations, the Syllabus was cited as proof that Catholicism could never reconcile itself with the guiding principles of the nineteenth century.

This identification of Catholicism with the Dark Ages was even more powerfully reinforced by an integral part of the Ubryk story as it was reported in both the United States and France, torture. Several newspapers noted that a group of investigators sent to search the convent in the wake of Ubryk's liberation had stumbled upon a hidden torture chamber containing, to cite one source:

> two huge crosses, weighing eighty pounds each, which guilty nuns had to wear on their backs as a punishment; two heavy stones of marble to be placed on the chest, and a number of 'crowns of thorns' with long and sharp iron nails. There were also several girdles, also fitted with nails pointing inward, which it is said were worn next the skin by penitents, and a sort of knout for flogging the refractory.[87]

The anticlerical press in France also referred to "an arsenal full of torture instruments worthy of the Inquisition" which had been found in Ubryk's convent.[88] Fictional accounts of the Ubryk story went further than the press in detailing the usage of such devices. In one scene in *Les amoureuses cloîtrées*, a nun is tied to an iron ring, stripped to the waist, and whipped mercilessly by the other nuns. In a frenzy of cruelty and sadism, the torturers then begin inflicting such punishments on each other. Ubryk, too, is whipped following an attempt to escape; such is the ferocity of her torturers that drops of blood splatter their faces.[89]

Such startling depictions of torture served to taint the modern-day church with the worst excesses of the medieval Inquisition. Indeed, at times the linkage was made explicit. One account of the Ubryk case that appeared in the United States was entitled "the Horrors of the Inquisition Revived." Nor was the Barbara Ubryk story the only example of such graphic descriptions of torture. Such scenes were common in American convent atrocity stories. Many reviewers, of course, expressed their repugnance at these descriptions of torture; others criticized them as likely to alienate well-meaning readers from the anti-Catholic cause. Some convent stories limited their description to spiritual rather than physical torment. Nevertheless, it remains true that many of these stories dwell on graphic and violent scenes of torture. In Maria Monk's *Awful Disclosures*, young nuns are whipped, their naked flesh is branded with hot irons and their cheeks pierced with pins. Ned Buntline's sensational novel *The Beautiful Nun* contained one scene in which, having been judged by a panel of Inquisitors for the crime of reading a Bible, the torturers strip the nun Ursulina to the waist, brand her flesh with a cross, and pull her hair out by the roots.[90]

The reportage of the torture chamber in Barbara Ubryk's convent suggests that this fascination with the physical punishment of young women in the cloister was not confined to the United States. In the Goncourt brothers' *Soeur Philomène*, the nun at the centre of the story repeatedly "mortified her flesh with private tortures... and with all sorts of scourges."[91] In Michon's *La religieuse*, a nun who has attempted to escape is driven into the *cachot* by two nuns armed with whips; the author then offers an extended and detailed account both of her pain and her tormentors' apparent delight.[92] The sadistic pleasure that some nuns take in the suffering of others was also vividly described by Jules Michelet in *La sorcière*, his narrative of the witchcraft trials at the Louviers convent in the eighteenth century. In one scene, the nuns strip an accused witch of her robes and veil and then force pins into her naked body in order to gauge if she is impervious to pain, a sure sign, in their eyes, of her guilt. Again, the pleasure they derive from torturing the nun is obvious: "Everywhere they found pain: if they didn't have the happiness to prove her a witch, at least they rejoiced in the tears and cries."[93] The tortured nun is then thrown into a rat-filled *cachot* where she is the victim of sexual assault by the bishop's jailors.

Such scenes, as I have argued, formed part of a wider argument that identified Catholicism as a remnant of the darkest aspects of the medieval past, particularly the Inquisition and its torture chambers. But a number of other factors contributed to this depiction of the convent as a site of torture. In part, the popular understanding of the convent as immune both to public scrutiny and to the restraint imposed by social sanction appeared to invite speculation of this kind. In a commentary on the fate of Barbara Ubryk, the *New York Observer and Chronicle* attributed the apparently unrestrained cruelty within the convent to precisely this lack of external supervision. "Such monsters men or women are," the paper observed, "when left to themselves."[94] Of course, as we have seen, the fastest-growing religious orders in this period did not follow the contemplative model, and their members were highly visible and active members of society. Nevertheless, the term "convent" seemed to denote, in both France and the United States, a closed, walled-off institution, and for that reason alone became an object of suspicion. In a letter to the *New York Herald* signed by "A Western Catholic," the following observation is made: "There is something secret and hidden in those dark convent halls which the multitude know nothing about; therefore, it is wrong."[95] Like the Middle-Eastern harem to which the convent was endlessly compared, the mere existence of a community of women screened from public view seemed to incite both fascination and repulsion.

Many scholars have suggested a more fundamental set of factors behind the popularity of such stories. In his analysis of sensational literature in antebellum America, David S. Reynolds has classified the convent atrocity story as part of the "immoral reform" genre. By announcing their intention to instruct readers in the unfortunate prevalence of socially deviant acts, whether taking place in the brothel, the saloon or the convent, such reformers were able, according to Reynolds, to contravene social taboos while deflecting the charge of lewdness.[96] Karen Halttunen has identified such works as part of what she terms a "pornography of pain." In the nineteenth century, she argues, pornographic works began to give greater emphasis to physical torture, and particularly flagellation. When set against an emerging humanitarian ethos which sought to minimize pain and suffering, the prominence of flagellation made pornographic works even more scandalous.[97] In a society increasingly uncomfortable with physical suffering, pornography, in its role as a violator of taboos, became increasingly concerned with its infliction. Other scholars have identified the popularity of such works in a set of concerns specific to masculinity. In reference to the United States, David H. Bennett has argued that the sadism portrayed in these tales reflected a deep insecurity among men in the face of economic instability and a growing women's rights movement. For Bennett, men sought in such literature "reassurance that they were still masterful in these years of social and economic challenge and uncertainty."[98]

All of these explanations have some validity. However, torture was also a convenient means of painting Catholicism as suffused with the somber spirit of the Middle Ages. As Émile de Laveleye charged, the Catholic Party feared "the light and the liberty of modern civilization. It wants, through whatever means, to bring back the regime of the Middle Ages, the golden age of its domination."[99] A constant theme in the campaign against Catholicism was that the church, understood as an institution governed by the principles of the medieval period, was an anachronism in the progressive modern age. In this view, the recourse to torture in convents, a recourse allegedly established by the Inquisition, was merely another manifestation of Catholicism's sinister and regressive spirit. The convent, then, like the church itself, was understood as a medieval fortress at the heart of an enlightened age.

* * *

Long after the outrage surrounding her discovery had subsided, the fate of Barbara Ubryk continued to interest the American and French public. On October 9, 1869, *Harper's Weekly* ran a portrait of Ubryk recuperating in her asylum. In February 1870, the same journal published the observations of a visitor to Ubryk's asylum. The ex-nun, the journal reported, "looks extremely well," and "conversed freely, though rather incoherently."[100] In 1872, *Appletons' Journal* announced the following good news to its readership:

> Barbara Ubryk, the nun, whose long imprisonment attracted so much attention a few years ago, has entirely recovered from the effects of her long sufferings, and lives now at Cracow, a picture of perfect health and happiness.[101]

In the United States, accounts of her captivity continued to appear; another was published in 1890. In May 1891, Ubryk's death afforded many newspapers the opportunity to repeat her story. The *Boston Daily Transcript*, for example, described her as "the innocent cause of the Cracow riots of July, 1869."[102] French anticlericals also continued to acknowledge the importance of the Ubryk affair. A review of the details of the case was included, for example, in André Mater's 1909 work, *La politique religieuse de la République Française*.[103]

The case of Barbara Ubryk opens a window onto contemporary understandings of the nature and vocation of womanhood. In making the case that the convent violated the precepts of true womanhood, French and American writers revealed their own vision of the proper balance between the sexes. A dichotomy was established: the true woman was compassionate, maternal and secure in the home; the nun was callous, domineering and contemptuous of domesticity. Yet the convent atrocity story exposed the fundamental instability at the heart of the cult of domesticity. On both sides of the Atlantic, female domesticity was under great strain as more and more women challenged its constraints. By enshrining the power of female influence, the cult of domesticity itself encouraged this trend. One of the most potent rivals to the home was, I have argued, the convent itself. But whether through reform movements, philanthropic societies or religious orders, the avenues for female activism outside the home were multiplying. In this context, the convent atrocity story served a clear purpose: persuading young women that the home was a sanctuary rather than a prison. Preventing the spread of convents was undoubtedly a crucial goal for opponents of the church. But the larger aim was to bolster a cult of domesticity which appeared to be under greater and greater threat.

The Ubryk affair occurred in the build-up to another crucial event in the development of an international case against the Catholic Church.

At exactly the moment that news of Ubryk's liberation appeared in the French and American press, preparations were under way for the first Vatican Council. Arguably the most significant religious event of the century, the Vatican Council would reveal the extent to which opponents of the church on both sides of the Atlantic understood themselves as allies in a great international campaign.

Conclusion: Father Hyacinthe and the Vatican Council

The construction, over the middle decades of the century, of a Transatlantic case against Catholicism culminated in the last months of 1869. Just weeks after the tale of Barbara Ubryk was hitting front pages, New Yorkers, as we have seen, flocked to greet a French Carmelite monk, Father Hyacinthe, who had resigned from his order and launched a public attack on the Vatican. Overshadowing both of these stories, however, was one of the most significant religious events of the nineteenth century, the first Vatican Council. The only ecumenical Council to be held since that of Trent in the sixteenth century, it was scheduled to open in Rome on December 8, 1869. Well before this date, the Council was provoking intense speculation and debate on both sides of the Atlantic. In part, this public interest in the Council was due to its size. A gathering of some 1,050 prelates, the Council was an unmistakable assertion of the strength of the Catholic Church. Furthermore, in an era in which religious matters were treated with great seriousness, such a gathering of senior church figures was bound to dominate public discussion, even in largely Protestant nations such as the United States. The Vatican Council, the *New York Times* predicted, would surely be the most "extraordinary event of the age."[1]

On both sides of the Atlantic, the Council was regarded with trepidation. The key issue was its purpose. For most commentators, the Council appeared to have two main objectives, both of which were highly controversial. The first was the transformation into church dogma of the 1864 "Quanta Cura" encyclical and its accompanying Syllabus of Errors. An encyclical is a guide to church teaching which does not carry the status of dogma; now many observers feared that the Council would elevate the encyclical and the syllabus to the level of church dogma. After all, the Bull of Convocation, "Aeterni Patris," had listed the correction of modern errors as one of the goals of the Council. For the editors of the *Nation*, there was little doubt that the

Syllabus would be the central concern of the Council. The ridicule which greeted the release of the Syllabus had angered Pius IX to such an extent, the paper alleged, that he had convoked the Council "for the purpose of giving the Syllabus the full weight of the authority of the whole Church."[2] Among French anticlericals, there was a similar belief that the Syllabus would emerge from the Council as a part of Catholic dogma. For the editors of the *Siècle*, the conversion of the articles of Syllabus into "articles of faith" was one of the Council's primary goals.[3]

The second key goal of the Council was thought to be the definition of papal infallibility, a prospect creating divisions within the church itself. The leading support for papal infallibility came from the Ultramontanes, with their conviction that the papacy should be the supreme and unchallenged authority on questions of church teaching and administration. Against the Ultramontane drive for an infallibility in the person of the pope stood a diverse group of figures. In Hyacinthe's France, several leading bishops expressed their opposition. For Bishop Félix Dupanloup of Orléans, an infallibility which lay in the papacy was contrary to church teaching and history. Rather than the papacy, infallibility was, in this argument, an attribute of the church as a whole.[4] Anticipating a hostile reaction on the part of governments and opponents of the church, other bishops argued that, even if true, a definition of papal infallibility was inopportune. Another point of dispute concerned the rights and prerogatives of the pontiff in the administration of the church. Though not questioning the pontiff's status as the head of the church, bishops such as Dupanloup expressed a belief in the independence of the episcopacy over certain matters of faith and administration. The French church was a good example of such limited episcopal autonomy. Under the four Gallican articles of 1682, papal power had been explicitly limited not only by the powers of the secular state, but by the authority of general councils and bishops, and the canons and customs of the French church. It was such remnants of ecclesiastical particularism that the Ultramontanes sought to abolish. The Council thus loomed as a key moment of conflict between the Ultramontanes, and the dissenting, or minority, bishops opposed, for a variety of reasons, to a definition of papal infallibility.

The arguments over papal infallibility were thus, in terms of theology and church history, highly complex. Yet outside the church, these theological and historical arguments were distilled into one fundamental issue: the relationship between Catholicism and the modern world. For the Boston *Daily Evening Bulletin*, the alternatives were clear: either the Council would devise a "progressive platform," or the church would "continue to regard as heresies the opinions that form the basis and inspiration of modern society."[5] The Syllabus, of course, had declared anathema many of the most cherished principles of the nineteenth century. No church which embraced such a document, critics argued, could claim to share any common ground with the modern era. The *New York Herald* declared that the approval of the principles of the Syllabus by the Council would "create such a breach—or, if you will, a gulf—between the Church and the world as has not existed in any former age."[6] Assessments of the Council's significance on the part of French anticlericals were highly similar. The *Siècle* described the future legacy of the Council as the church's retreat to the world of the Middle Ages.[7] *La Liberté* similarly outlined what was at stake in the forthcoming Council: "Is the Church going to allow itself to be carried along by the civilization of the modern world?"[8]

Of course, the church responded to such arguments. But in articulating its defense, the church perhaps inadvertently provided further support to the allegations made by its opponents. On the eve of his departure for the Council, the American Father Isaac Hecker, founder of the Paulist fathers, published his views in the influential journal of which he was editor-in-chief, the *Catholic World*. On the question of the Council's purpose, Hecker provided a response which might have done little to assuage the fears that the Syllabus would be dogmatized. The Council, he announced, "will do whatever the Holy Ghost dictates." Hecker then tackled the accusation that the church intended to reject the ideal of progress and the values of modern civilization. If these terms denoted the "dictatorial control of the state over education," or "the doctrine that the chief end of man is to establish railways and telegraphic lines" then, Hecker affirmed, the church opposed them. To the charge that the church opposed liberty, Hecker declared that it did, if such liberty included, among others, "the atheistic constitution of the political and social state."[9] Such views were consistent with the church's conception of progress and freedom, but invited the charge that Catholicism stood opposed to the representative symbols of American civilization—the schoolhouse, the railway, and the separation of church and state.

The doctrine of papal infallibility was also condemned for a range of reasons. For many Americans, the notion that a man could be considered infallible was simply an affront to common sense. Not only was it unreasonable to consider any man free of error, but the history of the papacy revealed just how laughable such a doctrine was. Throughout history, as the *North American and United States Gazette* argued, popes had been guilty of "crimes of every grade of atrocity," yet the church now proposed that "the office held by these great criminals is sure to render the occupant infallible."[10] Many also detected, beneath the theological arguments for infallibility, an entrenched Catholic aspiration for temporal as well as spiritual sovereignty. "That Church and State should still be one," as the *New York Herald* reminded its readers in an editorial on the Council, "is still a dogma dear to Rome."[11] Papal infallibility, in this view, was intended to persuade Catholics that their allegiance lay with the Vatican rather than with national governments. What the papacy and its Ultramontane supporters seemed intent on recreating, according to many commentators, was the theocratic regime of the medieval period. Infallibility, warned the *Revue des Deux Mondes*, would create an autocracy with no counterbalancing power.[12] The result of dogmatizing the Syllabus and infallibility, according to the *Siècle*, would be the mingling of the pope and church in the political and civil order as in the Middle Ages.[13] The *Opinion Nationale* detected an even more devious aspect of papal infallibility. It was surely not coincidental, the paper argued, that such a strong assertion of papal authority had appeared at exactly the moment that the personal authority of Napoléon III was beginning to wane. Pius IX, the paper claimed, intended to replace the declining power of the imperial regime with his own bold vision of personal primacy over Catholics and the church.[14]

Whether grounded in common sense, a defense of secularism or an appreciation for the frailties of human nature, attacks on papal infallibility ultimately returned to an essential point: that such a doctrine was out of step with the values of the modern age. In an editorial subsequently reprinted in the *Living Age*, the *Temps* warned that, by giving papal infallibility a dogmatic definition, the "separation between modern society and Ultramontanism will thereby become a little wider."[15] Opponents of infallibility within the church were in turn depicted as bravely striving to keep Catholicism in contact with modernity. The "crime" of dissenters such as Father Hyacinthe, the *Revue des Deux Mondes* argued, was to try to remain faithful sons of modern society.[16] For the *Opinion Nationale*, relations between Catholicism and the modern world had reached a kind of zero-sum game. Following the Council, the paper predicted, people would have a basic choice: either they could remain Catholic and thus alienated from the age, or they could abandon the church and seek a religious home which accommodated the great advances made by contemporary civilization. In short, the Council loomed as a key moment when the church's attitude to the modern age would be exposed. Any church that declared a mortal man infallible, the *Independent* of New York concluded "cannot claim to represent the nineteenth, but only the seventeenth century."[17]

In a further sign of the church's apparent intolerance, the Council was widely portrayed as little more than a rubber-stamp for Ultramontane principles. Far from encouraging genuine debate and discussion, the pope, along with his Ultramontane supporters, was viewed as intent on silencing all expressions of dissent. The aim of the Council, one paper reported, was "not to devise and discuss questions and points of belief, but to promulgate and establish those already determined on by His Holiness the Pope."[18] The Council had been convened, another paper declared, "to vote, not to argue"; any discussion, it concluded, "was out of the question."[19] Such fears were heightened by the rules of the Council, which were promulgated on November 27, 1869. Chapter II, for example, gave the pope the ultimate power to decide which questions might be put before the Council. Chapter III of the rules imposed secrecy on the Council; attendees were forbidden from making public the decrees, questions for examination and opinions of Council members. The effect of such provisions was to forestall, critics alleged, any expressions of opposition to papal domination of the Council.

As in any attack on the Catholic Church, the role of the Jesuits also came into question. Many commentators assumed that the Jesuits were the masterminds of the Council. The idea of papal infallibility was, in this view, another blow aimed by the Jesuits at the conventions of modern society. In an editorial which dismissed the Council as a "stupid, old fashioned medieval kind of thing," the *New York Herald* described the Jesuits as the "masters of the situation. Pius the Ninth is their tool and the proceedings of the solemn farce will be manipulated to suit their purposes."[20] For the *New York Times*, the Jesuits were using every means to secure a majority in favor of papal infallibility and the dogmatization of the Syllabus of Errors.[21] The only obstacle to their triumph was, in the view of many American commentators, rebels such as Father Hyacinthe. "What," asked the *Nation*, "is the hydra against which Father Hyacinthe has been struggling for the last five or six years? Jesuitism."[22] In France, opponents of the Council pointed to the articles in favor of infallibility which were published in the main Jesuit organ at Rome, the Civiltà Cattolica. The leaders of the Civiltà, the *Revue des Deux Mondes* declared, were determined to give the Syllabus of Errors a dogmatic definition and install the personal infallibility of the pope; their aim, the journal declared, was nothing less than refashioning the world to suit their medieval principles.[23]

In both France and the United States, then, the Vatican Council was understood as a key moment when Roman-Catholicism would either bow to the spirit of the age, or reveal its essentially backward, medieval nature. There was, however, one other possibility which struck many opponents of Catholicism as both a possible and desirable outcome: the church itself might break apart. The pressure on the Vatican came, in part, from outside the church. Newspapers reported at great length the reservations expressed by Catholic powers such as France and Austria in regard to the Council. Particularly disquieting from the perspective of these governments was the possibility, the press reported, that the Council would formally declare the pope's temporal authority over Catholics everywhere, thereby challenging the sovereignty of national governments. As the *North American and United States Gazette* reported, "The monarchs and statesmen of Europe reason shrewdly enough that if the Pope be set up above them as infallible, his interference in their affairs may be a source of endless trouble."[24] Such reports of official anxiety regarding the Council were not entirely fictitious. The governments of the major Catholic powers privately expressed their concern over infallibility to each other and to the Vatican. As early as April 5, 1869, the Minister of Foreign Affairs of the Kingdom of Bavaria, the Prince Hohenlohe, instructed his diplomats to propose to the governments of France and Austria a unified diplomatic stance in regards to the Council. These governments should, Hohenlohe suggested, jointly inform the Vatican of their anxieties concerning the doctrine of infallibility and its implications for church-state relations.[25]

This attempt to forge a united position failed, but individual efforts on the part of the Catholic powers to moderate the Vatican's ambitions continued. Prior to the opening of the Council, the French ambassador to the Papal States, the Marquis de Banneville, was instructed to warn the Vatican that any dogmatization of the Syllabus would threaten the Concordat, and might even jeopardize the maintenance of the French garrison at Rome. As the Minister of Justice and of Religion, Jean-Baptiste Duvergier, explained in a report to his colleague, the Minister for Foreign Affairs, any affirmation of personal infallibility would "modify the fundamental organization" of the church, and thus "seriously disrupt the reciprocal commitments contained in the Concordat."[26] The French government also closely watched the controversy over the Council in neighboring states; in September 1869, for example, the French foreign ministry received a report from its minister to the southern German state of Württemberg concerning the increasing hostility between the Protestant and Catholic communities caused by the approaching Council.[27] On February 20, 1870, the French foreign minister, Napoléon Daru, with the consent of the Emperor, instructed Banneville to forcefully protest against the proposed proclamation of infallibility on the grounds that it elevated religious over civil and political obedience.

The pressure on the Vatican which might, in the eyes of its opponents, lead to a split also came from within. Much of the press in the United States expressed the hope that the American bishops would resist any attempt to transform the principles of the Syllabus into dogma. The Boston *Daily Evening Bulletin* thought such a course of action unlikely but nonetheless expressed the hope that the American bishops might continue a "tacit compromise with rationalistic and republican tendencies" by means of a "discreet silence of speech and abstinence of action."[28] The opposition to infallibility on the part of Bishop Ignaz Döllinger, provost of St Cajetan and professor of church history at Munich, also attracted much interest. Döllinger's book-length attack on the doctrine of infallibility entitled, "The Pope and the Council," which was published under the pseudonym "Janus," was commended to the French and American public.[29] French opponents of the Council also suggested that American bishops might ally with their German counterparts to thwart the triumph of the Ultramontanes at the Council.[30] Opposition in Germany seemed particularly strong. In September 1869, twenty-two German bishops met at Fulda, and fourteen declared the declaration of papal infallibility to be "inopportune." Following the meeting, the *North American Gazette* reported that a schism involving the German bishops was likely.[31]

The French minority bishops attracted particular attention. In just one example, much of the American and French press reprinted a pastoral letter by Bishop Dupanloup in which he argued against the definition of infallibility at the Council.[32] A two-volume work which appeared prior to Hyacinthe's letter, *Du concile générale et de la paix religieuse* by the dean of the theological faculty of Paris, Bishop Maret, sparked a great deal of commentary in anti-Vatican circles. The book was extensively reviewed in leading organs of the anticlerical and republican press, and the Imperial government maintained a file on the reaction to its publication.[33] But were these bishops powerful enough to defeat the Ultramontanes? Many commentators were skeptical. For the more virulent organs of the French anticlerical press, a liberal Catholic was in fact a contradiction in terms. The terms "liberal" and "Catholic," according to the *Siècle*, had as much in common as fire and water. A true liberal could not remain in a church that would never shed its regressive nature, the paper concluded.[34]

Yet whatever the outcome of the Council, commentators on both sides of the Atlantic drew satisfaction from the prospect of the Catholic Church, a church that vaunted its unity and its tradition, beginning to fall apart. "Roman Catholicism," the editors of the *Siècle* declared, "is playing its last card, and the forthcoming Council will plainly show to all, friends and enemies, its divisions and its hatreds." The anticlerical *Démocratie* was just as scathing. The Council, declared its editor Charles-Louis Chassin, would offer free-thinkers "the divine spectacle of the suicide of a religion."[35]

* * *

But would Father Hyacinthe take the lead in any schism? In the wake of his dramatic resignation from his order on September 20, 1869, the American press scrambled for details of his life-story. Born at Orléans in 1827, he began his theological studies at the seminary of Saint-Sulpice in 1845, and was ordained in 1851. His first sermons at Saint-Sulpice foreshadowed many of the ideas which would lead to his break with the church. One sermon in particular, in which he invited Freemasons to work with the church, revealed a concern to overcome division as well as a willingness to court controversy that would arguably continue throughout his career. In 1858 he joined the Dominicans, but after only five months of training left for the Carmelite monastery of Broussais, near Bordeaux. Hyacinthe's talent as an orator, however, would draw him away from the contemplative life of the Carmelite. In 1864, having preached at the cathedral of Bordeaux and the Madeleine in Paris, Hyacinthe was chosen by Archbishop Darboy of Paris to deliver the Advent sermon at Notre-Dame cathedral, a position in which he would, over the next five years, win a reputation as one of the most accomplished and powerful orators of the day. A collection of his sermons was published in the United States in 1867, and American correspondents in Paris wrote occasionally of his charismatic and persuasive oratory.

Hyacinthe also won a reputation for liberalism. In July 1869, in a speech to the *Ligue Internationale et permanente de la paix*, Hyacinthe claimed that Catholicism, Protestantism, and Judaism were all equal before God, a speech which won him praise from the liberal and republican press, and a rebuke from his Carmelite Superior. In a letter dated July 23, Hycinthe's Superior denounced such views as heterodox, and formally ordered him to cease from publishing letters and giving speeches outside the church.[36] For Hyacinthe, as he explained in his letter of resignation, this marked a decisive moment. No longer could he accept any restriction on his freedom of speech, even when his views clashed with those of the church. The same month a correspondent of the *Univers* claimed that Protestant brochures were being distributed outside the Madeleine church following one of Hyacinthe's sermons. Even before his resignation in September, then, Hyacinthe had become an object of some suspicion among Ultramontanes, to the point that his resignation, though creating a sensation outside the church, came to be seen by his opponents as almost inevitable. The famous letter of resignation would not, in the words of Louis Veuillot, "surprise anyone." A long time before then, Veuillot continued, "this mediocre fruit had broken away."[37]

Hyacinthe's opposition to the Ultramontane party was certainly clear. In his letter, he had explicitly acknowledged the role of the Council in bringing him to abandon his order and to launch his protest. The church, he had declared, was "traversing one of the most violent, obscure and decisive crises of its existence." The cause of the crisis, Hyacinthe made clear, was the Ultramontane party and its determination to define papal infallibility. As Hyacinthe wrote, an "all-powerful party" was intent on overthrowing centuries of church tradition and teaching. Furthermore, Hyacinthe protested, the Ultramontanes were determined to silence all expressions of dissent from within the church itself. Like secular critics of the Council, Hyacinthe feared that there would be little opportunity for open discussion of doctrines such as papal infallibility:

> If fears which I will not share came to be realized, if the august assembly had not more liberty in its deliberations than it now has in its preparation; if, in a word, it were deprived of the characters essential to an Ecumenical Council, I would cry out to God and to men to demand another, truly brought together in the Holy Spirit—not the spirit of parties—really representing the Universal Church, and not the silence of some and the oppression of others.[38]

But could Hyacinthe rally other opponents of infallibility to form a significant force? Many commentators hoped that European bishops would join Hyacinthe in opposing papal infallibility at the Council. In October 1869, the New York *Independent* speculated that the French church might become independent from the Vatican under the leadership of Hyacinthe.[39] If he were to be treated as a heretic by the Vatican, the *Boston Daily Advertiser* warned, he would "carry away with him no inconsiderable body of the Catholic [C]hurch."[40] In France, Hyacinthe was also seen as a potential alternative both to Ultramontanism and to the dissenting bishops who, in the eyes of many anticlericals, lacked the required boldness to lead such a revolt. Again, the language of manliness was prominent. In an article reprinted in the *Living Age*, the *Temps* praised Hyacinthe for his manly courage in resisting the Ultramontane movement; his bold stand was, the paper declared, "an example and a lesson for everyone: an example in virile frankness, a lesson in firm courage."[41] The *Journal des Débats* drew an interesting contrast between Hyacinthe and Bishop Dupanloup. Unlike Hyacinthe, Dupanloup had not broken with the church; indeed, as the press in both nations reported, Dupanloup had implored Hyacinthe to retract his resignation and return to his monastery. For the *Journal*, the difference between Hyacinthe and Dupanloup was a question of manliness. Dupanloup was "only a bishop." Father Hyacinthe, on the other hand, was "a man."[42]

Hyacinthe was unlikely to form such a coalition of French bishops while visiting the United States, where he arrived just weeks after his resignation, and from which he would not depart until after the Council's opening. During his visit, he gave few clues as to his intentions. Throughout his stay in the United States, Hyacinthe stayed aloof from any speculation, and sought as far as possible to avoid the attention of crowds. Of course, Hyacinthe did not escape the public gaze entirely. On October 24, he attended a sermon by one of America's most famous preachers, Henry Ward Beecher, and when, at the end of the service, Beecher sought out the Frenchman, a small crowd gathered to observe the meeting between the two famous men. Yet for the most part Hyacinthe was content to meet privately with leading religious, political, and literary figures. Soon after his arrival Hyacinthe was visited by John Bigelow, and accepted his invitation to spend more than a week at Bigelow's country house. The two men, Bigelow later recalled, "spent about eighteen hours out of every twenty-four discussing the causes and history of his rupture with his Church, and in speculating upon the future which he had to confront."[43] On October 23, he dined with Harriet Beecher Stowe, and recorded in his journal his admiration for her project to teach ex-slaves in Florida.

On November 15, Hyacinthe traveled to Boston accompanied by the son of the Reverend Leonard W. Bacon, and the next day dined with the following members of the Massachusetts elite: Henry Wadsworth Longfellow, the scientist Louis Agassiz, the historian Charles Francis Adams, the Governor of Massachusetts William Claflin and the author and lawyer Richard Henry Dana. His journal, however, records little of their conversation, apart from the "remarkable discussion" over Agassiz's views on the plurality of human races. On November 22 he visited the home of Longfellow, where he also met the poet William Cullen Bryant. Longfellow was struck by Hyacinthe's modest and quiet bearing. "He did not even wear his Carmelite dress," Longfellow wrote to a French author, Louis Pierre Frédéric Dépret.[44] On November 25, he returned to New York, and in December spent half an hour with the poet Oliver Wendell Holmes Sr.[45] For the duration of his stay, however, Hyacinthe kept contact with the public to a minimum. It was almost as if Hyacinthe were returning to the solitary ways of the monk; for most of his stay in Boston he remained, as one paper noted, in "strict seclusion."

Perhaps even more puzzling for Americans was Hyacinthe's stance toward the Catholic Church. Was Hyacinthe still a Catholic? In a letter to Reverend Bacon which was read at a meeting of the Evangelical Alliance, Hyacinthe insisted that he remained a faithful servant of the Catholic Church.[46] Such a claim appeared to be confirmed by Hyacinthe's behavior; many commentators noted, for example, that he carried his breviary at all times. Yet few could resist speculating that Hyacinthe was, if not yet a Protestant, likely to become one in the near future. Why else would he resign from his order and launch an attack on Ultramontanism? Where else could he turn but Protestantism? Signs of an impending conversion were seized on. In an article reproduced in many papers, the New York *Sun* even carried a report that Hyacinthe had been observed eating a beefsteak on Friday.[47] Still, his supporters longed for a more explicit statement of Hyacinthe's position. This sentiment was captured in the concluding verse to a poem which appeared in the Protestant press:

> So Father Hyacinthe! Dear friend and brother,
> Will thou not, *please*, be one thing or the other?
> Jump off the fence! Thy bellowing foe's behind thee:
> Land on *our* side, and take the part assigned thee.[48]

The church itself seemed to have little sympathy for Hyacinthe. Henry Ward Beecher noted that although Hyacinthe longed to remain a Catholic, the church itself was sure to cast him out.[49] The reaction of American Catholics to the arrival of Hyacinthe was apparently mixed. Nothing in Hyacinthe's journal during his stay in America suggests any outward show of hostility toward him on the part of Catholics. Furthermore, on October 19 he received a visit from Father Isaac Hecker who, despite his own misgivings about papal infallibility, did not announce them to the public. Hecker was evidently shocked by Hyacinthe's resignation. "He hasn't had a good night's sleep since my letter," Hyacinthe recorded. However, much of the Catholic press ridiculed the notion that Hyacinthe might rally American Catholics to his cause. "This is a poor country," the *New York Tablet* warned, "for shaky, especially renegade Catholics. If Père Hyacinthe comes here expecting to induce any considerable number of Catholics, or even a single Catholic, to accept him as a leader, or to follow him on his most intemperate and silly attacks on the church, he will find that he has come on a fool's errand." The *Freeman's Journal* dismissed the interest in Hyacinthe as little more than a brief craze; the renegade monk was destined to fall "out of all public observation as completely as if he had retired to the remotest cell in a Carmelite garden." Interestingly, such attacks were quickly reprinted in the non-Catholic press, as if they were a badge of Hyacinthe's authenticity.[50] The leading Catholic journalist Orestes Brownson was also hostile. In a letter to his son, he wrote that Hyacinthe "has made a fool of himself." Furthermore, in a declaration which might have confirmed the widespread belief in the church's intolerance for other faiths, he continued, "He says he is a Catholic, but holds that he and Protestants all belong to the same brotherhood of faith...I regard him as lost."[51]

Hyacinthe, however, did not yet consider himself lost to Catholicism. Though he certainly found elements of Protestantism appealing, he was unable to renounce the church in which he had made his career. Throughout his stay in the United States he was struck by the spirit of tolerance among his Protestant companions; he recorded, for example, that the Reverend Joseph P. Thompson, editor of the *Independent*, had invited him to preach in his church, even if he remained a Catholic. In November 1869 he attended a Quaker meeting in the company of John Bigelow's wife, and expressed his admiration for the simple and pure devotion he witnessed there. Yet such admiration was balanced by criticism. None of the Protestant churches, he wrote in one journal entry dated October 27, really attracted him; Protestantism was too heavily marked by the spirit of the sixteenth century to offer a religion of the future. Converting from Catholicism to Protestantism would be, he concluded, a "false" and "sterile" path for him.

Rather than a move to Protestantism, Hyacinthe's vision was of a reformed Catholicism. In this sense his visit to the United States appeared to be decisive. Although he had resigned from his order before arriving, his decision to reject any return to the church came in the midst of his American stay. Following a long conversation with John Bigelow, where the two men discussed the issue of papal infallibility, Hyacinthe appears to have resolved much of his previous confusion and settled on his future path. November the third, he wrote, is a significant date—from this day on, he writes, "I am no longer Roman-Catholic." His mission, he declared, must be to purify the church of its abuses—of doctrine, discipline, and government—and thereby bring it into harmony with the principles of the modern age. Hyacinthe's American experience also seems to have stiffened his belief that theological distinctions were of little importance. He took care to note in his journal the number of his companions, among them John Bigelow, who professed no particular creed, but who lived exemplary Christian lives nonetheless. He also cited Henry Ward Beecher's observation that he was both a good Catholic and a true Protestant. After his visit to the Quaker meeting, he wrote, "I truly feel myself to be a member and minister of all the churches." On

December 6, just days before his departure, he stated, "I have never belonged more than today to the Church of Jesus-Christ."

The act which might seal forever Hyacinthe's break with Roman-Catholicism was, of course, marriage. Hyacinthe, it should be remembered, was in love with Emilie Meriman, the American widow he had converted to Catholicism. By late 1869 Hyacinthe appears to have entertained few doubts as to the legitimacy of his feelings for Meriman. Hyacinthe's journals and letters from this period attest not only to his love for Meriman, but the psychological security he derived from her. "The one thing," he wrote on October 26, "that I must never doubt—not more than God—is our Love. God revealed himself to us in this Love." At the same time, he wrote often, and with some longing, of the joyful family life he had witnessed among his American friends. Returning from his stay with the Bigelows in their country house, for example, he wrote on November 9, "How much good this life of country and of family has done me." Later he admits to being "surprised and gladdened to hear him [Bigelow] say, 'You must soon have your own family.'"

For the duration of his visit to the United States, Hyacinthe gave little public indication of these emotions and desires. There were, however, press reports that Hyacinthe had come to the United States in order to wed. Such rumors first appeared in the Catholic press, and were intended to tarnish Hyacinthe's reputation. The opposite, of course, occurred—the *Zion's Herald*, which relayed the rumor of an impending marriage for Hyacinthe, concluded that such an act would embellish rather than detract from Hyacinthe's standing in the United States. By marrying, the paper asserted, "he will do more to destroy the power of the papal Church than by any other step he can take."[52] Leading American Catholics were evidently aware of a possible relationship. Orestes A. Brownson, for example, in the letter to his son concerning Hyacinthe, wrote that "I am afraid there is a woman in the affair." Reports of Hyacinthe's wedding plans remained, however, scattered, and only became slightly more frequent once Hyacinthe had left the United States, when several papers reported that he had fallen in love with a Boston widow.[53]

If not to marry, however, why had Father Hyacinthe come to New York? Much of the press concluded that Hyacinthe was seeking a period of rest after the turmoil surrounding his resignation. By removing himself from Paris, Hyacinthe would be able, as one paper noted, to "cogitate over his plans for the future."[54] Other commentators thought Hyacinthe intended to study firsthand the American system of church-state relations. Some even speculated that Hyacinthe hoped to rally American bishops to the anti-Ultramontane cause.[55] Meriman had in fact motivated Hyacinthe's visit, but in a completely different manner: Hyacinthe had come to the United States to conclude a business affair on her behalf. As revealed in Hyacinthe's journal, Meriman had taken out a patent on a design for what she termed a "health corset"; the objective of the trip was to meet with potential American manufacturers (though given his limited English, it is difficult to imagine how Hyacinthe might have successfully concluded any arrangement.) Meriman thus remained in Paris throughout Hyacinthe's visit to America.

Hyacinthe left the United States on December 11, 1869, but the controversy over the Vatican Council continued unabated. Following its opening, the *New York Times* concluded that the Council was little more than the arraignment and trial of modern civilization.[56] By mid-1870, the results of the Council were becoming clearer. Contrary to the fears of many Americans, the Syllabus of Errors was not unequivocally adopted as church dogma. Papal infallibility was defined, though in less stringent terms than its Ultramontane supporters had hoped for. Many Ultramontanes wished that all of the pope's utterances would be declared infallible; in fact, as set out in the dogmatic Constitution that the Council approved on July 18, 1870, the pope would only be infallible when speaking *ex cathedra*, that is, when issuing a solemn doctrine concerning faith or morals. Whatever its precise form, the adoption of an infallibility residing in the person of the pope attracted widespread condemnation. In France, hostility to the Council was muted somewhat by the vital question of liberal reforms to the Empire; as Lucien Prévost-Paradol wrote to his friend John Bigelow, news of the Council's proceedings was given little attention in a country "where the question of revolution or no revolution is put every morning."[57] French reaction to the final vote was further muted by the news of the outbreak of the Franco-Prussian war just a day later; nonetheless, as the editors of the *Temps* took time to note, even if delayed in their realization by such an event, the consequences of the vote were likely to be considerable.[58]

In the United States, there was less to distract readers from the news of the vote. Even before the final approval of the Constitution, commentators were launching attacks on infallibility. In June 1870, the former anti-slavery campaigner William Lloyd Garrison ridiculed the idea that any man could be made infallible through a collective vote. Such a belief, he wrote, stood in "flagrant contempt of the common sense of mankind," and was "noticeably audacious in this stage of the world's progress." The decisions of the Council, he concluded, were not worth more than "the chatterings of the inmates of a lunatic asylum."[59] Aside from its absurdity, other commentators saw papal infallibility as a manifestation of Catholicism's intolerance for free speech and inquiry. By effectively silencing dissent within the church, the doctrine was also intended, in this view, to silence criticism from secular society. Infallibility was, the *New York Times* declared, "a denial of the principles upon which the liberties of all free nations of the world are founded."[60] The acceptance of papal infallibility, the *New York Tribune* concluded, had built a "Chinese wall between the world of modern progressive thought and the Roman Catholic Church."[61] The conclusion of many was that Catholicism had spurned the chance to reconcile itself with the modern age.

The much anticipated religious schism did not, of course, occur. Despite the expressions of opposition from within the church, the two Constitutions proposed to the Council were overwhelmingly approved by the assembled bishops. Only one American bishop voted against the Constitution which included the proclamation of papal infallibility: Bishop Edward Fitzgerald of Little Rock.[62] Rather than voting against the constitution, most of the dissenting bishops chose not to attend the session in which the vote occurred. The earnest hope that Father Hyacinthe might follow in the footsteps of Luther was also not met. Hyacinthe was not present at the Council. Despite being formally excommunicated following his refusal to return to his Carmelite order, he rejected the urgings of his supporters to embrace Protestantism. Far from being a new Luther, for the rest of his life Hyacinthe continued to view himself as a true Catholic faithfully serving a church which had lost touch, in his view, with its elemental spirit and principles. His mission, which he had discovered during his visit to America in 1869 and which he strove energetically to complete, was not to destroy the church, but to bring it into line with the dictates of modern civilization.

Father Hyacinthe thus never managed either to fully embrace Protestantism or to fully reject Catholicism. His personal turmoil over his relationship to Emilie Meriman, however, reached a more definite and happier conclusion. On September 3, 1872, Father Hyacinthe, under the name of Charles Loyson, married Emilie Meriman in London, and the couple had a son, Paul, the following year. In a letter which was published in the English, French and American press, Hyacinthe described his marriage as a crucial step in the great task, as he perceived it, of creating a Catholic Church in step with the modern age. Though a faithful servant of the church, Hyacinthe declared, he was not bound by its abuses, primary among which was the vow of celibacy. A married priesthood would not only give an example of conjugal happiness for secular society but, by linking the priest to wider society, enhance the influence and prestige of the church itself. The freedom to marry would, Hyacinthe concluded, reconcile priests "with the interests, the affections, the duties of human nature and of civil society."[63]

For the rest of his life Hyacinthe retained a certain public renown. In March 1871 he traveled to Rome with a letter of recommendation from the republican statesman Jules Favre. "He has honored the priesthood," Favre wrote to the French chargé d'affaires in Rome, "with an independence of character which is too rare these days."[64] In a letter to Monseigneur Lucien Lacroix, he would later claim that Léon Gambetta tried to convince him to launch a political career.[65] In 1879 he published a program of reform for the church that included, not surprisingly, the abolition of celibate vows and papal infallibility.[66] Hyacinthe also tried to create the sort of reformed Catholic Church that he had advocated for so long. In 1883 he obtained authorization, though not an official recognition, from the French state for what was called the Gallican Catholic Church in the Rue d'Arras, Paris; among its doctrines, as he wrote to the Minister of Religion, was a rejection of papal infallibility, and the insistence that its priests be at the same time loyal citizens of the nation.[67] His return to the United States for a lecture tour in 1884, a trip motivated in part by the need to raise funds for the church, attracted some interest, though far less than in 1869. American visitors to Paris, including Frederick Douglass and Elizabeth Cady Stanton, went to hear Hyacinthe preach. Mark Twain would cite Hyacinthe as a guide to the ills of ecclesiastical celibacy: "Pere Hyacinthe testifies that of a hundred priests confessed by him, ninety-nine had used the confessional effectively for the seduction of married women and girls. The official list of questions which the priest is required to ask," Twain concluded with typical wit, "will overmasteringly excite any woman who is not paralytic."[68]

This ongoing interest in Hyacinthe invites the question as to the extent to which the case against Catholicism which had been created in the middle decades of the century continued to serve opponents of the church after 1869. The period of the Third Republic lies outside the boundaries of this study, yet there are many grounds to suggest that republicans and liberals continued to draw on the fund of ideas that had been created in the preceding decades. Many of the leading oppositional figures of the Second Empire held important posts during the Third Republic. These included some of the most fervent admirers of the United States prior to 1870 such as Eugène Pelletan, Henri Allain-Targé, and Jules Ferry. Republicans remained obsessed with the two issues on which the United States appeared to have won such a decisive advantage: the separation of church and state and the establishment of a public education system. Key works from the middle decades of the century such as Michelet's *Du prêtre, de la femme et de la famille* remained popular. Once in power, French republicans continued to mine the discourse concerning Catholicism, gender, and domesticity that had been created in the middle decades of the century.

The body of ideas which had been elaborated in the decades preceding Hyacinthe's visit retained its usefulness for American anti-Catholics as well. Many of the great controversies surrounding Catholicism in the middle decades of the century would continue to reverberate decades later. As we have seen, the American press referred to Edgardo Mortara, Barbara Ubryk and Father Hyacinthe long after the controversies with which they were associated had passed from the front pages. French works from the middle decades of the century retained their appeal. Eugène Sue's *The Wandering Jew*, for example, enjoyed a new burst of popularity in the 1880s and 1890s. In 1878, for instance, Ellen Emerson left the following note for her father, Ralph Waldo: "Please get Eugene Sue's 'Wandering Jew' from the Athanaeum."[69] As this study has tried to argue, the case against Catholicism was always about more than just the church. On both sides of the Atlantic, many of the broader social tensions which fed anti-Catholic sentiment, such as fears of depopulation or an anxiety around masculinity, only increased in intensity in the latter decades of the century.

Emilie Meriman died on December 3, 1901. Up to his own death in February 1912, Hyacinthe continued to adhere to that resolution he had fixed in New York in 1869. "I have never," as he wrote in 1900 to Monseigneur Lucien Lacroix, "wished the destruction of the church; all that I want is to see it reformed and transformed."[70] The first volume of a biography of Hyacinthe appeared in France in 1920. Yet he never regained the prominence he had won in the last months of 1869, when he appeared to be the most formidable enemy of a church which was widely seen to be suffused with the intolerance and dogmatism associated with the Dark Ages.

Notes

Introduction: Father Hyacinthe in America

1. John Bigelow, "Father Hyacinthe and His Church," *Putnam's Monthly Magazine of American Literature, Science and Art* 15, no. 25 (January 1870): 96. The article was written by Bigelow at the request of George Putnam himself.
2. The letter appeared in full in, amongst others, the *New York Times*, *New York Herald*, *Boston Advertiser*, and *Milwaukee Herald*. For a review of Hyacinthe's career, see Lucienne Portier, *Christianisme, églises et religions. Le dossier Hyacinthe Loyson* (Louvain-la-Neuve: Centre d'histoire des religions, 1982).
3. *Moniteur Universel*, September 22, 1869.
4. *Tribune*, September 26, 1869; *Opinion Nationale*, September 29, 1869.
5. *New York Weekly Herald*, October 2, 1869.
6. *New York Times*, November 6, 1869; *New York Weekly Herald*, October 2, 1869.
7. *Independent*, October 7, 1869.
8. *Chicago Tribune*, October 28, 1869.
9. Ibid., October 18, 1869.
10. *Daily Central City Register*, October 20, 1869.
11. *Independent*, October 28, 1869.
12. *Milwaukee Daily Sentinel*, December 10, 1869.
13. George L. Prentiss, ed., *The Life and Letters of Elizabeth Prentiss* (New York: A.D.F. Randolph, 1882), December 10, 1869; Bryant to Leonice M.S. Moulton, December 10, 1869, in Thomas G. Voss, ed., *The Letters of William Cullen Bryant*, Vol. 5 (New York: Fordham University Press, 1990), 347.
14. *New York Times*, December 11, 1869.
15. *Daily Cleveland Herald*, December 10, 1869.
16. Ibid.
17. Charles Loyson papers, M.S. fr 3905, Manuscript Division, Bibliothèque de Genève.
18. Unpublished journal, Charles Loyson papers, Bibliothèque de Genève. The period covering Hyacinthe's visit to the United States is contained in M.S. fr 2862 and 2863. Capitals in original. All translations in this text are my own.
19. John Bigelow, *Retrospections of an Active Life*, vol 4 (New York: Doubleday Page, 1913), 328. Bigelow noted, however, that Hyacinthe's repeated questions on the subject of celibacy, and his approval of Bigelow's "Protestant" views on the matter, "made me suspicious that his interest in the discussion of that subject was not entirely evangelical or academical."

20. For critical discussions of the manner in which exceptionalism has hampered comparative or transnational approaches to American history, see: Raymond Grew, "The Case for Comparing Histories," *American Historical Review* 85 (October 1980): 763–778; George M. Frederickson, "Comparative History," in *The Past Before Us: Contemporary Historical Writing in the United States*, ed. Michael Kammen (Ithaca: Cornell University Press, 1980); Raymond Grew, "The Comparative Weakness of American History," *Journal of Interdisciplinary History* 16, no. 1 (Summer 1985): 87–101; Laurence Veysey, "The Autonomy of American History Reconsidered," *American Quarterly* 31, no. 4 (Autumn 1979): 455–477; John Higham, "The Future of American History," *Journal of American History* 80, no. 4 (March 1994): 1289–1309; George M. Frederickson, "From Exceptionalism to Variability: Recent Developments in Cross-National Comparative History," *Journal of American History* 82, no. 2 (September 1995): 587–604; David Thelen, "Of Audiences, Borderlands and Comparisons: Toward the Internationalization of American History," *Journal of American History* 79, no. 2 (September 1992): 432–462; Ian Tyrrell, "American Exceptionalism in an Age of International History," *American Historical Review* 96, no. 4 (October 1991): 1031–1055; Joyce Appleby, "Recovering America's Historical Diversity: Beyond Exceptionalism," *Journal of American History* (September 1992): 419–431; "The Nation and Beyond: A Special Issue. Transnational Perspectives on United States History," *Journal of American History* 86, no. 3 (December 1999); Daniel T. Rodgers, "Exceptionalism," in *Imagined Histories: American Historians Interpret the Past*, ed. Anthony Molho and Gordon S. Wood (Princeton: Princeton University Press, 1998); Thomas Bender, ed., *Rethinking American History in a Global Age* (Berkeley: University of California Press, 2002); Thomas Bender, *A Nation Among Nations: America's Place in World History* (New York: Hill and Wang, 2006).
21. Marc Bloch, "Pour une histoire comparée des sociétés européennes," *Revue de synthèse historique* 46 (1928): 15–50. For an analysis of Bloch's approach, see William H. Sewell, "Marc Bloch and the Logic of Comparative History," *History and Theory* 6, no. 2 (1967): 208–218.
22. See, for example, Bénédicte Zimmermann, Claude Didry, and Peter Wagener, eds., *Le travail et la nation; histoire croisée de la France et de l'Allemagne* (Paris: Maison des sciences et de l'homme, 1999). On European approaches to comparative and transnational history, see Deborah Cohen and Maura O'Connor, eds., *Comparison and History: Europe in Cross-National Perspective* (London: Routledge, 2004).
23. The classic work is Ray Allen Billington, *The Protestant Crusade 1800–1860* (New York: Rinehart and Company, 1938). For anti-Catholicism as a conspiracy, see Richard Hofstader, *The Paranoid Style in American Politics, and Other Essays* (New York: Knopf, 1965); David Brion Davis, "Some Themes of Countersubversion: An Analysis of Anti-Masonic, Anti-Catholic and Anti-Mormon Literature," *The Mississippi Valley Historical Review* 47, no. 2 (September 1960): 205–224. For a more recent approach that depicts anti-Catholicism as an expression of a recurring fear that the American Eden was under threat from hostile and alien forces, see David H. Bennett, *The Party*

of Fear: From Nativist Movements to the New Right in American History* (Chapel Hill: University of North Carolina Press, 1988).
24. Barbara Welter, "From Maria Monk to Paul Blanchard," in *Uncivil Religion: Interreligious Hostility in America*, ed. Robert N. Bellah and Frederick E. Greenspahn (New York: Crossroad, 1987), 44; Daniel A. Cohen, "Miss Reed and the Superiors: The Contradictions of Convent Life in Antebellum America," *Journal of Social History* 30, no. 1 (Fall 1996): 149–184; Daniel A. Cohen, "The Respectability of Rebecca Reed: Genteel Womanhood and Sectarian Conflict in Antebellum America," *Journal of the Early Republic* 16, no. 3 (Autumn 1996): 419–461; Susan M. Griffin, "Awful Disclosures: Women's Evidence in the Escaped Nun's Tale," *PMLA* 111, no. 1 (January 1996): 93–107; Tracey Fessenden, "The Convent, the Brothel, and the Protestant Woman's Sphere," *Signs* 25, no. 2 (Winter 2000): 451–478; Marie Anne Pagliarini, "The Pure American Woman and the Wicked Catholic Priest: An Analysis of Anti-Catholic Literature in Antebellum America," *Religion and American Culture* 9, no. 1 (Winter, 1999): 97–128; C. Walker Gollar, "The Alleged Abduction of Milly McPherson and Catholic Recruitment of Presbyterian Girls," *Church History* 65, no. 4 (December 1996): 596–608.
25. Jenny Franchot, *Roads to Rome: The Antebellum Protestant Encounter with Catholicism* (Berkeley: University of California Press, 1994), xx. On the influence of Mexico on American anti-Catholics, see John C. Pinheiro, "'Extending the Light and Blessings of the Purer Faith': Anti-Catholic Sentiment among American Soldiers in the U.S.-Mexican War," *Journal of Popular Culture* 35, no. 2 (Fall 2001): 129–152.
26. René Rémond, *L'anticléricalisme en France, de 1815 à nos jours* (Paris: Arthème Favard, 1999), esp. 5–7. A variation on this argument characterizes anticlericalism as a myth which allowed French people to construct a polarized vision of their society: Joseph N. Moody, *The Church as Enemy: Anticlericalism in Nineteenth Century French Literature* (Washington, DC: Corpus, 1968).
27. See, for example, William R. Keylor, "Anti-Clericalism and Educational Reform in the French Third Republic: A Retrospective Evaluation," *History of Education Quarterly* 21, no. 1 (1981): 95–103. See also Henri Guillemin, *Histoire des Catholiques français au XIXe siècle* (Genève: Éditions du Milieu du Monde, 1947), 323; Jérôme Grévy, *Le Cléricalisme? Voilà l'ennemi! Un siècle de guerre de religion en France* (Paris: Armand Colin, 2005), 77.
28. Jean Faury, *Cléricalisme et anticléricalisme dans le Tarn, 1848–1900* (Toulouse: Service des publications de l'Université de Toulouse-Le Mirail, 1980); Ralph Gibson, "Why Republicans and Catholics Couldn't Stand Each Other in the Nineteenth Century," in *Religion, Society and Politics in France Since 1789*, ed. Frank Tallet and Nicholas Atkin (London: Hambledon Press, 1991).
29. Theodore Zeldin, while conscious of the political conflict between the two sides, nonetheless suggests that their moral codes of conduct were almost identical. See his *France: 1848–1945*, Vol. 2, *Intellect, Taste and Anxiety* (Oxford: Clarendon, 1977), 1024–1039, esp. 1031. On the question of gender, the strongest case for the shared precepts of the church and its

enemies has been put by James F. McMillan in his *France and Women 1789–1914: Gender, Society and Politics* (New York: Routledge, 2000).
30. René Rémond, "Anticlericalism: Some Reflections by Way of Introduction," *European Studies Review* 13 (1983): 122.
31. Wolfram Kaiser, "'Clericalism—That Is Our Enemy!': European Anticlericalism and the Culture Wars," in *Culture Wars: Secular-Catholic Conflict in 19th Century Europe*, ed. Christopher Clark and Wolfram Kaiser (Cambridge: Cambridge University Press, 2003), 50. See also Owen Chadwick, *The Secularization of the European Mind in the Nineteenth Century* (Cambridge: Cambridge University Press, 1975). A more recent account of European secularisation is René Rémond, *Religion et société en Europe: la sécularisation aux XIXe et XXe siècles, 1789–2000* (Paris: Seuil, 2001).
32. John Lothrop Motley, *Democracy, the Climax of Political Progress and the Destiny of Advanced Races* (Melbourne: George Robertson, 1869), 6.
33. Cited in Emmanuel Godin and Tony Chafer, eds., *The French Exception* (New York: Bergahn Books, 2005), 5.
34. Edgar Quinet, *The Roman Church and Modern Society*, trans. C. Edwards Lester (New York: Gates and Stedman, 1845), 17.
35. See Austin Gough *Paris and Rome: The Gallican Church and the Ultramontane Campaign, 1848–1853* (Oxford: Clarendon Press, 1986).
36. *New York Times*, February 25, 1860.
37. J. Ryan Beiser, *The Vatican Council and the American Secular Newspapers, 1869–1870* (PhD diss., Catholic University of America, 1941).
38. John T. McGreevy, *Catholicism and American Freedom: A History* (New York: W.W. Norton, 2003), 103.
39. Sudhir Hazareesingh, "Religion and Politics in the Saint-Napoleon Festivity 1852–1870: Anti-Clericalism, Local Patriotism and Modernity," *English Historical Review* 119, no. 482 (June 2004): 616–617. See also his *From Subject to Citizen: The Second Empire and the Emergence of Modern French Democracy* (Princeton: Princeton University Press, 1998); Philip G. Nord, *The Republican Moment: Struggles for Democracy in Nineteenth-Century France* (Cambridge, MA: Harvard University Press, 1995).
40. Theodore Zeldin, "The Conflict of Moralities," in *Conflicts in French Society: Anticlericalism, Education and Morals in the Nineteenth Century* ed. Theodore Zeldin (London: Allen & Unwin, 1970).
41. Caroline Ford, *Divided Houses: Religion and Gender in Modern France* (Ithaca: Cornell University Press, 2005).
42. Ellen Carol DuBois and Vicki L. Ruiz, eds., *Unequal Sisters: A MultiCultural Reader in U.S. Women's History* (New York: Routledge, 1990), xi.
43. Michelle Perrot "Women, Power and History," in *Writing Women's History*, ed. Michelle Perrot, trans. Felicia Pheasant (Oxford: Blackwell, 1992), esp. 168–169. See also Dorothy O. Helly and Susan M. Reverby, eds., *Gendered Domains: Rethinking Public and Private in Women's History* (Ithaca: Cornell University Press, 1992); Kathy Peiss, "Going Public: Women in Nineteenth-Century Cultural History," *American Literary History* 3, no. 4 (Winter 1991): 817–828. On the history of female activism in the United States, see Lori D. Ginzberg, *Women and the Work of Benevolence: Morality, Politics, and Class in the Nineteenth-Century United States* (New Haven: Yale University Press,

1990); Nancy A. Hewitt, *Women's Activism and Social Change: Rochester, New York, 1822–1872* (Ithaca, Cornell University Press, 1984); Jean Fagan Yellin and John C. Van Horne, eds., *The Abolitionist Sisterhood: Women's Political Culture in Antebellum America* (Ithaca: Cornell University Press, 1994); Julie Roy Jeffrey, *The Great Silent Army of Abolitionism: Ordinary Women in the Antislavery Movement* (Chapel Hill: University of North Carolina Press, 1998).

1 The Transatlantic Case against Catholicism

1. Samuel Morse, preface to *Confessions of a French Catholic Priest, to which are Added Warnings to the People of the United States by the Same Author* (New York: John S. Taylor, 1837), x. Morse was a prominent nativist who had already written two pamphlets denouncing the Catholic Church and immigration: *Imminent Dangers to the Free Institutions of the United States through Foreign Immigration* (1835) and *Foreign Conspiracy against the Liberties of the United States* (1835).
2. See Gilbert Chinard, ed., *La vie américaine de Guillaume Merle d'Aubigné* (Baltimore: John Hopkins Press, 1935).
3. J.H. Merle d'Aubigné, *History of the Reformation of the Sixteenth Century* (New York: Robert Carter, 1847), 50.
4. *Circulation and Character of the Volumes of the American Tract Society for the Society's Colporteurs* (American Tract Society, 1848), 86. The historians Elizabeth-Fox Genovese and Eugene D. Genovese have found that many Southern women recorded their admiration for the book in their diaries and correspondence. *The Mind of the Master Class* (Cambridge: Cambridge University Press, 2005), 651–652.
5. Author's Preface, *History of the Reformation in Europe in the Time of Calvin*, Vol. 1 (New York: Carter and Brothers, 1863), iii.
6. Archives of James Harpers and Brothers, Contract Books, Vol. I, 146, Chadwyck-Healey Archives of British Publishers on microfilm.
7. F. Bungener, *The Priest and the Huguenot* (Boston: Gould and Lincoln, 1853), 156.
8. Peter Bloom, "Robert Schumann and Mary Potts," *Notes* 65, no. 2 (December 2008).
9. *New York Times*, February 9, 1854; *Methodist Quarterly Review* 37 (1855): 642–43; and *Literary World*, December 3, 1853.
10. *The Religious Magazine and Monthly Review* June 1855, 356–357. For a longer review, see "The Relations of Romanism and Protestantism to Civilization," *Methodist Quarterly Review* (July 1855). For articles by Roussel, "Conversion of Young Girls to Popery," *Zion's Herald and Wesleyan Journal*, October 27, 1847; "Romanism Changing Its Skin," *New York Evangelist*, April 3, 1851.
11. McGreevy, *Catholicism and American Freedom*, 35.
12. M.J. Spalding, *Miscellanea: Comprising Reviews, Lectures, and Essays, on Historical, Theological, and Miscellaneous Subjects*, (Baltimore: J. Murphy & Co, 1875), 460. First published 1853.
13. René Rémond, *Les Etats-Unis devant l'Opinion Française*, Vol. 1 (Paris: Armand Colin, 1962), 167–169.

14. César Pascal, *A travers l'Atlantique et dans le nouveau monde* (Paris: Grassart, 1870), 217.
15. Jean-Henri Grandpierre, *A Parisian Pastor's Glance at America* (Boston: Gould and Lincoln, 1854), 111–112.
16. On Michelet's influence in the United States, see Franchot, *Roads to Rome*, 121–123. A brief account of American reviews of Michelet and Quinet is provided in Howard Mumford Jones, *America and French Culture 1750–1848* (Chapel Hill: University of North Carolina Press, 1927; reprint, Westport: Greenwood Press, 1973), 442–443.
17. Louis le Guillou, ed., *Jules Michelet, Correspondance Générale*, Vol. 4 (Paris: Champion, 1994–96), 756. Hempel had met Michelet and his family during a trip to Europe, but was only a sporadic correspondent. His previous letter to Michelet dates from January 26, 1831.
18. Ronald A Bosco and Joel Meyerson, eds., *Emerson in His Own Time: A Biographical Chronicle of His Life* (Iowa City: University of Iowa Press, 2003), 161.
19. Ronald A. Bosco and Glen M. Johnson, eds., *The Journals and Miscellaneous Notebooks of Ralph Waldo Emerson*, Vol. 16 (Cambridge, MA: Belknap Press, 1982), 353.
20. See Genovese, *Mind of the Master Class*, 762.
21. *Harper's New Monthly Magazine* 19, no. 113 (October 1859): 702. A similar accusation was contained in the *Atlantic Monthly* 4, no. 23 (September 1859): 391–3. For further satirical portrayals of Michelet's theories about women, see the illustrations which appeared in *Vanity Fair*, January 7, 1860, as well as the chapter dedicated to *L'Amour* in Bret Harte's *Condensed Novels* (New York: G.W. Carleton, 1867).
22. J. Michelet, *Love* (New York: Rudd and Carleton, 1859), 46.
23. To Charles Sumner, Andrew Hilen, ed., *The Letters of Henry Wadsworth Longfellow*, Vol. IV (Cambridge, MA: Belknap Press, 1966), p. 133.
24. Theodore Parker and John Weiss, *Life and Correspondence of Theodore Parker*, Vol. 2 (New York: Appleton, 1864), 312.
25. J.C. Derby, *Fifty Years among Authors, Books and Publishers* (New York: G.W. Carleton, 1884), 240.
26. Translator's Preface, *Love*, vi.
27. Cited in Luke White, *Henry William Herbert and the American Publishing Scene 1831–58* (Newark: Carteret Book Club, 1943), 11. See also Catherine Seville, *The Internationalisation of Copyright Law: Books, Buccaneers and the Black Flag in the Nineteenth Century* (Cambridge: Cambridge University Press, 2006).
28. Derby, *Fifty Years among Authors*, 240–241.
29. D'Aubigné, *Reformation in Europe in the time of Calvin*, vi.
30. Michelet, *Correspondance Générale*, Vol. 9, 369.
31. Michelet to Palmer, March 17, 1860, *J.W. Palmer Collection*, Special Collections, University of Virginia.
32. Michelet to Palmer, April 26, 1860. A longer account of the adventurous life of Michelet's father-in-law is contained in Athénais Michelet, *The Story of My Childhood* (Boston: Little, Brown & Co, 1867).
33. Michelet, *Correspondance Générale*, Vol. 9, 535.
34. Ibid., 539.

35. Ibid., Vol. 8, 195.
36. Ibid., 330.
37. Ibid., 349.
38. Michelet, *Du prêtre, de la femme et de la famille* (Paris: Hachette, 1845), 14.
39. Charles Cocks, *Bordeaux, Its Wines and the Claret Country*. The French translation by Jean-Baptiste Féret remains the classic reference work on the topic, and is known as the *Cocks & Féret*.
40. *Princeton Review* 17, no. 4 (1845): 643.
41. *Methodist Quarterly Review*, January 1846, 7.
42. *Littell's Living Age*, May 17, 1845, 336–340; *Anglo American, a Journal of Literature, News, Politics, the Drama*, October 11, 1845.
43. John Angell James, *Female Piety, or the Young Woman's Friend and Guide through Life to Immortality* (New York: Robert Carter and Brothers, 1854), 109–110.
44. Orvilla S. Belisle, *The Arch Bishop, or, Romanism in the United States* (Philadelphia: WM White Smith, 1855), 180, note 50; Julia McNair Wright, *Secrets of the Convent and Confessional* (Chicago: Jones, 1872), 208–209.
45. Catharine Beecher, *An Address to the Protestant Clergy of the United States* (New York: Harper and Brothers, 1846), 20.
46. Spalding, *Miscellanea*, 441.
47. Orestes A. Brownson, "The Madness of Antichristians," in *The Works of Orestes A. Brownson* Vol. 14 (New York: CAMS Press, 1966), 415.
48. *New York Times*, September 8, 1867.
49. *National Repository, Devoted to General and Religious Literature*, November 1877, 422.
50. *North American Review* 59, no. 125 (October 1844): 412.
51. C.F. Lester, *The Glory and Shame of England*, Vol.1 (New York: Harpers, 1841), viii.
52. *Liberator*, March 18, 1842.
53. *New York Times*, February 23, 1853.
54. Michelet, *Correspondance Générale*, Vol. 5, 204.
55. Ibid., 282.
56. *Encyclopaedia Americana: Supplementary Volume*, Vol. 14 (Boston: B.B. Mussey, 1851), 443.
57. *United States and Democratic Review*, 17, no. 90 (December 1845): 478.
58. *Methodist Quarterly Review*, January 1846. See also "The Jesuits in France," *New York Evangelist*, April 24, 1845.
59. *Biblical Repository and Classical Review*, January 1846, 184.
60. See the collection of reviews printed in Charles Billings Smith, *The Philosophy of Reform* (New York: Gates & Stedman, 1846).
61. Archives of James Harper and Brothers, Series I (Correspondence), Box 30.
62. *New York Herald*, January 12, 1845.
63. *Southern Quarterly Review* 9, no. 17, January 1846, 73.
64. Sir Charles Lyell, *A Second Visit to the United States of America*, Vol. 2 (London: John Murray, 1849), 340.
65. In S.E. Meats, "The Letters of Henry William Herbert" (PhD diss., University of South Carolina, 1972), 210. For a complete list of Herbert's many publications, see William Mitchell van Winkle and David A. Randall, *Henry*

William Herbert (Frank Forester): A Bibliography of his Writings (New York: B. Franklin, 1971).
66. Cited in Sterling F. Delano, *The Harbinger and New England Transcendentalism* (Cranbury: Associated University Presses, 1983), 20.
67. *The American Review: A Whig Journal of Politics, Literature, Art and Science*, March 1846.
68. *Daily Atlas*, August 24, 1846. *Milwaukee Daily Sentinel*, February 4, 1845.
69. Ruth Miller Elson, *Guardians of Tradition: American Schoolbooks in the Nineteenth Century* (Lincoln: University of Nebraska Press, 1964), esp. 46–48.
70. Henry C. Lea, "Monks and Nuns in France," *Putnam's Magazine of Literature, Science, Art, and National Interests* 4, no. 21 (September 1869): 265. Lea was the Protestant grandson of Mathew Carey, a Catholic publisher and economist. See also "Shall the Bible or the Pope be Schoolmaster," *Zion's Herald*, December 16, 1869.
71. *Harper's Weekly*, November 27, 1869.
72. *Revue du Monde Catholique* 9 (April–July 1864): 408.
73. *Temps*, January 5, 1864.
74. In addition to *Le maudit* and *La religieuse*, Michon wrote a number of scandalous novels. He is perhaps best remembered today as a pioneer of graphology. See Claude Savart, *L'Abbé Jean-Hippolyte Michon: Contribution à l'étude du libéralisme catholique au XIX siècle* (Paris: Les Belles Lettres, 1971); Philip Spencer, *Politics of Belief in Nineteenth-Century France: Lacordaire, Michon, Veuillot* (London: Faber, 1954).
75. *Harper's Monthly Magazine* 30, no. 176 (January 1865): 259. *New York Times*, November 12, 1864. See also *Boston Daily Advertiser*, November 24, 1864; *Harper's Weekly*, December 17, 1864; *Christian Advocate and Journal*, December 22, 1864.
76. *New York Observer and Chronicle*, December 12, 1867. For further reviews, see *Zion's Herald and Wesleyan Journal*, November 30, 1864; *Independent*, August 9, 1866; *American Presbyterian and Theological Review*, January 1865; *Christian Examiner*, January 1865; *Christian Advocate and Journal*, May 4, 1865.
77. *Pope, or President? Startling Disclosures of Romanism as Revealed by its Own Writers* (New York: R.L. Delisser, 1859), 60. See also "Count de Lasteyrie's Auricular Confession," *Living Age* 17, no. 203, April 1, 1848, 20–21; Howard Malcolm, *Theological Index: References to the Principal Works in every Department of Religious Literature* (Boston: Gould and Lincoln, 1868), 39.
78. Enrichetta Caracciolo, *Mystères des couvents de Naples* (Paris: Dentu, 1865), 94.
79. Pierre Larousse, *Grand dictionnaire universel du XIXe siècle*, Vol. 5 (Paris: Administration du Grand Dictionnaire, 1869), 419.
80. *Daily Evening Bulletin*, October 23, 1867. Two lengthier reviews of the book from British journals were reprinted in America. See James Picciotti, "A Peep at a Neapolitan Nunnery," *The Eclectic Magazine of Foreign Literature* (January 1870); "An Italian Nun," *Living Age* 83, no. 1071 (December 10, 1864): 572–574.
81. *New York Observer and Chronicle*, October 17, 1867.

82. Despite charting the appreciation on the part of the French cultural elite for the works of Hawthorne, Edgar Allan Poe, and Walt Whitman in this period, Blumenthal notes that "even favorable reviews of the works of the most outstanding American poets did not induce large numbers of Frenchmen to acquaint themselves with nineteenth-century American authors." *American and French Culture, 1800–1900: Interchanges in Art, Science, Literature, and Society* (Baton Rouge: Louisiana State University Press, 1975), 231. On Howe, see her *Is Polite Society Polite?* (Boston: Lamson, Wolffe), 51.
83. Eugène Pelletan, Auguste Colin, Hippolyte-Michel de la Morvonnais, and Victor Hennequin, *Les dogmes, le clergé et l'état* (Paris: Librairie Sociétaie, 1844), 16. See also his *Profession de foi du dix-neuvième siècle*, 4th edition (Paris: Pagnerre, 1857), 306–308.
84. Agénor de Gasparin, *America before Europe: Principles and Interests* (New York: Scribner, 1862), 9.
85. For Booth's career, see Harriet Spofford, *A Little Book of Friends* (Boston: Little Broan and Company, 1916), 117–131; Edward T James et al., *Notable American Women, 1607–1950* (Cambridge, MA: Harvard University Press, 1971), 207–208. After the Civil War, Booth became the first editor of *Harper's Bazaar*, a position she held for twenty-two years.
86. *Speech of Hon. Charles Sumner, of Massachusetts on Maritime Rights*, January 9, 1862, 13.
87. Roy P. Basler, ed., *Collected Works of Abraham Lincoln*, Vol. 5 (New Brunswick: Rutgers University Press, 1953).
88. Ibid., 355–356.
89. Edgar Quinet, *Œuvres complètes*, Vol. 14, *L'Enseignement du peuple* (Paris: Hachette, 1870), 12. Quinet, like so many other French republicans, was married to a Protestant. On the appeal of Protestantism for the French left, see Philippe Boutry, "La gauche et la religion," in *Histoire des gauches en France*, Vol. 1, *L'héritage du XIXe siècle*, ed. Jean-Jacques Becker and Gilles Candar (Paris: Découverte, 2004), esp. 324–328.
90. E. Laboulaye, *Histoire des Etats-Unis*, 5th edition (Paris: Charpentier, 1870), 215–216.
91. For his comments on the relationship between religious faith and political systems, see *Lettres sur l'Amérique du Nord*, Vol. 2, 4th edition (Brussels: Wouters, 1844), 160. Chevalier's book was translated and published as *Society, Manners and Politics in the United States* (Boston: Weeks & Jordan, 1839).
92. *Investigator and Advocate of Independence*, December 1846; *Christian Observer*, August 19, 1848; *New York Times*, October 24 1851; *Christian Watchman and Reflector*, May 4, 1854; *National Magazine; Devoted to Literature, Art, and Religion*, December 1854; *Methodist Quarterly Review*, July 1855.
93. On Laboulaye, see Walter D. Gray, *Interpreting American Democracy in France: The Career of Édouard Laboulaye, 1811–1883* (Newark: University of Delaware Press, 1994).
94. Translator's Preface, *Paris in America* (New York: Scribner, 1863), iii.

95. On these connections, see Gray, *Interpreting American Democracy*. On the career of Walsh, see Sister M. Frederick Lochemes, *Robert Walsh: His Story* (Washington, DC: Catholic University Press, 1941).
96. E.L. Pierce, ed., *Memoirs and Letters of Charles Sumner*, Vol. 3 (London: Sampson Low & Marston, 1893), 566.
97. Pelletan, *Heures de travail* (Paris: Pagnerre, 1854), 372–392. On the admiration for Channing among liberal French Protestants, see Nord, *The Republican Moment*, 113.
98. Edgar Quinet, *Lettres sur la question religieuse en 1856* (Bruxelles: Mélines and Cans, 1857), 18. On Channing's influence on French republicans, see Juda Tchernoff, *Le parti républicain au coup d'état et sous le Second Empire* (Paris: Pedone, 1906), 307; Georges Weill, *Histoire du parti républicain en France 1814–1870* (Paris: Librairie Félix Alcan, 1928), 348.
99. Letter to Maurice Sand, September 1, 1861, in *Correspondance*, Vol. 4 (Paris: Calmann-Lévy, 1883).
100. Jules Simon, *La politique radicale* (Brussels: Lacroix, Verboeckhoven, 1868) 157. The debate concerned Article 8 of the Law of May 17, 1819.
101. For Renan, see "Channing et le mouvement unitaire aux Etats-Unis," *Revue des Deux Mondes* 8, October-December 1854, 1085–1107. For Chasles, see *Études sur la littérature et les mœurs des Anglo-Américains au XIXe siècle* (Paris: Amyot, 1851), 64–66.
102. Henri Baudrillart, *Des rapports de la morale et de l'économie politique* (Paris: Guillaumin, 1860), 43. Gambetta quoted Channing in a speech in Bordeaux in 1871: J.C. Chaplain, ed., *Discours et plaidoyers choisis de Léon Gambetta* (Paris: E. Fasquelles, 1909), 71.
103. Émile de Laveleye, *Questions contemporaines* (Bruxelles: A. Lacroix, Verboeckhoven, 1863), 35–37.
104. Jules Simon, *La liberté de conscience*, 2nd edition (Paris: Hachette, 1857), 241, note 2; Pierre Joseph Proudhon, *De la justice dans la révolution et dans l'église* Vol. 2 (Paris: Garnier Frères, 1858), 363.
105. Henri Allain-Targé, *La république sous l'empire* (Paris: Bernard Grasset, 1939), 39.
106. Charles Sauvestre, *Les congrégations religieuses dévoilées* (Paris: E. Dentu, 1870), 65.
107. Eyma, *Les deux Amériques, histoire, mœurs et voyages* (Paris: D. Giraud, 1853), 81.
108. Émile de Laveleye, "De l'instruction du peuple au XIXe siècle—i.—l'enseignement populaire dans les écoles américaines," *Revue des Deux Mondes*, November 15, 1865.
109. Ralph Gibson, *A Social History of French Catholicism 1789–1914* (New York: Routledge, 1989), 122.
110. "L'éducation des femmes et des affranchis en Amérique," *Revue des Deux Mondes* 83 (September–October 1869): 450–476. See also Françoise Mayeur, *L'éducation des filles en France au XIXe siècle* (Paris: Hachette, 1979), 135. On Duruy's reforms, see Sandra Ann Horvath, "Victory Duruy and the Controversy over Secondary Education for Girls," *French Historical Studies* 9, no. 1 (Spring, 1975): 83–104.
111. Célestin Hippeau, *L'instruction publique aux Etats-Unis* (Paris: Didier, 1870), ix.

112. Olympe Audouard, A travers l'Amérique (Paris: Dentu, 1870), 53–54.
113. Ibid., 92; Démocratie, 6 February 1870. See also Tribune, October 11 and October 18, 1868, and October 31, 1869.
114. Hippeau, L'instruction publique, 190.
115. de Laveleye, "De l'instruction du peuple," esp. 291–292.
116. Sauvestre, Les congrégations religieuses, 62.
117. Paul Robriquet, Discours et opinion de Jules Ferry, Vol. 1 (Paris: Armand Colin, 1893), 305.
118. Boston Daily Advertiser, March 5, 1868.
119. Gustave de Beaumont, Marie: ou, L'esclavage aux États-Unis, tableau de mœurs américaines (Paris: C. Gosselin, 1836), 289–301.
120. E. Laboulaye, De la constitution Américaine et de l'utilité de son étude: Discours prononcé, le 4 décembre 1849, à l'ouverture du cours de législation comparée (Paris: Hennuyer, 1850), 15–16.
121. E. Laboulaye, Le parti libéral: son programme et son avenir (Paris: Charpentier, 1865), 50.
122. Jean Maurain, La politique ecclesiastique du Second Empire (Paris: Félix Alcan, 1930).
123. Annales de l'Association internationale pour le progrès des sciences sociales (Paris: Guillaumin, 1863), 206.
124. De Gasparin, America before Europe, 346.
125. Revue du monde colonial 2nd series, no. 6, January-June 1862, 213.
126. Tribune, June 14, 1868.
127. Démocratie, May 9, 1869.
128. [italics added] Siècle, August 18, 1869. See also Voix du Peuple, July 10, 1869.
129. See Rémond, Les Etats-Unis devant l'opinion française, Vol. 2, 756–62.
130. Lucien Prevost-Paradol, La France nouvelle (Paris: Ressources, 1979), 234.
131. Laveleye, Questions contemporaines, 34.
132. Chevalier, Lettres sur l'Amérique du Nord, 122; see also his La liberté aux Etats-Unis (Paris: Capelle, 1949), 51.
133. De Beaumont, Marie, 270–272.
134. Sauvestre, Les congrégations religieuses, 95.
135. Oscar Comettant, L'Amérique telle qu'elle est (Paris: Achille Faure, 1864), 222. On Catholic views of the Know-Nothings, see, for example, "Nouveaux détails sur les excès des Know-Nothings," L'Ami de la religion et du Roi, 170, Oct-Dec 1855, 75–76.
136. Grandpierre, Parisian Pastor's Glance at America, 131.
137. J.J. Ampère, Promenade en Amérique (Paris: Michel Levy, 1860), 193.
138. Ernest Duvergier de Hauranne, Huit mois en Amérique, Vol. 2 (Paris: A. Lacroix, Verboeckhoven, 1866), 131.
139. Edouard Laboulaye, Etudes morales et politiques (Paris: Charpentier, 1866), 151.
140. Rodgers, Atlantic Crossings, 3–4.
141. Thomas A Sancton, "America in the Eyes of the French Left." (PhD diss., Oxford, 1978).
142. Philippe Roger, The American Enemy: A Story of French anti-Americanism, trans. Sharon Bowman (Chicago: University of Chicago Press, 2005).

188 Notes

143. Eyma, *La Republique Americaine—ses institutions, ses hommes*, Vol. 1 (Paris: Michel Lèvy, 1861), 8.
144. *North American Review* 83, no. 173 (October 1856): 490–491.
145. Henry T. Tuckerman, *America and Her Commentators* (New York: Scribner, 1864), 138.

2   Catholicism, Slavery, and the Family—The Mortara Affair

1. For a narrative of these events, David I. Kertzer, *The Kidnapping of Edgardo Mortara* (New York: Alfred A. Knopf, 1997).
2. *National Era*, December 12, 1858.
3. *New York Herald*, November 21, 1858.
4. *New York Times*, December 16, 1858. A comprehensive account of the American reaction is provided in Bertram Wallace Korn, *The American Reaction to the Mortara Case* (Cincinnati: American Jewish Archives, 1957). Korn's focus, however, is the significance of the Affair for the Jewish community in America, rather than the case against Catholicism itself.
5. *Journal des Débats*, September 29, 1858.
6. *Revue des Deux Mondes*, November 1, 1858.
7. *Edgar Mortara, dedié aux pères et aux mères* (Paris: E Dentu, 1860), 10.
8. *Journal des Débats*, September 29, 1858. For a brief survey of French reactions, see George J. Weill, "L'affaire Mortara et l'anticléricalisme en Europe à l'époque du Risorgimento," in *Aspects de l'anticléricalisme du Moyen-Age à nos jours*, ed. Jacques Marx (Bruxelles: Éditions de l'Université de Bruxelles, 1988). The controversy over the Affair, particularly within the Imperial Administration, is briefly discussed in Maurain, *La politique ecclesiastique du Second Empire*, 230–231. The file on the Affair in the French Ministry of Religion archives, F19 1937, contains little material.
9. *Philadelphia Public Ledger*, November 23, 1858.
10. *New York Times*, November 3, 1858.
11. *New York Times*, November 12, 1858.
12. *Harper's Weekly*, November 20, 1858.
13. *New York Tribune*, November 10, 1858.
14. See Cecil Roth, "Forced Baptisms in Italy," *Jewish Quarterly Review* 27, no. 2 (October 1936): 117–136.
15. According to Roger Aubert, the pope's refusal to return Edgardo Mortara played a key role in convincing the French emperor to support the cause of Italian unification: *Le pontificat de Pie IX* (Paris: Bloud and Gay, 1952), 87.
16. *New York Tribune*, December 2, 1858.
17. Edmond About, *La question romaine* (Bruxelles: Meline et Cans, 1859). Due to censorship restrictions in France, About's book was published in Belgium. The work was published as *The Roman Question* in New York in 1859, and contained the following: "The Roman Catholic Church...consists of one hundred and thirty-nine millions of individuals—without counting little Mortara." Edmond About, *The Roman Question* (New York: D. Appleton & Company, 1859), 7.

18. *New York Herald*, January 12, 1859.
19. *New York Times*, November 9, 1858.
20. *New York Evangelist*, January 20, 1859.
21. *Boston Daily Evening Transcript*, December 10, 1858.
22. *New York Observer and Chronicle*, January 6, 1859.
23. *Journal des Débats*, October 11, 1858.
24. *La Presse*, October 24, 1858.
25. *Domestic Revolutions: A Social History of American Family Life* (New York: Macmillan, 1988), 44. A similar point is made in Mary P. Ryan, *Cradle of the Middle Class: The Family in Oneida County, 1790–1865* (Cambridge: Cambridge University Press, 1981).
26. Paul Janet, *La famille: Leçons de philosophie morale* (Paris: Ladrange, 1856), 293. Janet was appointed to the chair of philosophy at the Sorbonne in 1864.
27. Eugène Buisson, *L'homme, la famille et la société considérés dans leurs rapports avec le progrès moral de l'humanité*, Vol. 2, *La famille* (Paris: Joel Cherbuliez, 1857), 15–16.
28. *Appletons' Journal: A Magazine of General Literature* 1, no. 4 (April 24, 1869): 115.
29. Jacques Donzelot, *The Policing of Families*, trans. Robert Hurley (London: Hutchinson, 1980).
30. Larousse, *Grand dictionnaire universel*, Vol. 8, 75.
31. *Brownson's Quarterly Review*, New York Series 4, no. 14 (1859): 227.
32. *L'Univers*, October 14, 1858.
33. See Tyler Anbinder, *Nativism and Slavery: The Northern Know Nothings and the Politics of the 1850's* (New York: Oxford University Press, 1992); Stephen Maizlish, "The Meaning of Nativism and the Crisis of the Union: The Know-Nothing Movement in the Antebellum North," in *Essays on American Antebellum Politics 1840–1860*, ed. S. Maizlish and J. Kushma (Austin: University of Texas Press, 1982).
34. The notion that whiteness was not a biological given but was socially and culturally constructed has proven particularly useful in understanding the adoption of white supremacist beliefs by Irish immigrants to the United States. However, my own research suggests that scholarship in this field has tended to overestimate the ease with which Irish immigrants were accepted as true members of the white race. In particular, I would argue that enduring suspicion of the Catholicism of the Irish counteracted any possible racial affinity. Such appeals to racial solidarity may have proven effective in certain regions, particularly the South, but throughout much of the North true acceptance as a member of the white race remained conditional throughout the nineteenth century on an allegiance to Protestantism. See the chapter entitled "Irish Americans and Race" in Timothy Meagher, *The Columbia Guide to Irish-American History* (New York: Columbia University Press, 2005).
35. Eric Foner, "The Meaning of Freedom in the Age of Emancipation," *Journal of American History* 81, no. 2 (September 1994): 438.
36. Quoted in Maizlish, "The Meaning of Nativism and the Crisis of the Union," 178.

37. Foner, "The Meaning of Freedom," 446.
38. Eugène Pelletan, *An Address to King Cotton*, trans. Leander Starr (New York: H. de Mareil, 1863), 6.
39. Michelet, *Du prêtre, de la femme et de la famille*, 325.
40. Caracciolo, *Mystères des couvents*, 347.
41. Michon, *La religieuse*, Vol. 1 (Paris: La Croix, Verboeckhoven, 1864), 326.
42. *Siècle*, August 16/17, 1857.
43. Louis Jourdain, preface to *Le nouveau monde. Scènes de la vie américaine* by Oscar Comettant (Paris: Pagnerre, 1861), xiv.
44. On Stowe's influence, see Edith E. Lucas, *La littérature anti-esclavagiste au 19ème siècle: Étude sur Mme Beecher Stowe et son influence en France* (Bordeaux: J. Bière, 1930).
45. Cited in Korn, *American Reactions to the Mortara Case*, 107.
46. *Liberator*, December 31, 1858.
47. *Chicago Tribune*, November 2, 1858.
48. *Journal des Débats*, October 16, 1858.
49. *Siècle*, November 20, 1858.
50. *Journal des Débats*, October 22, 1858.
51. Reprinted in the *Chicago Tribune*, December 7, 1858.
52. *Brownson's Quarterly Review*, New York Series 4, no. 14, 1859, 237.
53. *Independent*, January 6, 1859.
54. *Independent*, April 14, 1859.
55. *Zion's Herald and Wesleyan Journal*, December 22, 1858.
56. Prosper Mérimée, *Lettres à M. Panizzi, 1850–1870*, Vol. 2 (Paris: Calmann Lévy, 1881), 43. Panizzi was Chief Librarian at the British Museum Library from 1856 until 1866.
57. *Harper's Weekly*, November 11, 1876.

3 Natural or Unnatural? Doctors and the Vow of Celibacy

1. [E. Joy Morris], *Remarks of the Honorable E. Joy Morris of Philadelphia in the House of Representatives of Pennsylvania, Feb. 12, 1856* (Harrisburg: 1856), 9.
2. *The Natural Fruits of Popery* (Philadelphia: Presbyterian Board of Publications, 1842), 24.
3. *Opinion Nationale*, October 4, 1869.
4. Cited in F.W.J. Hemmings, *Emile Zola* (Oxford: Clarendon Press, 1966), 105. Zola's solution was to complicate the issue of celibacy by having his priest, Serge Mouret, suffer from amnesia. Mouret therefore breaks his vows without knowing he is a priest.
5. For example, Charles Sauvestre in *La Liberté*, October 11, 1869.
6. Antoine Jay, cited in *Ce qu'on a dit du mariage et du célibat*, ed. Larcher and P.J. Jullien (Paris: Éditions Hetzel, 1858), 187.
7. *Pope or President? Startling Disclosures of Romanism as Revealed by Its Own Writers* (New York: R.L. Delisser, 1859), 46–48. The Mingrat case was also brought to the attention of the American public through the Count de Lasteyrie's *Auricular confession*. See, for example, *Littell's Living Age* 17, no. 203 (April 1848): 20–21.

8. Michel Foucault, *The History of Sexuality*, Vol. 1, *An Introduction*, trans. Robert Hurley (New York: Vintage Books, 1985).
9. Jacques Léonard has noted the resentment of physicians at the competition provided by Catholic religious women. See *La médicine entre les pouvoirs et les savoirs* (Paris: Aubier Montaigne, 1981), esp. 74–79. The same rivalry was evident in the psychiatric profession. See Jan Goldstein, *Console and Classify: The French Psychiatric Profession in the Nineteenth Century* (Cambridge: Cambridge University Press, 1987), esp. 210–230.
10. Jan Goldstein, "The Hysteria Diagnosis and the Politics of Anticlericalism in Late Nineteenth-Century France," *Journal of Modern History* 54, no. 2 (June 1982): 209–239; Jack D. Ellis, *The Physician-Legislators of France: Medicine and Politics in the Early Third Republic 1870–1914* (Cambridge: Cambridge University Press, 1990).
11. Théodore Perrin, *Nature et virginité, considérations physiologiques sur le célibat religieux, par Jean-Ennemond Dufieux. Rapport fait à la Société de Médecine de Lyon* (Lyon: A. Vingtrinier, 1855), 16.
12. For testimony of the appeal of the French medical system for American doctors, see G. de Bertier de Sauvigny, *La France et les Français vus par les voyageurs Américains 1814–1848*, Vol. 2 (Paris: Flammarion, 1985), esp. 154. For a comprehensive account of the influence of French medical practice and training on American physicians, see John H. Warner, *Against the Spirit of the System: The French Impulse in Nineteenth-Century Medicine* (Princeton: Princeton University Press, 1998); R.M. Jones, "American Doctors and the Parisian Medical World 1830–1840," *Bulletin of the History of Medicine* 47, no. 2 (1973): 177–204.
13. Dr. Claude-Francois Lallemand, *Des pertes séminales involontaires*, Vol. 2 (Paris: Bêchet Jeune, 1839), 258.
14. Dr. Menville de Ponsan, *Histoire philosophique et médicale de la femme*, Vol. 1 (Paris: J.B. Baillière, 1858), 336.
15. Dr. Louis Seraine, *Les préceptes du mariage, traduits du Grec de Plutarque* (Paris: F. Savy, 1861), 84.
16. Dr. Seth Pancoast, *The Ladies' Medical Guide* (Philadelphia: John E. Potter, 1865), 230.
17. Robert James Culverwell, *The Institutes of Marriage, its Intent, Obligations and Physical and Constitutional Disqualifications, Anatomically, Physiologically, and Medically Considered* (New York: 1846), 43.
18. O.S. Fowler, *Creative and Sexual Science, or, Manhood, Womanhood, and Their Mutual Interrelations* (Grand Rapids: C.R. Parish, 1870), 599.
19. Léopold Deslandes, *De l'Onanisme et des autres abus vénériens* (Paris: Lelarge, 1835), 49–50.
20. Charles Knowlton, *Fruits of Philosophy; or, the private companion of young married people* (New York: 1832), 18. The Library Company of Philadelphia holds a rare first edition of this fascinating work.
21. The popularity of such works is difficult to establish with precision. In the United States, many scholars have concluded that despite legislative prohibition and the efforts of public prosecutors, guides to contraception circulated widely. In her study of contraceptive practices in the United States, Janet Farrell Brodie has identified a "boom" in the publication

and sale of guides to contraception after 1850. See Janet Farrell Brodie, *Contraception and Abortion in Nineteenth-Century America* (Ithaca: Cornell University Press, 1994), esp. Chapter 6. Carl Degler reaches a similar conclusion; see Carl N Degler, *At Odds: Women and the Family in America from the Revolution to the Present* (New York: Oxford University Press, 1980), 210–220.
22. Dr. J. Soule, *Science of Reproduction and Reproductive Control* (New York: 1856; reprint, New York: Arno Press, 1974), 26. Italics in original. According to Janet Farrell Brodie, Dr. Soule was probably a businessman, Asa J Soule.
23. Cited in the *Boston Medical and Surgical Journal*, September 18, 1844. In a review of a later work purportedly written by a physician, one reviewer referred to Becklard's work as among those sold "on the sly." *Medical and Surgical Reporter* 21, no. 3 (July 17, 1869): 60. Later scholars have continued to refer to Becklard as an influential French physician. Both Carl Degler and Janet Farrell Brodie, for example, failed to detect that the work was a forgery.
24. *Dictionaire des sciences médicales*, Vol. 4 (Paris: C.L.F. Panckoucke, 1813), 404.
25. Frederick Hollick, *The Marriage Guide, or Natural History of Generation* (New York: T.W. Strong, 1850), 362. On those medical writers in America who celebrated the sexual instinct, see Helen Lefkowitz Horowitz, *Rereading Sex: Battles over sexual knowledge and suppression in nineteenth-century America* (New York: Alfred A. Knopf, 2002), especially Chapter 12. On Hollick's trial, April Haynes, "The Trials of Frederick Hollick: Obscenity, Sex Education, and Medical Democracy in the Antebellum United States," *Journal of the History of Sexuality* 12, no. 4 (October 2003): 543–574.
26. Ibid., 363.
27. Ibid., 364.
28. Deslandes, *De l'onanisme*, 518. The American title was *A Treatise on the Diseases Produced by Onanism, Masturbation, Self-pollution and other Excesses*. Another work by Deslandes, *Manhood: The Causes of its Premature Decline*, reached its fifth American edition just four years after its first publication in 1838.
29. Claude-Franc‚ois Lallemand, *A Practical Treatise on the Causes, Symptoms and Treatment of Spermatorrhœa* (Philadelphia: Blanchard & Lea, 1861), 246.
30. Dr. Hector Landouzy, *Traité complet de l'hystérie* (Paris: Baillière, 1846), 186.
31. Ibid., 185.
32. Gunning S. Bedford, *Clinical Lectures on the Diseases of Women and Children* (New York: Samuel S. and William Wood, 1857), 371.
33. Auguste Debay, *Hygiène et physiologie du mariage* (Paris: E. Dentu, 1859), 18.
34. *Dictionaire des sciences médicales*, 407.
35. *Nation*, October 31, 1867. Deparcieux's work was entitled *Essai sur les probabilités de la durée de la vie humaine* (Paris: Guérin frères, 1746).
36. Buffon published the letter in the *Histoire naturelle générale et particulière: Supplément. Tome quatrième* (Paris: Imprimerie Royale, 1777), 383–394.
37. Dr. Felix Roubaud, *Traité de l'Impuissance et de la stérilité*, Vol. 1 (Paris: J.-B. Baillière, 1855), 372.

38. Michel Lèvy, *Traité d'hygiène publique et privée*, Vol. 1 (Paris: J.-B. Baillière, 1869), 146.
39. Benedict-Auguste Morel, *Traité des maladies mentales* (Paris: V. Masson, 1860), 181.
40. Jean-Ennemond Dufieux, *Nature et virginité: Considérations physiologiques sur le célibat religieux* (Paris: Julien et Lanier, 1854), 373.
41. Lallemand, *Des pertes séminales involontaires*, 225.
42. Ibid., 256.
43. Deslandes, *De l'Onanisme*, 518.
44. Ibid.
45. Dr. Louis Seraine, *De la santé des gens mariés, ou Physiologie de la génération de l'homme* (Paris: F. Savy, 1865), 233.
46. Soule, *Science of Reproduction and Reproductive Control*, 24.
47. Becklard, *KNOW THYSELF: The Physiologist; or, Sexual Physiology Revealed* (Boston: Bela Marsh, 1859; reprint, New York: Arno Press, 1974), 43.
48. *Dictionaire des sciences médicales*, 405.
49. Debay, *Hygiène et physiologie du mariage*, 17. Although Debay might be classified less a physician than a popularizer of medical theories, his works were cited by other doctors. Dr. Menville de Ponsan, for example, relied heavily on Debay's case studies in his own work on female diseases.
50. Ibid., 18.
51. Ibid., 211.
52. Hollick, *The Marriage Guide*, 363; James Ashton, *The Book of Nature: Containing Information for Young People who Think of Getting Married* (New York: Brother Jonathan Office, 1865; reprint New York: Arno Press, 1974), 36.
53. Dr. Frederick Hollick, *Facts for the feeble! Or Professional Notes of Curious Medical Consultations relating to the various peculiarities, disabilities and forms of decay of the Sexual System* (New York: American News, 1855), 377.
54. Dr. George Henry Napheys, *The Physical Life of Woman* (Toronto: Maclean, 1871), 232.
55. Pancoast, *Ladies' Medical Guide*, 232.
56. Ibid., 233.
57. Edward Bliss Foote, *Plain Home Talk* (Boston: Thayer and Eldridge, 1860), 167.
58. Stark's findings were published in France as "De l'influence du mariage sur la mortalité moyenne des deux sexes," *Annales d'hygiène*, series 2, no. 29 (1868): 34–49.
59. *Dictionnaire encyclopédique des sciences médicales,* second series, Vol. 5 (Paris: G. Masson and P. Asselin, 1874), 49.
60. *Medical and Surgical Reporter*, December 24, 1859.
61. "The Hygienic Relations of Celibacy," *Nation*, October 31, 1867.
62. Isabel V. Hull, *Sexuality, State and Civil Society in Germany, 1700–1815* (Ithaca: Cornell University Press, 1997), 241. In *The Sexual Contract*, Carole Pateman argues that such sexual criteria were employed by male writers to justify the exclusion of women from citizenship. For Pateman, masculine theorists of gender relations from Rousseau to Freud claimed that women, who were considered unable to fully master their sexual passions, were

thereby deemed unsuitable to take part in the social contract. *The Sexual Contract* (Cambridge: Polity, 1988), esp. 100–102.
63. Mark E. Kann, *A Republic of Men: The American Founders, Gendered Language, and Patriarchal Politics* (New York: New York University Press, 1998); Suzanne Desan, *The Family on Trial in Revolutionary France* (Berkeley: University of California Press, 2004), 55–56. On the nineteenth-century, see Jean Borie, *Le célibataire français* (Paris: Le Sagittaire, 1976).
64. Robert A. Nye, *Masculinity and Male Codes of Honor in Modern France* (New York: Oxford University Press, 1993), 65–67; Judith Surkis, *Sexing the Citizen: Morality and Masculinity in France, 1870–1920* (Ithaca: Cornell University Press, 2006), 49.
65. For the American figures, see Degler, *At Odds*, 181. The French figures are based on a study by the historian Emile Lavisseur, cited in Peter Gay, *The Bourgeois Experience: Victoria to Freud*, Vol. 1, *The Education of the Senses* (New York: Oxford University Press, 1984), 266. Carl Degler has drawn attention to the similarity of France and the United States in relation to their decline in fertility. As he has written, "Among European countries in the middle of the nineteenth century, only France resembled the United States in having a steady decline." Degler, *At Odds*, 180.
66. See Angus McLaren, *Sexuality and Social Order* (New York: Holmes & Meier, 1983), 11; Nye, *Masculinity and Male codes of Honor*, 76–82. The term demography was in fact invented in France in this period.
67. Lèvy, *Traité d'hygiène publique*, Vol. 2, 704.
68. *Dictionnaire encyclopédique des sciences médicales*, 14.
69. Dr. Edward M. Dixon, *Scenes in the Practice of a New York Surgeon* (New York: DeWitt & Davenport, 1855), 186.
70. Ibid., 185.
71. *New York Times*, January 24, 1869.
72. Catharine E. Beecher and Harriet Beecher Stowe, *The American Woman's Home* (New Brunswick: Rutgers University Press, 2002), 25.
73. de Ponsan, *Histoire philosophique et médicale de la femme*, 319.
74. Thomas Low Nichols, *Esoteric Anthropology* (New York: Stringer and Townsend, 1853), 407.
75. Thomas Low and Mary Gove Nichols, *Marriage* (New York: T.L. Nichols, 1854), 315.
76. Thomas Low Nichols, *Esoteric Anthropology* (Malvern: T.L. Nichols, 1872), 113.
77. Thomas Low Nichols, *Human Physiology* (London: Trubner, 1872), 273.
78. Stephen Nissenbaum, *Sex, diet and debility in Jacksonian America* (Chicago: Dorsey Press, 1988), 161. Nissenbaum, I would argue, unfairly diminishes the radical nature of the Nichols' philosophy. For another analysis which casts Nichols more as an iconoclast, see Jean Silver-Isenstadt, "Passions and Perversions: The radical ambition of Dr Thomas Low Nichols" in Charles Rosenberg, ed., *Right-living: An Anglo-American tradition of self-help medicine and hygiene* (Baltimore: John Hopkins Univ. Press, 2003), 186–205.
79. Augustus K. Gardner, *The French Metropolis: Paris; as Seen during the Spare Hours of a Medical Student* (New York: C.S. Francis & Co, 1850), 93–94.

80. Dr. Xavier Bourgeois, *Les passions dans leurs rapports avec la santé et les maladies* (Paris: J.B. Baillière, 1863), 35. The American title was *The Passions in Their Relations to Health and Diseases*; a second edition was published in 1876.
81. William Alcott, *The Physiology of Marriage* (Boston: John P. Jewett, 1856), 71.
82. Ibid., 116–117. Graham was, of course, the inventor of the Graham cracker, which he intended as an aid to abstinence. See Jayme A. Sokolow, *Eros and Modernization: Sylvester Graham, Health Reform, and the Origins of Victorian Sexuality in America* (Rutherford: Fairleigh Dickinson University Press, 1983).
83. Dr. Nicholas Cooke, *Satan in Society, by a Physician* (Cincinnati: C.F. Vent, 1876; reprint New York: Arno Press, 1974), 202. The work was first published in 1870.
84. Dr. Alfred Becquerel, *Traité élémentaire d'hygiène privée et publique*, 6th edition (Paris: P. Asselin, 1877), 795. The first edition appeared in 1851.
85. Dr. Pierre Briquet, *Un traité clinique et thérapeutique de l'hystérie* (Paris: J.B. Baillière, 1859), 132.
86. Augustus K. Gardner, *Conjugal Sins Against the Laws of Life and Health* (New York: J.S. Redfield, 1870; reprint New York: Arno Press, 1974), 41.
87. Ibid., 67.
88. Cooke, *Satan in Society*, 202.
89. Dr. L.F.F. Bergeret, *Des fraudes dans l'accomplissement des fonctions génératrices* (Paris: J.B.Baillère, 1868). By 1926, the book had reached its twentieth edition. The American edition was entitled *The Preventive Obstacle, or Conjugal Onanism* (New York: Turner and Mignard, 1870; reprint New York: Arno Press, 1974).
90. Dufieux, *Nature et virginité*, iv.
91. Ibid., 10.
92. Cited in Dio Lewis, *Chastity, or Our Secret Sins* (Philadelphia: George Maclean & Co., 1874; reprint New York: Arno Press, 1974), 246. Lewis (1823–1886) played an important role in introducing physical exercise into the education system. In 1861 he opened the Normal Institute of Physical Education in Boston, which was designed to train teachers in the principles of physical education. He was later active in the temperance movement. On the French belief in semen's life-giving power, see Angus McLaren, "Doctor in the House," Medicine and Private Morality in France, 1800–1850," *Feminist Studies* 2, no. 2/3 (1975): 45–47.
93. Francis Devay, *De la physiologie humaine et de la médicine* (Paris: Pitois, 1840), 170.
94. Bergeret, *The Preventive Obstacle*, 163.
95. Briquet, *Traité clinique et thérapeutique*, 136.
96. *American Journal of the Medical Sciences* (Philadelphia: Blanchard and Lea, 1858) 35, 253.
97. J.B.F. Descuret, *La médicine des passions, ou les passions considérées dans leurs rapports avec les maladies, les lois et la religion* (Paris: Labé, 1860), 473.
98. Bourgeois, *Les passions dans leur rapports avec la santé et les maladies*, 45.
99. Ibid., 36.

100. Becquerel, *Traité élémentaire d'hygiène*, 334.
101. Horatio Robinson Storer, *Why Not? A Book for Every Woman* (Boston: Lee & Shepard, 1866), 64. Storer pioneered the use of chloroform in surgery and childbirth in America, and was one of the founders of gynecology as a separate medical discipline. He was also one of the leaders of the crusade against abortion. His conversion to Roman Catholicism took place in 1876. Medical journals occasionally quoted with approval the condemnations of abortion issued by leading Catholics. See, for example, the report of such an address by Archbishop Spaulding contained in the *Medical and Surgical Reporter*, May 29, 1869.
102. Bergeret, *Preventive Obstacle*, 161.
103. Dr. Paul Diday, *Examen de l'ouvrage de m. le docteur dufieux, intitulé nature et virginité, considérations physiologiques sur le célibat religieux* (Lyon: Aimé Vingtrinier, 1855), 8.
104. *Dictionnaire encyclopédique des sciences médicales*, fourth series, Vol. 5 (Paris: G. Masson and P. Asselin, 1879), 858.
105. *Medical and Surgical Reporter*, May 28, 1870.
106. Cited in Gardner, *Conjugal Sins*, 43.
107. O.S. Fowler, *Sexual Science, Including Manhood, Womanhood and Their Mutual Interrelations* (National Publishing Company, Philadelphia, 1870), 278. Emphasis in original.
108. Lewis, *Chastity*, 227.
109. Gardner, *Conjugal Sins*, 15.

4 Neither Male nor Female—The Jesuit as Androgyne

1. Francis Parkman, *The Jesuits in North America* (Boston: Little, Brown, 1922), 99 [originally published in 1867].
2. Michel Leroy, *Le mythe Jésuite: de Béranger à Michelet* (Paris: Presses Universitaires, 1992) and Geoffrey Cubitt, *The Jesuit Myth: Conspiracy Theory and Politics in Nineteenth Century France* (Oxford: Oxford University Press, 1993).
3. Róisín Healy, "Anti-Jesuitism in Imperial Germany: The Jesuit as Androgyne," in *Protestants, Catholics and Jews in Germany 1800–1914*, ed. H.W. Smith (Oxford: Berg, 2001), 160.
4. Ibid., 174.
5. Thomas Laqueur, *Making Sex: Body and Gender from the Greeks to Freud* (Cambridge, MA: Harvard University Press, 1990).
6. Léopold Deslandes, *Manhood, the Causes of Its Premature Decline* (Boston: Otis, Broaders and Company, 1843), 17.
7. Sara Jospeha Hale, *Woman's Record; or, Sketches of All Distinguished Women, from the Creation to A.D. 1854* (New York: Harper and Brothers, 1855), xxxvii.
8. Michelet, *Love*, 45.
9. Ernest Legouvé, *The Moral History of Women*, trans. J.W. Palmer (New York: Rudd & Carleton, 1860), 284. On Legouvé, see Karen Offen, "Ernest Legouvé and the Doctrine of 'Equality in Difference' for Women: A

Case Study of Male Feminism in Nineteenth-Century French Thought," *Journal of Modern History* 58, no. 2 (June 1986): 452–484.
10. O.S. Fowler, *The Family*, Vol. 2, *Matrimony* (New York: O.S. Fowler, 1859), 31.
11. Alice Dreger, *Hermaphrodites and the Medical Invention of Sex* (Cambridge, MA: Harvard University Press, 1998) and Elizabeth Reis, "Impossible Hermaphrodites: Intersex in America 1620–1960," *Journal of American History* 92, no. 2 (September 2005): 411–443.
12. *Dictionaire des sciences médicales*, Vol. 21 (Paris: C.L.F. Pancoucke, 1817), 91. Ornella Moscucci has argued that hermaphroditism "enabled bio-medical writers to explore the meaning of a human nature common to both sexes." See "Hermaphroditism and Sex Difference: The Construction of Gender in Victorian England" in Andrew H. Miller and James Eli Adams, eds., *Sexualities in Victorian Britain* (Bloomington: Indiana University Press, 1996), 176.
13. *Godey's Lady's Book and Magazine*, April 1870, 339.
14. George Sand, *Gabriel*, trans. Gay Manifold (Westport: Greenwood Press, 1992), 105. This conception of androgyny was equally present in another famous literary depiction, Honoré de Balzac's *Séraphîta*. In Balzac's novel, the androgynous represents the union of the rational, intellectual, masculine *Séraphîtüs* with the intuitive, sentimental, feminine *Séraphîta*.
15. Catharine Beecher, *A Treatise on Domestic Economy for the Use of Young Ladies at Home and at School* (New York: Harper Brothers, 1850), 28–29.
16. *New York Times*, September 8, 1853; *Putnam's Monthly: A Magazine of Literature, Science and Art* 1, no. 1 (March 1853): 314.
17. Madame Romieu, *La femme au XIX siècle* (Paris: Amyot, 1858), 187.
18. Rebecca Reed, *Six Months in a Convent* (Boston: Russell, Odiorne & Metcalf, 1835), 166.
19. Maria Monk, *The Awful Disclosures of Maria Monk* (New York: Howe and Bates, 1836), 183.
20. *Atlantic Monthly* 5, no. 29, March 1860, 270.
21. Horace Greeley, *Glances at Europe* (New York: DeWitt and Davenport, 1851), 135.
22. Mark Twain, *The Innocents Abroad, or, the New Pilgrim's Progress* (Hartford: American Publishing Company, 1869), 235.
23. *New York Evangelist*, February 5, 1846.
24. Pierre Larousse, *Grand dictionnaire universel*, Vol. 9, 959.
25. *Ladies' Repository* 10, no. 2 (February 1850), 44.
26. Sauvestre, cited in Larousse, *Grand dictionnaire universel*, 961.
27. Abbate Leone, *The Jesuit Conspiracy, the Secret Plan of the Order Detected and Revealed by the Abbate Leone* (London: Chapman & Hall, 1858), 40.
28. Michelet and Quinet, *Des Jésuites*, 33.
29. Ibid., 71.
30. *New York Observer and Chronicle*, June 1, 1844.
31. Cited in Larousse, *Grand Dictionnaire Universel*, 958.
32. *Princeton Review* 22, no. 1 (Jan. 1850): 152. Emphasis added.
33. Parkman, *Jesuits in North America*, 188.

34. Helen Dhu, *Stanhope Burleigh: The Jesuits in our Homes* (New York: Stringer and Townsend, 1855), 113. "Helen Dhu" was, as noted in Chapter One, a pseudonym of Charles Edward Lester, the American translator of *Des Jésuites*.
35. *New York Times*, April 25, 1853.
36. François Laurent, *Lettres sur les Jésuites* (Paris: A. Lacroix, Verboeckhoven, 1864), 364.
37. Noah Porter, *The Educational System of the Puritans and Jesuits Compared: A Premier Essay* (New York: M.W. Dodd, 1851), 81.
38. Georges Dairnwaell, *Code des Jésuites, d'après plus de trois cents ouvrages* (Paris: 1845), 9.
39. Jean-Claude Pitrat, *Americans Warned of Jesuitism, or, the Jesuits Unveiled* (New York: J.S. Redfield, 1851), 34.
40. Ibid., 37.
41. Leone, *The Jesuit Conspiracy*, 56. Italics added.
42. *Dictionaire des sciences médicales*, Vol. 24, 26.
43. See Ann Taves, *The Household of Faith: Roman-Catholic Devotions in Mid-Nineteenth Century America* (Notre-Dame: University of Notre Dame, 1986).
44. Josephine M. Bunkley, *The Testimony of an Escaped Novice from the Sisterhood of St Joseph, Emmetsburg* (New York: Harper and Brothers, 1855), 14.
45. Gustave Flaubert, *Madame Bovary*, trans. Alan Russell (Harmondsworth: Penguin, 1950), 48.
46. Michelet and Quinet, *Des Jésuites*, 169.
47. Pitrat, *Americans Warned of Jesuitism*, 75.
48. Casimir Bouis, *Calottes et soutanes. Jésuites et Jésuitesses* (Paris: Lacroix, Verboeckhoven, 1870), 110.
49. Dhu, *Stanhope Burleigh*, 24.
50. Michelet and Quinet, *Des Jésuites*, 13.
51. Larousse, *Grand dictionnaire universel*, 966.
52. "Thus shall we dive into every secret, and have a finger in every affair transacted in the family." *Secret Instructions of the Jesuits* (Philadelphia: F.C. Wilson, 1844), 24.
53. *New York Observer and Chronicle*, January 5, 1854.
54. See, for example, the review of the sequel which appeared in the *Ladies' Repository*. Although the truthfulness of the first book had been in some doubt, the reviewer conceded, the sequel "seemed to settle that question, as names of parties, dates and places are here given." *Ladies' Repository* 13, no. 4 (April 1853), 189. Luke cited Michelet's work extensively in both books.
55. See, for example, the *Code des Jésuites*, 44–45.
56. Quoted in Cubitt, *The Jesuit Myth*, 239.
57. Michel Foucault, *Herculine Barbin: Being the Recently Discovered Memoirs of a Nineteenth Century French Hermaphrodite*, trans. Richard McDougall (Brighton: Harvester Press, 1980).
58. The pioneering French anatomist Isidore Geoffroy Saint-Hilaire coined the term "teratology" to denote the scientific study of monstrosities such

as hermaphrodites. As Alice Dreger has argued, doctors remained steadfast in their view that "there did exist two distinct sexes and only two sexes, and that, accordingly, each body ought to be limited to one, in theory and in practice." See Dreger, *Hermaphrodites and the Medical Invention of Sex*, 109. As in the case against ecclesiastical celibacy, French physicians greatly influenced their American counterparts: Reis, "Impossible Hermaphrodites," 422.

59. On Fuller and her notion of androgyny, see Theresa Freda Nicolay, *Gender Roles, Literary Authority and Three American Writers* (New York: P. Lang, 1995), Ch. 3.
60. On Ballanche, as well as the importance of androgyny to French social theorists, see A.J.L. Busst, "The Image of the Androgyne in the Nineteenth Century," in *Romantic Mythologies*, ed. I. Fletcher (London: Routledge, 1967). On page 16, Busst writes that "many, indeed, of the historical and political philosophies of early nineteenth-century France are based to a large extent on the conception of androgynous universal man." For the uses of androgyny amongst French Romantic Socialists, see Naomi J. Andrews, "Utopian Androgyny: Romantic Socialists Confront Individualism in July Monarchy France," *French Historical Studies* 26, no. 3 (2003): 437–457.
61. Jean Molino, "Le mythe de l'androgyne," in *Aimer en France 1760–1860: Actes du Colloque Internationale de Clermont-Ferrand*, ed. Paul Viallaneix and Jean Ehrard, Vol. 1 (Clermont-Ferrand: Publications de la Faculté des Lettres de l'Université de Clermont Ferrand, 1980), 401.
62. Eugène Pelletan, *La femme au XIXe siècle* (Paris: Pagnorre, 1869), 14.
63. *North American Review* 94, no.195 (April 1862): 342–343.
64. Jules Michelet, *Les femmes de la Revolution* (Paris: A Delahays, 1854).
65. *North American Review* 42, no. 91 (October 1836): 513. Italics in original.
66. Andreas Huyssen, "Mass Culture as Woman: Modernism's Other," in *After the Great Divide: Modernism, Mass Culture, Postmodernism* (Bloomington: Indiana University Press, 1986).
67. Gustave le Bon, *The Crowd: A Study of the Popular Mind* (Georgia: Norman S. Berg), 20. Tarde made the same point: "By its whimsy, its revolting docility, its credulity, its nervousness, its brusque psychological leaps from fury to tenderness, from exasperation to laughter, the crowd is feminine, even when it is composed, as is usually the case, of males." Cited in Susanna Barrows, *Distorting Mirrors: Visions of the Crowd in Late Nineteenth-Century France* (New Haven: Yale University Press, 1981), 47. See also Robert A. Nye, *The Origins of Crowd Psychology: Gustave Le Bon and the Crisis of Mass Democracy in the Third Republic* (London: Sage, 1975).
68. Dorinda Outram, *The Body and the French Revolution: Sex, Class and Political Culture* (New Haven: Yale University Press, 1989); Geneviève Fraisse, *Reason's Muse: Sexual Difference and the Birth of Democracy* (Chicago: University of Chicago Press, 1994); Joan Landes, *Women and the Public Sphere Age in the Age of the French Revolution* (Ithaca: Cornell University Press, 1998).
69. *New York Observer and Chronicle*, November 4, 1843.

70. Greeley, *Glances at Europe*, 125.
71. *New York Observer and Chronicle*, June 1, 1844.
72. *Littell's Living Age*, December 21, 1867. Parkman himself made a similar point: "As for the religion which the Jesuits taught them, however Protestants may carp at it, it was the only form of Christianity likely to take root in their crude and barbarous natures." *Jesuits in North America*, 418.
73. Eugène Sue, *The Wandering Jew*, Vol. 3 (New York: Routledge, 1889), 447. Italics added.
74. Ibid., 441–442; 489–493.
75. Pierre Larousse, *La femme sous tous ses aspects* (Paris: Administration du Grand Dictionnaire, 1871), v.
76. *Southern Quarterly Review* 12, no. 1, July 1855, 14.
77. Larousse, *Grand dictionnaire universel*, 961.
78. Dhu, *Stanhope Burleigh*, ix.
79. Michelet and Quinet, *Des Jésuites*, 11.
80. Thomas R. Whitney, *A Defence of the American Policy* (New York: DeWitt & Davenport, 1856), 329.
81. Ibid., 100. Italics in original.
82. *Natural Fruits of Popery*, 26.
83. As Ralph Gibson has noted, "In every diocese where we have information, more women than men took Easter communion." *Social History of French Catholicism*, 180–181.
84. *Catholic World* 10:55 (October 1869), 95.
85. See Ann Douglas, *The Feminization of American Culture* (New York: Avon, 1977).
86. Michelet and Quinet, *Des Jésuites*, 7.
87. Dhu, *Stanhope Burleigh*, 135.
88. Jean-Hippolyte Michon, *Le Jésuite*, Vol. 1 (Paris: A. Lacroix, Verboeckhoven et Cie, 1865), 274.
89. *Grand dictionnaire universel*, 959. Anticlerical newspapers regularly denounced the manner in which the Jesuits were apparently trying to undermine state-run schools. In 1867, for instance, *Le Temps* contained a story of a public school in the town of Vannes that was threatened with closure because the bulk of its pupils had transferred to a recently established Jesuit school. "We know," the author of the article lamented, "how artfully the members of the too-famous Company manage to seduce families, to attract young people, and to dominate them by whatever means." *Temps*, May 18, 1867.
90. Porter, *Education System of the Puritans and Jesuit Compared*, 80.
91. *Southern Quarterly Review*, 33.
92. *New York Observer and Chronicle*, September 30, 1843.
93. Michon, *Le Jésuite*, 166.
94. Sue, *Wandering Jew*, Vol. 1, 126.
95. Parkman, *Jesuits in North America*, 96.
96. *Encyclopaedia Americana, a Popular Dictionary of Arts, Sciences, Literature, History, Politics and Biography*, vol. 7 (Boston: B.B. Mussey and Co., 1851), 201.
97. Michon, *Le Jésuite*, 102.

98. Michelet and Quinet, *Des Jésuites*, 128.
99. Victor Considérant, Preface to *The Jesuit Conspiracy* by Leone, xv.
100. Parkman, *Jesuits in North America*, 100.
101. William Reddy, *The Invisible Code: Honor and Sentiment in Post-Revolutionary France* (Berkeley: University of California Press, 1997); Robert A. Nye, *Masculinity and Male Codes of Honor*.
102. E. Anthony Rotundo, *American Manhood: Transformations in Masculinity from the Revolution to the Modern Era* (New York: Basic Books, 1993).
103. On the late nineteenth century, see Christopher E. Forth, *The Dreyfus Affair and the Crisis of French Manhood* (Baltimore: John Hopkins University Press, 1994); Edward Berenson, *The Trial of Madame Caillaux* (Berkeley: University of California Press, 1992); Kristin L. Hoganson, *Fighting for American Manhood: How Gender Politics Provoked the Spanish-American and Philippine-American Wars* (New Haven: Yale University Press, 1998).
104. Reddy, *Invisible Code*, 22.
105. Nye, *Masculinity and Male Codes of Honor*, 71.
106. Benjamin Gasteau, *La guerre des Jésuites* (Paris: Bordenave, 1845), 20.
107. French anticlericals made great use of the Jesuit historian Lorriquet's *Histoire de France*, which appeared to celebrate Bonaparte's defeat at Waterloo as a sign of Divine Justice. In his denunciation of one such history produced by the Society, Michelet accused the Jesuits of "calumnies" against France. "Everywhere," Michelet alleged, "the English heart, the glory of Wellington." Michelet and Quinet, *Des Jésuites*, 58.
108. Griffin, *Anti-Catholicism and Nineteenth Century Fiction*, 96.

5 The Captivity of Sister Barbara Ubryk

1. The nun's exact words were a matter of dispute. According to much of the press, the nun had implored her liberators to "Please give me meat. I will be obedient." In other accounts, her first words are recorded as being "Why don't you give me the cup of coffee you promised me two years ago?" For the latter, see *La Liberté*, July 27, 1869.
2. For reports of the liberation of Ubryk, see *Philadelphia Public Ledger*, August 12, 1869; *Chicago Tribune*, August 13, 1869; *New York Times* August 15, 1869; *The Constitution* (Atlanta) August 18, 1869; *New York Observer and Chronicle* August 19, 1869; *New York Evangelist* August 26, 1869. In France, the first lengthy report was published in *Le Temps* and *La Liberté* on July 27, 1869, and the following day in *Le Siècle*, *Le Journal des Débats*, *Le Moniteur Universel*, and *L'Opinion Nationale*.
3. *New York Times*, August 16, 1869; *New York Weekly Herald*, August 14, 1869.
4. *Journal des Débats*, August 10, 1869; *Siècle*, August 6, 1869.
5. *The Convent Horror: or, the True Narrative of Barbara Ubryk* (Philadelphia: C.W. Alexander, 1869); *Les amoureuses cloîtrées: Barbara Ubryk* (Paris: Librairie Générale, 1871).
6. *Univers*, August 8, 1869. A letter allegedly written by the Superior to Ubryk's sister in which she describes Ubryk's mental illness and complains

of the cost of treating her was published in the *New York Times* on August 24, 1869, as well as the *Charleston Courier* of August 31. For a description of the contested versions of the Ubryk narrative, particularly in an English context, see Rene Kollar, "The Myth and Reality of Sr. Barbara Ubryk, the Imprisoned Nun of Cracow: English Interpretations of a Victorian Religious Controversy," in *Victorian Churches and Churchmen: Essays Presented to Vincent Alan McClelland*, ed. Sheridan Gilley (London: Catholic Record Society, 2005).
7. *Philadelphia Public Ledger*, August 12, 1869.
8. *Moniteur Universel*, July 28, 1869. Reprinted in the *New York Times*, August 15, 1869.
9. Ibid., August 10, 1869.
10. *ROMISH CONVENTS, as Regulated by Papal Laws and Usages, Incompatible with Individual Rights and Public Welfare and Ought to Be Subjected to Legislative Supervision and Control*, 4.
11. *Chicago Tribune*, July 19, 1855; *New York Times*, July 24, 1855.
12. *Harper's Weekly*, May 22, 1869.
13. See, for example, le Petit-Picpus in Victor Hugo's *Les misérables*. Though appearing to be a pleasant house, the successive entrances to the interior of the convent are protected by iron grills and trellises. In *L'Abbesse de Castro*, Stendhal portrays the Convent of the Visitation as a "vast building ringed by dark walls, and quite similar to a fortress." *Oeuvres complètes: Chroniques Italiennes*, Vol. 1 (Geneva: Édito-Service, 1968), 172. Stendhal's story is set in the sixteenth century, but most opponents of the convent considered that such institutions had barely evolved since the Middle Ages.
14. Alfred Villeneuve, *Les mystères du cloître*, Vol. 2 (Paris: Alexandre Cadot, 1846), 503.
15. Jean-Hippolyte Michon, *La religieuse*, Vol. 2, 400–401.
16. *Tribune*, July 31, 1869.
17. Michelet Papers, A4745, Bibliothèque Historique de la Ville de Paris. See Caroline Ford, *Divided Houses*, Ch 3, for an extended analysis of the case.
18. Sauvestre, *Les congrégations religieuses*, 112.
19. Ibid., 89; *Opinion Nationale*, July 15, 1869.
20. Soeur X, *Le couvent: Mémoires d'une religieuse* (Paris: Degorce-Cadot, 1868), 261.
21. *Opinion Nationale*, July 27, 1869.
22. *Siècle*, August 12, 1869.
23. *Journal des Débats*, August 10, 1869.
24. *Avenir National*, August 13, 1869. In *La Démocratie*, Ch.-L Chassin used the case to argue for the separation of church and state, August 1, 1869.
25. *Albion, a Journal of News, Politics and Literature*, August 28, 1869.
26. Ubryk's captivity appeared to hold a similar significance for German-speaking liberals. See Michael Gross, *The War against Catholicism: Liberalism and the Anti-Catholic Imagination in Nineteenth-Century Germany* (Ann Arbor: University of Michigan Press, 2004), 157–170.
27. James, *Female Piety*, 298.

28. Cited in Larcher, *Les femmes jugées par les hommes* (Paris: Hertzel, 1859), 63.
29. Legouvé, *Moral History of Women*, 296.
30. Daniel C. Eddy, *The Young Woman's Friend, or, The Duties, Trials, Loves, and Hopes of Woman* (Boston: Wentworth, 1857), 23.
31. For French approaches to the feminine private sphere, see Laura S. Strumingher, "L'Ange de la Maison: Mothers and Daughters in Nineteenth Century France," *International Journal of Women's Studies* 2, no. 1 (1979): 51–61; Yvonne Knibiehler, *La sexualité et l'histoire* (Paris: Odile Jacob, 2002), 156–159.
32. Madame Romieu, *La femme au XIXè siècle* (Paris: Amyot, 1858), 24. Catholic writers on domesticity, it should be noted, often agreed with this sentiment. The Abbé Jean Gaume, for example, declared that "The woman is the queen of the domestic foyer." Abbé Jean Gaume, *Histoire de la société domestique chez tous les peuples anciens et modernes, où Influence du Christianisme sur la famille* (Paris: Gaume Frères, 1854), II.
33. Joan Burbick, *Healing the Republic: The Language of Health and the Culture of Nationalism in Nineteenth-Century America* (New York: Cambridge University Press, 1994), 190.
34. Bunkley, *Testimony of an Escaped Novice*, 99–100.
35. Victor Hugo, *Les misérables* (Paris: Gallimard, 1951), 504.
36. Bunkley, *Testimony of an Escaped Novice*, 61.
37. Michon, *La religieuse*, Vol. 2, 39; Soeur X, *Le couvent*, 113.
38. Given in, among others, the *New York Times* report of August 15, and the *Moniteur Universel* of July 28, 1869.
39. *New York Weekly Herald*, August 14, 1869.
40. *New York Observer and Chronicle*, August 19, 1868.
41. *Temps*, July 28, 1869.
42. Isaac Kelso, *Danger in the Dark: A Tale of Intrigue and Priestcraft* (Cincinnati: Moore, Anderson, Wilstach & Keys, 1854), 9.
43. *Nunneries in France: Comprising a Series of Letters between a Nun, a Novice and Her Friend* (New York: 1846), 35.
44. Jane Dunbar Chaplin, *The Convent and the Manse* (Boston: John P. Jewett, 1853), 42. Chaplin used the pseudonym Hyla.
45. *Remarks of the Honorable E. Joy Morris*, 10.
46. *Revue des Deux Mondes*, June 19, 1864. In his survey of stereotypes of Americans which appear in French drama and fiction, Simon Jeune has observed that the two stock figures were the grasping businessman and the forthright young girl. Simon Jeune, *De F.T. Graindorge à A.O. Barnabooth: Les types américains dans le roman et le théâtre français* (Paris: Didier, 1963).
47. Gabrielle Houbre, *La discipline de l'amour: L'éducation sentimentale des filles et des garçons à l'âge du romantisme* (Paris: Plon, 1997), 256–257. See also Yvonne Knibiehler, *De la Pucelle à la Minette: Les jeunes filles de l'âge classique à nos jours* (Paris: Temps actuels, 1983).
48. For a discussion of the parallels between the two, see James R. Lewis, "'Mind-Forged Manacles': Anti-Catholic Convent Narratives in the

Context of the American Captivity Tradition," *Mid-America* 72, no. 3 (1990): 149–167. In many of the Puritan narratives, captivity occurs at the hands of tribes directed by French Catholics, thus serving, as one scholar has noted, both anti-French and anti-Catholic purposes. See Kathryn Zabelle Derounian-Stodola and James Arthur Levernier, *The Indian Captivity Narrative 1550–1900* (New York: Twain, 1993), 27–28. At least one female captive joined the Catholic Church. Esther Wheelwright, captured in Wells, Maine in 1703, eventually became the Superior of the Ursuline Convent in Quebec. See Laurel Thatcher Ulrich, *Good Wives: Image and Reality in the Lives of Women in Northern New England, 1650–1750* (New York: Knopf, 1982), 211.
49. *Les amoureuses cloîtrées*, 118.
50. June Namias, *White Captives: Gender and Ethnicity on the American Frontier* (Chapel Hill: University of North Carolina Press, 1993), 139.
51. Franchot, *Roads to Rome*, 120.
52. *Harper's Weekly*, March 20, 1869.
53. Scholars of feminism have argued about the role of Protestantism and Catholicism in fostering or discouraging organized women's movements. In his *The Feminists: Women's Emancipation Movements in Europe, America and Australasia 1840–1920*, Richard Evans argues strongly that Catholicism acted as a brake on feminist movements. Patrick Kay Bidelman also characterizes the Catholic Church as an obstacle to the development of feminism. See *Pariahs Stand Up! The Founding of the Liberal Feminist Movement in France, 1858–1889* (Connecticut: Greenwood Press, 1982), 6–9. Evans and Bidelman's argument is disputed by James McMillan in "Clericals, Anticlericals and the Women's Movement in France under the Third Republic," *The Historical Journal* 24, no. 2 (1981): 361–376. McMillan notes, amongst other points, that leading republicans were just as opposed to female suffrage as the Catholic Church. See also Evans' response "Feminism and Anticlericalism in France, 1870–1922," *The Historical Journal* 25, no. 4 (December 1982): 947–949. Jane Rendall's *The Origins of Modern Feminism: Women in Britain, France and the United States, 1780–1860* (London: MacMillan, 1985) argues that the "more positive Protestant evaluation of women's domestic and religious role which...brought women to take a more active part in sects and churches, in religious and charitable activity outside the home, in the formation of voluntary associations. For Catholics the possibility of such initiatives was limited by their own theology, and by the role allocated to them by an established and hierarchical church." (p. 101.) A far more nuanced analysis has been provided by Steven Hause and Anne Kenney, who cite a range of factors in addition to religion—legal tradition, demography, and the rate of industrialization—in accounting for the strength of suffrage campaigns in different nations. Steven Hause and Anne Kenney, *Women's Suffrage and Social Politics in the French Third Republic* (Princeton: Princeton University Press, 1984), esp. 18–27.
54. Sarah A. Curtis, "Charitable Ladies: Gender, Class and Religion in Mid Nineteenth-Century Paris," *Past and Present* 177 (November 2002): 121–156;

Christine Adams, "Maternal Societies in France: Private Charity Before the Welfare State," *Journal of Women's History* 17, no. 1 (2005): 87–111.
55. McMillan concludes that "the Catholic religion...cannot be viewed exclusively as the constraining influence on women's experience which some historians, too ready to endorse the discourse of nineteenth-century anticlericals, have made it out to be." *France and Women*, 54. Ralph Gibson had made a similar argument. The *congregations*, he suggests, were the only institutions in France to offer women not only a vocation, but a "very real career." Gibson, *Social History of French Catholicism*, 118.
56. Claude Langlois, *Le catholicisme au féminin: Les congrégations françaises à supérieure générale au XIXe siècle* (Paris: Éditions du Cerf, 1984).
57. Hazel Mills, "'Saintes Soeurs' et femmes fortes': Alternative Accounts of the Route to Womanly Civic Virtue, and the History of French Feminism," in *Wollstonecraft's Daughters: Womanhood in England and France 1780–1920*, ed. Clarissa Campbell Orr (Manchester: Manchester University Press, 1996), 141–142. Mills, it should be noted, tempers this picture somewhat by suggesting that Catholicism constricted as much as it expanded the range of choices and activities open to French women. See her comments in "Negotiating the Divide: Women, Philanthropy and the 'Public Sphere' in Nineteenth-Century France" in *Religion, Society and Politics in France since 1789*, ed. Frank Tallet and Nicholas Atkin, 52.
58. Legouvé, *The Moral History of Women*, 328.
59. George Sand, *Mademoiselle la Quintinie* (Paris: Michel Lévy Frères, 1863), 65.
60. Michon, *La religieuse*, Vol. 1, 162.
61. Mary Ewens, "Women in the Convent," in *American Catholic Women: A Historical Exploration*, ed. Karen Kennelly (New York: Macmillan, 1989), 21.
62. *New York Daily Times*, Feb. 20, 1856.
63. Mary Ewens, *The Role of the Nun in Nineteenth-Century America* (New York: Arno, 1978), 102–103.
64. Ibid., 231.
65. Isaac Kelso, *Danger in the Dark*, 132.
66. Cohen, "The Respectability of Rebecca Reed," 441.
67. Elizabeth Blackwell, *Medicine as a Profession for Women* (New York: W.H. Tinson, 1860), 12. On the appeal of the convent for American women, see Fessenden, "The Convent, the Brothel, and the Protestant Woman's Sphere," 461–462.
68. Catharine Beecher and Harriet Beecher Stowe, *The American Woman's Home*, 331.
69. Catharine Beecher, *An Address to the Protestant Clergy of the United States*, 33.
70. Christopher Castiglia, *Bound and Determined: Captivity, Culture-Crossing and White Womanhood from Mary Rowlandson to Patty Hearst* (Chicago: University of Chicago Press, 1996), 4.
71. *Moniteur Universel*, August 10, 1869. Ulrich, *Good Wives*, makes a similar argument, esp. 170.
72. Susan M. Griffin has suggested that the escaped nun's tale reveals "the fundamental weakness of the female self on which the future of American Protestantism rests." See Susan M. Griffin, "Awful Disclosures: Women's Evidence in the Escaped Nun's Tale," *PMLA* 111, no. 1 (January 1996): 105.

73. *Les amoureuses cloîtrées*, 8. In a melodramatic twist, the suitor rejected by Ubryk's father on the grounds of his poverty turns out to be none other than the investigating magistrate who eventually liberates her.
74. Charles Frothingham, *The Haunted Convent* (Boston: Graves & Weston, 1854), 22.
75. See Ward M. McAfee, *Religion, Race, and Reconstruction: The Public School in the Politics of the 1870's* (New York: SUNY Press, 1998); Tracy Fessenden, "The Nineteenth-Century Bible Wars and the Separation of Church and State," *Church History* 74, no. 4 (December 2005): 784–811. See also Diane Ravitch, *The Great School Wars, New York City 1805–1973* (New York: Basic Books, 1973).
76. Sœur X, *Le couvent*, 6.
77. Hugo, *Les misérables*, 906.
78. Caracciolo, *Mystères des couvents*, 177.
79. Carol K. Coburn and Martha Smith, *Spirited Lives: How Nuns Shaped Catholic Culture and American Life, 1836–1920* (Chapel Hill: University Of North Carolina Press, 1999), 171–172.
80. Ibid., 161.
81. Gollar, "The Alleged Abduction of Milly McPherson," 597.
82. Cited in Ewens, *Role of the Nun*, 141.
83. *Chicago Daily Tribune*, August 13, 1869.
84. *Siècle*, August 12, 1869.
85. *New York Daily Times,* January 21, 1865.
86. Allain-Targé, *La République sous l'Empire*, 8.
87. *New York Weekly Herald*, August 21, 1869.
88. *Siècle*, August 8, 1868.
89. *Les amoureuses cloîtrées*, 253.
90. Ned Buntline, *The Beautiful Nun* (Philadelphia: T.B. Peterson, 1866), 80.
91. Edmond and Jules de Goncourt, *Sister Philomène*, trans. Madeline Jay (London: Chatto & Windus, 1989), 152–154.
92. Michon, *La religieuse*, Vol. 2, 400.
93. Jules Michelet, *La sorcière* (Paris: E. Dentu, 1862), 299.
94. *New York Observer and Chronicle*, August 19, 1869.
95. *New York Weekly Herald*, November 20, 1869.
96. David S. Reynolds, *Beneath the American Renaissance: The Subversive Imagination in the Age of Emerson and Melville* (New York: Alfred A. Knopf, 1988), esp. Chapter 2.
97. Karen Halttunen, "Humanitarianism and the Pornography of Pain in Anglo-American Culture," *The American Historical Review* 100, no. 2 (April 1995): 303–334.
98. Bennett, *Party of Fear*, 47.
99. Laveleye, *Questions contemporaines*, 8.
100. *Harper's Weekly*, February 26, 1870.
101. *Appletons' Journal: A Magazine of General Literature* 7, no. 162 (May 1872): 503.
102. *Boston Daily Transcript*, May 15, 1891.
103. André Mater, *La politique religieuse de la République Française* (Paris: Emile Nourry, 1909), 109–110.

Conclusion: Father Hyacinthe and the Vatican Council

1. *New York Times*, July 21, 1868.
2. *Nation*, October 7, 1869.
3. *Siècle*, August 18 1869.
4. On the opposition of these French bishops, see O'Gara, *Triumph in Defeat: Infallibility, Vatican I, and the French Minority Bishops* (Washington, DC: Catholic University of America Press, 1988). On the Council itself, Roger Aubert, *Vatican I* (Paris: Éditions de l'Orante, 1964).
5. *Daily Evening Bulletin*, October 5, 1869.
6. *New York Weekly Herald*, October 9, 1869.
7. *Siècle*, August 18, 1869.
8. *Liberté*, July 31, 1869.
9. *Catholic World* 10, no. 57 (December 1869): 290 and 292.
10. *North American and United States Gazette*, December 10, 1869.
11. *New York Herald*, August 15, 1869.
12. *Revue des Deux Mondes*, October 1, 1869.
13. *Le Siècle*, August 18, 1869.
14. *Opinion Nationale*, September 26, 1869.
15. *Temps*, Sept. 22, 1869. Reprinted in the *Living Age* 103, no 1327 (November 6, 1869): 346–347.
16. *Revue des Deux Mondes*, October 1, 1869.
17. *Independent*, July 29, 1869.
18. *Daily Central City Register*, October 20, 1869.
19. *Albion*, November 27, 1869.
20. *New York Weekly Herald*, September 25, 1869.
21. November 12, 1869.
22. *Nation*, October 28, 1869.
23. *Revue des Deux Mondes*, December 15, 1869.
24. *North American and United States Gazette*, December 10, 1869.
25. Maurain, *La politique ecclésiastique du Second Empire*, 899.
26. October 11, 1869, Series F^{19} 1940, Archives Nationales, Paris.
27. September 10, 1869, Series F^{19} 1941, Archives Nationales, Paris.
28. *Daily Evening Bulletin*, 5 October 1869. Such hopes were not unfounded. According to the Catholic scholar James Hennesey, four-fifths of the forty-nine American bishops at the Council judged the dogma of papal infallibility to be at least "inopportune." *A History of the Roman Catholic Community* (Kansas: Sheed, Andrews and McMeel, 1977), 169.
29. For example, the *Independent*, December 30, 1869; *Nation*, December 30, 1869.
30. For example, the *Journal des Débats*, September 24, 1869.
31. *North American and United States Gazette*, September 7, 1869.
32. On Dupanloup's letter, see the *Nation*, December 16, 1869; *Chicago Tribune*, December 2, 1869; *New York Times*, November 17, 1869.
33. Series F^{19} 1941, Archives Nationales, Paris.
34. *Siècle*, 1 October 1, 1869.
35. Ibid., September 23, 1869; *Démocratie*, March 14, 1869.

36. July 23, 1869, Charles Loyson papers, MS f.r. 2967, Manuscript Department, Bibliothèque de Genève.
37. *Univers*, July 28, 1869; September 22, 1869.
38. *New York Times*, October 5, 1869.
39. *Independent*, October 7, 1869.
40. *Boston Daily Advertiser*, October 7, 1869.
41. *Temps*, September 22, 1869.
42. *Journal des Débats*, September 30, 1869.
43. John Bigelow, *Retrospections of an Active Life*, Vol. 4 (New York: Doubleday Page & Co., 1913), 327.
44. Hilen, ed., *The letters of Henry Wadsworth Longfellow*, Vol. 5, 320.
45. See Holmes' letter to Bigelow, in Bigelow, *Retrospections of an Active Life*, 338.
46. *Boston Daily Advertiser*, November 6, 1869.
47. *Boston Investigator*, November 3, 1869.
48. *Congregationalist and Boston Recorder*, November 11, 1869.
49. Beecher's article on Hyacinthe in the Christian *Union* was subsequently reprinted in, among others, the *Lowell Daily Citizen and News*, November 20, 1869.
50. See, for example, the *Daily Cleveland Herald*, October 26, 1869; *Nation*, October 7, 1869.
51. Henry Francis Brownson, *Orestes A. Brownson's Later Life* (Detroit: H.F. Brownson, 1900), 512.
52. *Zion's Herald*, November 18, 1869. The source of the rumor was the *Pittsburgh Advocate*, a Catholic paper.
53. Brownson, *Brownson's Later Life*, 512; *Chicago Tribune*, January 1, 1870; *Harper's* Weekly, January 22, 1870. The report also appeared in the *New York News*, the *San Antonio Express*, and the *Daily Standard* (Raleigh).
54. *Daily Cleveland Herald*, October 19, 1869.
55. *Daily Arkansas Gazette*, October 24, 1869.
56. *New York Times*, December 31, 1869.
57. Bigelow, *Retrospections of an Active Life*, 343.
58. *Temps*, July 20, 1870.
59. *Independent*, June 9, 1870.
60. *New York Times*, July 17, 1870.
61. Reprinted in the *Albion*, August 6, 1870.
62. The American bishops returned home, according to Sydney E. Ahlstrom, "with a new apologetic burden to bear in democratic America." *A Religious History of the American People* (New Haven: Yale University Press, 1972), 826.
63. Charles Loyson, *Lettre sur mon mariage* (Paris: Sandoz and Fischbacher, 1872), 13.
64. Charles Loyson papers, MS f.r. 2967, Bibliothèque de Genève.
65. October 19, 1900. Letters addressed to Monseigneur L. Lacroix, Nouvelles Acquisitions Francaises 24401, Manuscripts Division, Bibliothèque Nationale de France.
66. Charles Loyson, *Programme de la réforme Catholique* (Paris: Grassart, 1879). On Hyacinthe's later career, see Albert Houtin, *Le Père Hyacinthe. Réformateur Catholique 1869–189* (Paris: Emile Nourry, 1922).
67. Series F^{19} 6069. Archives Nationales, Paris.

68. Bernard de Voto, ed., *Mark Twain, Letters from the Earth* (New York: Harper and Row, 1962), 52–53.
69. Bosco and Johnson, *Journals and Miscellaneous Notebooks of Ralph Waldo Emerson*, Vol. 16, 505.
70. September 25, 1900. Letters addressed to Monseigneur L. Lacroix, Nouvelles Acquisitions Francaises 24401, Manuscripts Division, Bibliothèque Nationale de France.

Selected Bibliography

Archival and Manuscript Sources

Archives of James Harper and Brothers, Chadwyck-Healey archives of British publishers.
Charles Loyson Papers, Manuscript Division, Biliothèque de Genève.
Documents concerning the first Vatican Council, F[19] 1939–1942, Ministry of Religion, Archives Nationales, Paris.
Documents concerning Hyacinthe Loyson, F[19] 6069, Ministry of Religion, Archives Nationales, Paris.
John Williamson Palmer Collection, Special Collections, University of Virginia.
Jules Michelet Papers, Bibliothèque Historique de la Ville de Paris.
Letters addressed to Monseigneur L. Lacroix, N.A.F. 24401, Manuscripts Division, Bibliothèque Nationale de France.

Selected Newspapers and Journals

Albion, a Journal of News, Politics and Literature (New York)
Appletons' Journal: A Magazine of General Literature
Atlantic Monthly
L'Avenir National
Boston Daily Advertiser
Boston Recorder
Brownson's Quarterly Review
Chicago Tribune
Constitution (Atlanta)
La Démocratie
Harper's Weekly
Independent (New York)
Le Journal des Débats Politiques et Littéraires
Liberator
La Liberté
Littell's Living Age
Methodist Quarterly Review
Milwaukee Daily Sentinel
Le Moniteur Universel
Nation
New York Evangelist

New York Herald
New York Observer and Chronicle
New York Tribune
North American and United States Gazette
North American Review
L'Opinion Nationale
Philadelphia Public Ledger
Putnam's Magazine of Literature, Science, Art, and National Interests
La Presse
La Revue des Deux Mondes
Le Siècle
La Tribune
Le Temps
United States and Democratic Review
L'Univers

Selected Primary Sources

About, Edmond. *La question romaine*. Bruxelles: Meline et Cans, 1859.
Alcott, William. *The Physiology of Marriage*. Boston: John P. Jewett, 1856.
Allain-Targé, Henri. *La république sous l'empire*. Paris: Bernard Grasset, 1939.
Ampère, Jean-Jacques. *Promenade en Amérique*. Paris: Michel Levy, 1860.
Assézat, Jules. *Affaire Mortara: Le droit du père*. Paris: Dentu, 1858.
Audouard, Olympe. *A travers l'Amérique*. Paris: E. Dentu, 1871.
Becquerel, Dr. Alfred. *Traité élémentaire d'hygiène privée et publique*. 6th ed. Paris: P. Asselin, 1877.
Bedford, Gunning S. *Clinical Lectures on the Diseases of Women and Children*. New York: Samuel S. and William Wood, 1857.
Beecher, Catharine. *An Address to the Protestant Clergy of the United States*. New York: Harper and Brothers, 1846.
———. *The Duty of American Women to Their Country*. New York: Harper and Brothers, 1845.
———. *A Treatise on Domestic Economy for the Use of Young Ladies at Home and at School*. New York: Harper Brothers, 1850.
Beecher, Catharine E. and Harriet Beecher Stowe. *The American Woman's Home*. Edited by Nicole Tonkovich. New Brunswick: Rutgers University Press, 2002.
Bergeret, Dr. L.F.E. *Des fraudes dans l'accomplissement des fonctions génératrices*. Paris: J.B. Baillière, 1868.
Bouis, Casimir. *Calottes et soutanes. Jésuites et jésuitesses*. Paris: Lacroix, Verboeckhoven, 1870.
Bourgeois, Dr. Xavier. *Les passions dans leurs rapports avec la santé et les maladies*. 2nd ed. 2 vols. Paris: J.B. Baillière, 1863.
Bouvet, Francisque. *De la confession et du célibat des prêtres, où la politique du pape*. Paris: Comptoir des Imprimeurs-Unis, 1845.
Briquet, Dr. Pierre. *Un traité clinique et thérapeutique de l'hystérie*. Paris: J.B. Baillière, 1859.
Brownson, Henry F., ed. *The Works of Orestes A. Brownson*. 20 vols. New York: CAMS Press, 1966.

Bunkley, Josephine. *The Testimony of an Escaped Novice from the Sisterhood of St Joseph*. New York: Harper and Brothers, 1856.
Buntline, Ned. *The Beautiful Nun*. Philadelphia: T.B. Peterson, 1866.
Caracciolo, Enrichetta. *Mystères des couvents*. Paris: E. Dentu, 1865.
Chaplin, Jane Dunbar. *The Convent and the Manse*. Boston: John P. Jewett, 1853.
Chevalier, Michel. *La liberté aux Etats-Unis*. Paris: Capelle, 1849.
———. *Lettres sur l'Amérique du Nord*. 4th ed. 2 vols. Brussels: Wouters, 1844.
Comettant, Oscar. *L'Amérique telle qu'elle est: Voyage anecdotique de Marcel Bonneau dans le nord et le sud des Etats-Unis*. Paris: Achille Faure, 1864.
———. *Le nouveau monde, scènes de la vie américaine*. Paris: Pagnerre, 1861.
Cooke, Dr. Nicholas. *Satan in Society, by a Physician*. Cincinnati: C.F. Vent, 1876. Reprint, New York: Arno Press, 1974.
Culverwell, Robert James. *The Institutes of Marriage, Its Intent, Obligations and Physical and Constitutional Disqualifications, Anatomically, Physiologically, and Medically Considered*. New York, 1846.
Dairnwaell, Georges. *Code des Jésuites, d'après plus de trois cents ouvrages*. Paris, 1845.
Debay, Auguste. *Hygiène et physiologie du mariage*. 16th ed. Paris: E. Dentu, 1859.
de Beaumont, Gustave. *Marie; où, l'esclavage aux Etats-Unis*. 4th ed. Paris: Charles Gosselin, 1840.
Dechambre, A., ed. *Dictionnaire encyclopédique des sciences médicales*. 28 vols. Paris: G. Masson and P. Asselin, 1868–1889.
de Gasparin, Count Agènor. *America before Europe: Principles and Interests*. Translated by Mary L. Booth. 3rd ed. New York: Charles Scribner, 1862.
———. *Uprising of a Great People: The United States in 1861*. Translated by Mary L. Booth. New York: C. Scribner, 1861.
de Hauranne, Ernest Duvergier. *Huit mois en Amérique*. 2 vols. Paris: A. Lacroix, Verboeckhoven, 1866.
de Laveleye, Émile. *Questions contemporaines*. Bruxelles: A. Lacroix, Verboeckhoven, 1863.
de Ponsan, Dr. Menville. *Histoire philosophique et médicale de la femme*. 2 ed. 3 vols. Paris: J.B. Baillière, 1858.
Derby, J.C. *Fifty Years among Authors, Books and Publishers*. New York: G.W. Carleton, 1884.
Descuret, J.B.F. *La médicine des passions, ou les passions considérées dans leurs rapports avec les maladies, les lois et la religion*. Paris: Labé, 1860.
Deslandes, Léopold. *De l'onanisme et des autres abus vénériens*. Paris: Lelarge, 1835.
———. *Manhood, the Causes of Its Premature Decline: With Directions for Its Perfect Restoration: Addressed to Those Suffering from the Destructive Effects of Excessive Indulgence, Solitary Habits*. Boston: Otis, Broaders and Company, 1843.
de Tocqueville, Alexis. *Democracy in America*. Chicago: University of Chicago Press, 2000.
Devay, Francis. *De la physiologie humaine et de la médicine*. Paris: Pitois, 1840.
Dhu, Helen. *Stanhope Burleigh: The Jesuits in Our Homes*. New York: Stringer and Townsend, 1855.
Dictionaire des sciences médicales. 60 vols. Paris: C.L.F. Panckoucke, 1812–1822.

Dictionnaire encyclopédique des sciences médicales. Paris : Masson : P. Asselin: [then] Asselin et Houzeau, 1864–1888.

Diday, Dr. Paul. *Examen de l'ouvrage de m. le docteur dufieux, intitulé nature et virginité, considérations physiologiques sur le célibat religieux*. Lyon: Aimé Vingtrinier, 1855.

Diderot, Denis. *La religieuse*. London: Bristol Classical Press, 2000.

Dixon, Dr. Edward M. *Scenes in the Practice of a New York Surgeon*. New York: DeWitt & Davenport, 1855.

Dufieux, Jean-Ennemond. *Nature et virginité: Considérations physiologiques sur le célibat religieux*. Paris: Julien et Lanier, 1854.

Eyma, Louis-Xavier. *La république américaine—ses institutions, ses hommes*, Vol. 1. Paris: Michel Lèvy, 1861.

Flaubert, Gustave. *Madame Bovary*. Translated by Alan Russell. Harmondsworth: Penguin, 1950.

Foote, E.B. *Plain Home Talk*. Boston: Thayer and Eldridge, 1860.

Frothingham, Charles. *The Haunted Convent*. Boston: Graves & Weston, 1854.

Gardner, Augustus K. *Conjugal Sins against the Laws of Life and Health*. New York: J.S. Redfield, 1870. Reprint, New York: Arno Press, 1974.

———. *The French Metropolis: Paris; as Seen During the Spare Hours of a Medical Student*. New York: C.S. Francis & Co, 1850.

Goncourt, Edmond and Jules. *Sister Philomène*. Translated by Madeline Jay. London: Chatto & Windus, 1989.

Grandpierre, Jean-Henri. *A Parisian Pastor's Glance at America*. Boston: Gould and Lincoln, 1854.

Hollick, Frederick. *The Marriage Guide, or Natural History of Generation*. New York: T.W. Strong, 1850.

James, John Angell. *Female Piety: Or the Young Woman's Friend and Guide through Life to Immortality*. New York: Robert Carter and Brothers, 1854.

Kelso, Isaac. *Danger in the Dark: A Tale of Intrigue and Priestcraft*. Cincinnati: Moore, Anderson, Wilstach & Keys, 1854.

Knowlton, C. *Fruits of Philosophy; or, the Private Companion of Young Married People*. New York, 1832.

Laboulaye, Edouard. *Paris en Amérique*. Paris: Charpentier, 1863.

———. *De la constitution américaine et de l'utilité se son étude: discours prononcé, le 4 décembre 1849, à l'ouverture du cours de législation comparée*. Paris: Hennuyer, 1850.

Lallemand, Dr. Claude-Francois. *Des pertes séminales involontaires*. 3 vols. Paris: Bêchet Jeune, 1836–1842.

Landouzy, Dr. Hector. *Traité complet de l'hystérie*. Paris: Baillière, 1846.

Larcher, Jullien, ed. *Ce qu'on a dit du mariage et du célibat*. Paris: Éditions Hetzel, 1858.

Larousse, Pierre, ed. *La femme sous tous ses aspects*. Paris: Administration du Grand Dictionnaire, 1871.

Larousse, Pierre, ed. *Grand dictionnaire universel du XIXe siècle: français, historique, géographique, biographique, mythologique, bibliographique, littéraire, artistique, scientifique, etc*. 17 vols. Paris: Administration du Grand Dictionnaire, 1866–1876.

Laurent, François. *Lettres sur les Jésuites*. Paris: A. Lacroix, Verboeckhoven, 1864.

Le Bon, Gustave. *The Crowd: A Study of the Popular Mind*. Georgia: Norman S. Berg.
Legouvé, Ernest. *The Moral History of Women*. Translated by J.W. Palmer. New York: Rudd & Carleton, 1860.
Leone, Abbate. *The Jesuit Conspiracy, the Secret Plan of the Order Detected and Revealed by the Abbate Leone*. London: Chapman & Hall, 1858.
Les amoureuses cloîtrées: Barbara Ubryk. Paris: Librairie Générale, 1871.
Lèvy, Michel. *Traité d'hygiène publique et privée*. 5th ed. 2 vols. Paris: J.-B. Baillière, 1869.
Lewis, Dio. *Chastity, or Our Secret Sins*. Philadelphia: George Maclean & Co, 1874. Reprint, New York: Arno Press, 1974.
Loyson, Hyacinthe. *Programme de la réforme catholique*. Paris: Grassart, 1879.
Michelet, Jules. *Du prêtre, de la femme et de la famille*. Paris. Hachette & Paulin, 1845
———. *La sorcière*. Paris: E. Dentu, 1862.
———. *Les femmes de la revolution*. Paris: A Delahays, 1854.
———. *Love*. Translated by J.W. Palmer. New York: Rudd & Carleton, 1860.
Michelet, Jules and Edgar Quinet. *Des Jésuites*. Paris: Hachette & Paulin, 1843.
Michon, Jean-Hippolyte. *Le Jésuite*. 2 vols. Paris: A. Lacroix, Verboeckhoven et Cie, 1865
———. *Le maudit*. 2 vols. Paris: La Croix, Verboeckhoven, 1863.
———. *La religieuse*. 2 vols. Paris: La Croix, Verboeckhoven, 1864.
Monk, Maria. *The Awful Disclosures of Maria Monk, and the Mysteries of a Convent*. Philadelphia: T.B. Peterson, 1854.
Morel, Benedict-Auguste. *Traité des maladies mentales*. Paris: V. Masson, 1860.
Morris, E. Joy. *Remarks of the Honorable E. Joy Morris of Philadelphia in the House of Representatives of Pennsylvania, February 12 1856, against the Introduction of the Monastic System and the Secret Religious Orders of the Church of Rome*. Harrisburg, 1856.
Morse, Samuel. *Confessions of a French Catholic Priest, to which are added Warnings to the People of the United States by the same author*. New York: John S. Taylor, 1837.
Natural Fruits of Popery. Philadelphia: Presbyterian Board of Publications, 1842.
Nunneries in France: Comprising a Series of Letters between a Nun, a Novice and Her Friend. New York, 1846.
Nichols, T.L. *Esoteric Anthropology*. New York: Stringer and Townsend, 1853.
Pancoast, Dr. Seth. *The Ladies' Medical Guide*. Philadelphia: John E. Potter, 1865.
Parkman, Francis. *The Jesuits in North America*. Boston: Little, Brown, 1922.
Pascal, César. *A travers l'atlantique et dans le nouveau monde*. Paris: Grassart, 1870.
Pelletan, Eugène. *An Address to King Cotton*. Translated by Leander Starr. New York: H. de Mareil, 1863.
———. *Heures de travail*. Paris: Pagnerre, 1854.
———. *La femme au XIXe siècle*. Paris: Pagnorre, 1869.
Perrin, Théodore. *Nature et virginité, considérations physiologiques sur le célibat religieux, par Jean-Ennemond Dufieux. Rapport fait à la société de médecine de Lyon*. Lyon: A. Vingtrinier, 1855.

Pitrat, Jean-Claude. *Americans Warned of Jesuitism, or, the Jesuits Unveiled*. New York: J.S. Redfield, 1851.
Pope, or President? Startling Disclosures of Romanism as Revealed by Its Own Writers. New York: R.L. Delisser, 1859.
Porter, Noah. *The Educational System of the Puritans and Jesuits Compared: A Premier Essay*. New York: M.W. Dodd, 1851.
Quinet, Edgar. *Oeuvres complètes*. Vol. 2, *Les Jesuites, L'ultramontanisme*. Paris: Hachette, 1912.
———. *Œuvres complètes*, Vol. 14, *L'enseignement du peuple*. Paris: Hachette, 1912.
———. *The Roman Church and Modern Society*. Translated by C. Edwards Lester. New York: Gates and Stedman, 1845.
Reed, Rebecca. *Six Months in a Convent*. Boston: Russell, Odiorne and Metcalf, 1835.
Romieu, Madame. *La femme au XIX siècle*. Paris: Amyot, 1858.
Romish Convents, as Regulated by Papal Laws and Usages, Incompatible with Individual Rights and Public Welfare and Ought to Be Subjected to Legislative Supervision and Control.
Sand, George. *Correspondance*. 5 vols. Paris: Calmann-Lévy, 1883.
———. *Gabriel*. Translated by Gay Manifold. Westport: Greenwood Press, 1992.
———. *Mademoiselle La Quintinie*. Paris: Michel Lévy Frères, 1863.
Sauvestre, Charles. *Sur les genoux de l'église*. Paris: E. Dentu, 1868.
———. *Les congrégations religieuses dévoilées*. Paris: E. Dentu, 1870.
Secret Instructions of the Jesuits. Philadelphia: F.C. Wilson, 1844.
Seraine, Dr. Louis. *De la santé des gens mariés, ou physiologie de la génération de l'homme*. Paris: F. Savy, 1865.
———. *Les préceptes du mariage, traduits du grec de Plutarque*. Paris: F. Savy, 1861.
Sex for the Common Man: Nineteenth Century Marriage Manuals. New York: Arno Press, 1974.
Sœur X. *Le couvent: Mémoires d'une religieuse*. Paris: Degorce-Cadot, 1868.
Simon, Jules. *La liberté de conscience*. Paris: Hachette, 1857.
Soule, Dr. J. *Science of Reproduction and Reproductive Control*. New York, 1856. Reprint, New York: Arno Press, 1974.
Spalding, M.J. *Miscellanea: Comprising Reviews, Lectures, and Essays, on Historical, Theological, and Miscellaneous Subjects*. Baltimore: J. Murphy & Co, 1875.
Storer, Horatio Robinson. *Why Not? A Book for Every Woman*. Boston: Lee & Shepard, 1866.
Sue, Eugène. *The Wandering Jew*. 11 vols. New York: Routledge, 1889.
The Convent Horror: Or, the True Narrative of Barbara Ubryk. Philadelphia: C.W. Alexander, 1869.
Tuckerman, Henry T. *America and Her Commentators, with a Critical Sketch of Travel in the United States*. New York: Scribner, 1864.
Twain, Mark. *The Innocents Abroad, or, the New Pilgrim's Progress*. Hartford: American Publishing Company, 1869.
Villeneuve, Alfred. *Les mystères du cloître*. 2 vols. Paris: Alexandre Cadot, 1846.
Whitney, Thomas. *A Defence of the American Policy, as Opposed to the Encroachments of Foreign Influence, and Especially to the Interference of the*

Papacy in the Political Interests and Affairs of the United States. New York: DeWitt and Davenport, 1856.
Wright, Julia McNair. *Secrets of the Convent and Confessional.* Chicago: Jones, 1872.
Zola, Emile. *A Priest in the House.* Translated by Brian Rhys. London: Elek Books, 1957.

Selected Secondary Sources

Adams, Christine. "Maternal Societies in France: Private Charity before the Welfare State." *Journal of Women's History* 17, no. 1 (2005): 87–111.
Ahlstrom, Sydney E. *A Religious History of the American People.* New Haven: Yale University Press, 1972.
Anbinder, Tyler. *Nativism and Slavery: The Northern Know Nothings and the Politics of the 1850's.* New York: Oxford University Press, 1992.
Andrews, Naomi J. "Utopian Androgyny: Romantic Socialists Confront Individualism in July Monarchy France." *French Historical Studies* 26, no. 3 (2003): 437–457.
Atkin, Nicholas and Frank Tallet, eds. *Religion, Society and Politics in France since 1789.* London: Hambledon, 1991.
Aubert, Roger. *Le pontificat de Pie IX (1846–1873).* Paris: Bloud and Gay, 1952.
Barrows, Susanna. *Distorting Mirrors: Visions of the Crowd in Late Nineteenth-Century France.* New Haven: Yale University Press, 1981.
Becker, Jean-Jacques and Gilles Candar, eds. *Histoire des gauches en France.* 2 vols. Paris: Découverte, 2004.
Beiser, J. Ryan. "The Vatican Council and the American Secular Newspapers, 1869–1870." PhD dissertation, Catholic University of America, 1941.
Bellah, Robert N. and Frederick E. Greenspahn, eds. *Uncivil Religion: Interreligious Hostility in America.* New York: Crossroad, 1987.
Bennett, David H. *The Party of Fear: From Nativist Movements to the New Right in American History.* Chapel Hill: University of North Carolina Press, 1988.
Bernstein, Susan. *Confessional Subjects: Revelations of Gender and Power in Victorian Literature and Culture.* Chapel Hill: University of North Carolina Press, 1997.
Bertocci, Philip A. *Jules Simon: Republican Anticlericalism and Cultural Politics in France, 1848–1886.* Columbia: University of Missouri Press, 1978.
Billington, Ray Allen. *The Protestant Crusade 1800–1860.* New York: Rinehart and Company, 1938.
Bloch, Marc. "Pour une histoire comparée des sociétés européennes." *Revue de synthèse historique* 46 (1928): 15–50.
Blumenthal, Henry. *American and French Culture, 1800–1900: Interchanges in Art, Science, Literature, and Society.* Baton Rouge: Louisiana State University Press, 1975.
Borie, Jean. *Le célibataire français.* Paris: Le Sagittaire, 1976.
Brodie, Janet Farrell. *Contraception and Abortion in Nineteenth-Century America.* Ithaca: Cornell University Press, 1994.
Castiglia, Christopher. *Bound and Determined: Captivity, Culture-Crossing and White Womanhood from Mary Rowlandson to Patty Hearst.* Chicago: University of Chicago Press, 1996.

Chadwick, Owen. *The Secularization of the European Mind in the Nineteenth Century*. Cambridge: Cambridge University Press, 1975.

Cholvy, Gérard and Yves-Marie Hilaire. *Histoire religieuse de la France*. 3 vols. Toulouse: Privat, 2000.

Clark, Christopher and Wolfram Kaiser, eds. *Culture Wars: Secular-Catholic Conflict in 19th Century Europe*. Cambridge: Cambridge University Press, 2003.

Coburn, Carol K. and Martha Smith. *Spirited Lives: How Nuns Shaped Catholic Culture and American Life, 1836–1920*. Chapel Hill: University of North Carolina Press, 1999.

Cohen, Daniel A. "Miss Reed and the Superiors: The Contradictions of Convent Life in Antebellum America." *Journal of Social History* 30, no. 1 (Fall 1996): 149–184.

———. "The Respectability of Rebecca Reed: Genteel Womanhood and Sectarian Conflict in Antebellum America." *Journal of the Early Republic* 16, no. 3 (Autumn 1996): 419–461.

Cubitt, Geoffrey. *The Jesuit Myth: Conspiracy Theory and Politics in Nineteenth Century France*. Oxford: Oxford University Press, 1993.

Curtis, Sarah A. "Charitable Ladies: Gender, Class and Religion in Mid Nineteenth-Century Paris." *Past and Present* 177 (November 2002): 121–156.

Dansette, Adrien. *Histoire religieuse de la France contemporaine*. 2nd ed. Paris: Flammarion, 1965.

Davis, David Brion. *The Fear of Conspiracy: Images of Un-American Subversion from the Revolution to the Present*. Ithaca: Cornell University Press, 1971.

de Bertier de Sauvigny, G. *La France et les français vus par les voyageurs américains*. 2 vols. Paris: Flammarion, 1982.

Degler, Carl N. *At Odds: Women and the Family in America from the Revolution to the Present*. New York: Oxford University Press, 1980.

Derounian-Stodola, Kathryn Zabelle, and James Arthur Levernier. *The Indian Captivity Narrative 1550–1900*. New York: Twain, 1993.

Donzelot, Jacques. *The Policing of Families*. Translated by Robert Hurley. London: Hutchinson, 1980.

Douglas, Ann. *The Feminization of American Culture*. New York: Farrar, Straus and Giroux, 1998.

Dreger, Alice. *Hermaphrodites and the Medical Invention of Sex*. Cambridge, MA: Harvard University Press, 1998.

DuBois, Ellen Carol and Vicki L. Ruiz, eds. *Unequal Sisters: A MultiCultural Reader in U.S. Women's History*. New York: Routledge, 1990.

Dufeuille, Eugène. *L'anticléricalisme avant et pendant notre république*. Paris: Calmann-Lévy, 1910.

Echeverria, Durand. "L'Amérique devant l'opinion française, 1734–1870: Questions de méthode et d'interprétation." *Revue D'Histoire Moderne et Contemporaine* 9, no. 1 (1962): 51–62.

Ellis, Jack D. *The Physician-Legislators of France: Medicine and Politics in the Early Third Republic 1870–1914*. Cambridge: Cambridge University Press, 1990.

Elson, Ruth Miller. *Guardians of Tradition: American Schoolbooks in the Nineteenth Century*. Lincoln: University of Nebraska Press, 1964.

Espagne, Michel. *Bordeaux-Baltique: La présence culturelle allemande à Bordeaux aux XVIIIe et XIXe siècles*. Paris: Editions du CNRS, 1991.
Ewens, Mary. *The Role of the Nun in Nineteenth-Century America*. New York: Arno, 1978.
Faguet, Emile. *L'anticléricalisme*. Paris: Société française d'Imprimerie, 1906.
Faury, Jean. *Cléricalisme et anticléricalisme dans le Tarn (1848–1900)*. Toulouse: Service des publications de l'Université de Toulouse-Le Mirail, 1980.
Fessenden, Tracey. "The Convent, the Brothel, and the Protestant Woman's Sphere." *Signs* 25, no. 2 (Winter 2000): 451–478.
———. "The Nineteenth-Century Bible Wars and the Separation of Church and State." *Church History* 74, no. 4 (December 2005): 784–811.
Fletcher, I., ed. *Romantic Anthologies*. London: Routledge and Kegan Paul, 1967.
Foley, Susan K. *Women in France since 1789: The Meanings of Difference*. New York: Palgrave, 2004.
Foner, Eric. "The Meaning of Freedom in the Age of Emancipation." *Journal of American History* 81, no. 2 (September 1994):435–460.
Ford, Caroline. *Divided Houses: Religion and Gender in Modern France*. Ithaca: Cornell University Press, 2005.
Foucault, Michel. *Herculine Barbin: Being the Recently Discovered Memoirs of a Nineteenth Century French Hermaphrodite*. Translated by Richard McDougall. Brighton: Harvester Press, 1980.
———. *The History of Sexuality*. Translated by Robert Hurley. Vol. 1. New York: Vintage Books, 1985.
Franchot, Jenny. *Roads to Rome: The Antebellum Protestant Encounter with Catholicism*. Berkeley: University of California Press, 1994.
Gavronsky, Serge. *The French Liberal Opposition and the American Civil War*. New York: Humanities Press, 1968.
Gay, Peter. *The Bourgeois Experience: Victoria to Freud*. New York: Oxford University Press, 1984–1999.
Gibson, Ralph. *A Social History of French Catholicism, 1789–1914*. London: Routledge, 1989.
Giraud, Victor. *Anticléricalisme et catholicisme*. Paris: Bloud, 1906.
Goldstein, Jan. *Console and Classify: The French Psychiatric Profession in the Nineteenth Century*. Cambridge: Cambridge University Press, 1987.
———. "The Hysteria Diagnosis and the Politics of Anticlericalism in Late Nineteenth-Century France." *Journal of Modern History* 54, no. 2 (June 1982): 209–239.
Gollar, C. Walker. "The Alleged Abduction of Milly Mcpherson and Catholic Recruitment of Presybterian Girls." *Church History* 65, no. 4 (1996): 596–608.
Gough, Austin. *Paris and Rome: The Gallican Church and the Ultramontane Campaign, 1848–1853*. Oxford: Clarendon Press, 1986.
Gray, Walter D. *Interpreting American Democracy in France: The Career of Édouard Laboulaye, 1811–1883*. Newark: University of Delaware Press, 1994.
Grévy, Jérôme. *Le cléricalisme? Voilà l'ennemi! Une guerre de religion en France*. Paris: A. Colin, 2005.
Griffin, Susan M. *Anti-Catholicism and Nineteenth-Century Fiction*. Cambridge: Cambridge University Press, 2004.

Griffin, "Awful Disclosures: Women's Evidence in the Escaped Nun's Tale." *PMLA* 111, no. 1 (January 1996): 93–107.

Gross, Michael B. *The War against Catholicism: Liberalism and the Anti-Catholic Imagination in Nineteenth-Century Germany*. Ann Arbor: University of Michigan Press, 2004.

Halttunen, Karen. "Humanitarianism and the Pornography of Pain in Anglo-American Culture." *American Historical Review* 100, no. 2 (April 1995): 303–334.

Harrigan, Patrick and Raymond Grew. *School, State and Society: The Growth of Elementary Schooling in Nineteenth-Century France*. Ann Arbor: University of Michigan Press, 1991.

Hazareesingh, Sudhir. *From Subject to Citizen: The Second Empire and the Emergence of Modern French Democracy*. Princeton: Princeton University Press, 1998.

———. "Religion and Politics in the Saint-Napoleon Festivity 1852–1870: Anti-Clericalism, Local Patriotism and Modernity." *English Historical Review* 119, no. 482 (June 2004): 614–649.

Healy, Róisín. *The Jesuit Specter in Imperial Germany*. Boston: Brill Academic Publishers, 2003.

Hemmings, F.W.J. *Emile Zola*. Oxford: Clarendon Press, 1966.

Hennesey, James. *A History of the Roman Catholic Community in the United States*. Kansas: Sheed, Andrews and McMeel, 1977.

Hofstadter, Richard. *The Paranoid Style in American Politics, and Other Essays*. New York: Knopf, 1965.

Horowitz, Helen Lefkowitz. *Rereading Sex: Battles over Sexual Knowledge and Suppression in Nineteenth-Century America*. New York: Alfred A. Knopf, 2002.

Horvath, Sandra Ann. "Victory Duruy and the Controversy over Secondary Education for Girls." *French Historical Studies* 9, no. 1. (Spring, 1975): 83–104.

Houbre, Gabrielle. *La discipline de l'amour: L'éducation sentimentale des filles et des garçons à l'âge romantique*. Paris: Plon, 1997.

Houtin, Albert. *Le P. Hyacinthe dans l'eglise romaine 1827–1869: Avec un portrait*. Paris: Emile Nourry, 1920.

———. *Le Père Hyacinthe. Réformateur Catholique 1869–1893*. Paris: Emile Nourry, 1922.

———. *Le Père Hyacinthe, Prêtre solitaire 1893–1912*. Paris: Emile Nourry, 1924.

Jeune, Simon. *De F.T. Graindorge à A.O. Barnabooth: Les types américains dans le roman et le théâtre français (1861–1917)*. Paris: Marcel Didier, 1963.

Jones, Howard Mumford. *America and French Culture, 1750–1848*. Chapel Hill: University of North Carolina Press, 1927. Reprint. Westport: Greenwood Press, 1973.

Jones, R.M. "American Doctors and the Parisian Medical World 1830–1840." *Bulletin of the History of Medicine* 47, no. 2 (1973): 177–204.

Kann, Mark E. *A Republic of Men: The American Founders, Gendered Language, and Patriarchal Politics*. New York: New York University Press, 1998.

Kennelly, Karen, ed. *American Catholic Women: A Historical Exploration*. New York: Macmillan, 1989.

Kertzer, David I. *The Kidnapping of Edgardo Mortara.* New York: Alfred Knopf, 1997.
Keylor, William R. "Anti-Clericalism and Educational Reform in the French Third Republic: A Retrospective Evaluation." *History of Education Quarterly* 21, no. 1 (1981): 95–103.
Kimmel, Michael. *Manhood in America: A Cultural History.* New York: Free Press, 1996.
Knibiehler, Yvonne. *De la pucelle à la minette: Les jeunes filles de l'âge classique à nos jours.* Paris: Temps actuels, 1983.
———. *La sexualité et l'histoire.* Paris: Odile Jacob, 2002.
Korn, Bertram Wallace. *The American Reaction to the Mortara Case.* Cincinnati: American Jewish Archives, 1957.
Kselman, Thomas. "The Perraud Affair: Clergy, Church, and Sexual Politics in Fin-De-Siècle France." *Journal of Modern History* 70, no. 3 (September 1998): 588–618.
Lalouette, Jacqueline. *La république anticléricale XIXe–XXe siècles.* Paris: Seuil, 2002.
———. "Laïcité et séparation des églises et de l'état: Esquisse d'un bilan historiographique." *Revue Historique* 307, no. 4 (2005): 849–870.
Langlois, Claude. *Le catholicisme au féminin: Les congrégations françaises à supérieure générale au XIXe siècle.* Paris: Éd. du Cerf, 1984.
Laqueur, Thomas W. *Making Sex: Body and Gender from the Greeks to Freud.* Cambridge, MA: Harvard University Press, 1990.
———. *Solitary Sex: A Cultural History of Masturbation.* New York: Zone Books, 2003.
Léonard, Jacques. *La médicine entre les pouvoirs et les savoirs.* Paris: Aubier Montaigne, 1981.
Leroy, Michel. *Le mythe Jésuite: De Béranger à Michelet.* Paris: Presses universitaires, 1992.
Leroy-Beaulieu, Anatole. *Les doctrines de haine: L'antisémitisme, l'antiprotestantisme, l'anticléricalisme.* Paris: C. Lévy, 1902.
Lewis, James R. "'Mind-Forged Manacles': Anti-Catholic Convent Narratives in the Context of the American Captivity Tradition." *Mid-America* 72, no. 3 (1990): 149–167.
Lucas, Edith E. *La littérature anti-esclavagiste au 19ème siècle: Étude sur Mme Beecher Stowe et son influence en France.* Bordeaux: J. Bière, 1930.
Marx, Jacques, ed. *Aspects de l'anticléricalisme du moyen âge à nos jours: Hommage à Robert Joly: Colloque de Bruxelles, juin 1988.* Bruxelles: Université de Bruxelles, 1988.
Maurain, Jean. *La politique ecclésiastique du Second Empire de 1852 à 1869.* Paris: Librairie Félix Alcan, 1930.
Mayeur, Françoise. *L'éducation des filles en France au XIXe siècle.* Paris: Hachette, 1979.
McGreevy, John T. *Catholicism and American Freedom: A History.* New York: W.W. Norton, 2003.
McLaren, Angus. "Doctor in the House: Medicine and Private Morality in France, 1800–1850." *Feminist Studies* 2, nos. 2/3 (1975): 39–54.
———. *Sexuality and Social Order.* New York: Holmes & Meier, 1983.

McMillan, James F. "Clericals, Anticlericals, and the Women's Movement in France under the Third Republic." *Historical Journal* 24, no. 2 (June 1981): 361–76.

———. *France and Women, 1789–1914: Gender, Society and Politics*. London; New York: Routledge, 2000.

Mellor, Alec. *Histoire de l'anticléricalisme français*. Paris: Henri Veyrier, 1978.

Mintz, Steven and Susan Kellogg. *Domestic Revolutions: A Social History of American Family Life*. New York: Macmillan, 1988.

Moody, Joseph N. *The Church as Enemy: Anticlericalism in Nineteenth Century French Literature*. Washington, DC: Corpus, 1968.

Moreau, Thérese. *Le sang de l'histoire: Michelet, l'histoire et l'idée de la femme au XIXe siècle*. Paris: Flammarion, 1982.

Nord, Philip G. *The Republican Moment: Struggles for Democracy in Nineteenth-Century France*. Cambridge, MA: Harvard University Press, 1995.

Nye, Robert A. *Masculinity and Male Codes of Honor in Modern France*. New York: Oxford University Press, 1993.

———. The Origins of Crowd Psychology : Gustave Le Bon and the Crisis of Mass Democracy in the Third Republic. London: Sage, 1975.

Offen, Karen. "Ernest Legouve and the Doctrine of "Equality in Difference" for Women: A Case Study of Male Femininism in Nineteenth-Century French Thought." *Journal of Modern History* 58, no. 2 (June 1986): 452–484.

Outram, Dorinda. *The Body and the French Revolution: Sex, Class and Political Culture*. New Haven: Yale University Press, 1989.

Pagliarini, Maria Anne. "The Pure American Woman and the Wicked Catholic Priest: An Analysis of Anti-Catholic Literature in Antebellum America." *Religion and American Culture* 9, no. 1 (Winter 1999): 97–128.

Pateman, Carol. *The Sexual Contract*. Cambridge: Polity, 1988.

Perrot, Michelle, ed. *Les femmes, ou les silences de l'histoire*. Paris: Flammarion, 1998.

———. *Writing Women's History*. Oxford: Blackwell, 1992.

Ponton, Jeanne. *La religieuse dans la littérature française*. Quebec: Presses de l'Université Laval, 1969.

Portier, Lucienne. *Christianisme, églises et religions: Le dossier Hyacinthe Loyson*. Louvain-la-Neuve: Centre d'histoire des religions, 1982.

Reddy, William. *The Invisible Code: Honor and Sentiment in Post-Revolutionary France*. Berkeley: University of California Press, 1997.

Reis, Elizabeth. "Impossible Hermaphrodites: Intersex in America 1620–1960." *Journal of American History* 92, no. 2 (September 2005): 411–443.

Rémond, René. "Anticlericalism: Some Reflections by Way of Introduction." *European Studies Review* 13 (1983): 121–126.

———. *L'anticléricalisme en France, de 1815 à nos jours*. Paris: Artheme Favard, 1999.

———. *Les États-Unis devant l'opinion française*. 2 vols. Paris: A. Colin, 1962.

———. *Religion and Society in Modern Europe*. Translated by Antonia Nevill. Oxford: Blackwell Publishers, 1999.

Reville, Jean. "Anticlericalism in France." *American Journal of Theology* 9, no. 4 (1905): 605–620.

Reynolds, David S. *Beneath the American Renaissance: The Subversive Imagination in the Age of Emerson and Melville*. New York: Alfred A. Knopf, 1988.

Rodgers, Daniel T. *Atlantic Crossings: Social Politics in a Progressive Age.* Cambridge, MA; London: Belknap Press of Harvard University Press, 1998.

Roger, Philippe. *The American Enemy: A Story of French Anti-Americanism.* Chicago: University of Chicago Press, 2005.

Rogers, Rebecca. *From the Salon to the Schoolroom: Educating Bourgeois Girls in Nineteenth-Century France.* University Park: Pennsylvania State University Press, 2005.

———. "Retrograde or Modern? Unveiling the Teaching Nun in Nineteenth-Century France." *Social History* 23, no. 2 (May 1998): 146–164.

Rotundo, E. Anthony. *American Manhood: Transformations in Masculinity from the Revolution to the Modern Era.* New York: Basic Books, 1993.

Sanchez, José M. *Anticlericalism; a Brief History.* Notre Dame: University of Notre Dame Press, 1972.

Sancton, Thomas A. "America in the Eyes of the French Left." D. Phil, Oxford, 1978.

Savart, Claude. *L'abbé Jean-Hippolyte Michon: Contribution à l'étude du libéralisme catholique au XIXe siècle.* Paris: Les Belles Lettres, 1971.

Schapiro, J. Salwyn. *Anticlericalism: Conflict between Church and State in France, Italy and Spain.* Princeton: Van Nostrand, 1967.

Sewell, William H. "Marc Bloch and the Logic of Comparative History." *History and Theory* 6, no. 2 (1967): 208–218.

Sklar, Kathyrn Kish. *Catharine Beecher: A Study in American Domesticity.* New Haven: Yale University Press, 1973.

Smith, Bonnie G. *Ladies of the Leisure Class: The Bourgeoises of Northern France in the Nineteenth Century.* Princeton: Princeton University Press, 1981.

Smith, Helmut Walser, ed. *Protestants, Catholics, and Jews in Germany, 1800–1914.* New York: Berg, 2001.

Spencer, Philip. *Politics of Belief in Nineteenth-Century France; Lacordaire, Michon, Veuillot.* London: Faber and Faber, 1954.

Strumingher, Laura S. "'L'ange de la maison': Mothers and Daughters in Nineteenth Century France." *International Journal of Women's Studies* 2, no. 1 (1979): 51–61.

Surkis, Judith. *Sexing the Citizen: Morality and Masculinity in France, 1870–1920.* Ithaca: Cornell University Press, 2006.

Tchernoff, Juda. *Le parti républicain au coup d'état et sous le Second Empire.* Paris: Pedone, 1906.

Viallaneix, Paul and Jean Ehrard, eds. *Aimer en France 1760–1860: Actes du Colloque Internationale de Clermont-Ferrand.* 2 vols. Clermont-Ferrand: Publications de la Faculté des Lettres de l'Université de Clermont Ferrand, 1980.

Warner, John H. *Against the Spirit of the System: The French Impulse in Nineteenth-Century Medicine.* Princeton: Princeton University Press, 1998.

Weill, Georges. *Histoire de l'idée laïque en France au XIXe siècle.* Paris: F. Alcan, 1925.

———. *Histoire du parti républicain en France 1814–1870.* Paris: F. Alcan, 1928.

Welter, Barbara. "The Cult of True Womanhood: 1820–1860." *American Quarterly* 18 (Summer 1966): 151–174.

———. *Dimity Convictions: The American Woman in the Nineteenth Century.* Athens: Ohio University Press, 1976.

White, Elizabeth Brett. *American Opinion of France from Lafayette to Poincaré.* New York: A.A. Knopf, 1927.

Zeldin, Theodore. *Conflicts in French Society: Anticlericalism, Education and Morals in the Nineteenth Century.* London: Allen & Unwin, 1970.

———. *France 1848–1945.* Vol. 2: *Intellect, Taste and Anxiety.* Oxford: Oxford University Press, 1977.

Zimmermann, Bénédicte, Claude Didry, and Peter Wagener, eds. *Le travail et la nation; histoire croisée de la France et de l'Allemagne.* Paris: Maison des sciences et de l'homme, 1999.

Index

About, Edmond 61
Abstinence, sexual
  Catholic clergy 83–88, 96–100
  medical theories of effects 78–79, 81–83, 92–96
  and social decline 88–90
Alcott, William (Dr.) 94, 96
Allain-Targé, Henri 43, 44, 134, 152
American Tract Society 20, 36
Ampère, Jean-Jacques 52
Androgyny
  challenge to two-sex model 104–5, 116–7
  challenge to social order 116
  in literature 106
  in medical texts 105
  see also Jesuits; masculinity
Anti-Catholicism
  and gender 13–15
  historical writings on 6–7
  international phenomenon 8–9
  as response to Vatican initiatives 12–13
Anticlericalism
  historical writings on 6–7
  in Second Empire 13
  and gender 13–15
Anti-semitism 11
Assollant, Alfred 76

Bachelors
  hostility to 89–90
Baird, Robert 20–21, 22, 38
Baudrillart, Henri 43
Becklard, Eugene (pseud.) 80
Becquerel, Alfred (Dr.) 94–5
Bedford, Gunning S. (dr) 82
Beecher, Catharine 91, 106, 136
  attitude to convents 146

Beecher, Henry Ward 168, 169
Bigelow, John 1, 5, 42, 168, 170, 171, 172
Bloch, Marc 6
Booth, Mary L. 39, 41
Bourgeois, Xavier (Dr.) 94, 97, 98
Briquet, Pierre (Dr.)
  on causes of hysteria 95
  and Catholic clergy 97
Brownson, Orestes
  on Father Hyacinthe 170, 171
  on Michelet 29
  reaction to Mortara Affair 66, 72
Buffon, comte de (George-Louis Leclerc)
  on celibacy of clergy 84–5
Bungener, Félix 21
Bunkley, Josephine 113, 136, 137
Buntline, Ned 153

Captivity in convent
  compared to Indian 140–1
  and cult of domesticity 141–142, 147–9
  and female heart 135–9
  France compared to United States 139–140
  political symbolism of 135
  torture 152–55
Caracciolo, Enrichetta 36–7, 68, 150
Carmelites 144
Catholic Church
  and Know-Nothings 52
  position in United States and France 9, 51
  response to attacks 22, 29
  see also Brownson, Orestes; Celibacy, Catholic; Pius IX; Vatican Council; Veuillot, Louis.

225

Celibacy, Catholic
  attacks on 75–6
  and citizenship 90–92
  life expectancy rates 88–89
  and medical writers 77–78
  see also abstinence, sexual
Channing, William Ellery
  popularity in France 40–43, 69
Chassin, Charles-Louis
  on American education 46
  and Vatican Council 166
Chevalier, Michel
  on American attitudes to
    Catholicism 51
  on superiority of Protestantism 40
Cluseret, Gustave 50
Cocks, Charles C. 28
Comettant, Oscar 52, 68
Concordat of 1801 9, 48, 51, 164
Confessional
  polemics against 27–9, 35, 36, 99,
    122, 174
Contraception 80
Convents
  appeal to women 143, 145–6
  expansion of in France and
    U.S. 143–45
  hostile descriptions of 132–33
  see also captivity; education
Cooke, Nicholas (Dr.) 92, 94, 96
Copyright Act (1790) 25

de Beaumont, Gustave 48, 51
de Gasparin, Agénor 38–9, 49
de Hauranne, Ernest Duvergier 52,
  139
de Laveleye, Émile 43, 45, 46, 51,
  155
de Ponsan, Dr Melville 79, 92,
de Tocqueville, Alexis 50, 54–5, 106
Debay, Auguste 83, 86–7, 96
Descuret, J.B.F. 97
Des Jésuites (Michelet and
  Quinet) 29
  reception in United States 30–31
  see also Michelet, Jules; Quinet,
    Edgar

Deslandes, Léopold
  on celibacy 81, 85–6
  on sexual desire in women 79–80
  on sexual difference 104
Diderot, Denis 120, 133, 139, 143
Döllinger, Ignaz (Bishop)
  opposition to papal
    infallibility 165
Domesticity, cult of 136–7, 141
  and captive nun 147–51
  convent as rival to 143–6
  French and American views 64
  in Mortara Affair 61–63
  and social stability 64
  State intervention in 65–66
  see also separate spheres
Dreger, Alice 105
Dufieux, Jean-Ennemond 96–7
Dupanloup, Félix
  opposition to papal
    infallibility 160, 165
  opposition to state-run
    schools 45
Duruy, Victor 45

Education
  in America 33–34
  American views of French 34
  Catholic role in France 44–45
  and celibacy 76
  in convent 149–151
  female 45
  French admiration for American
    system 45–48
  and Jesuits 111, 123
  see also convents; Lea, Henry;
    Sauvestre, Charles; de Laveleye,
    Emile de
Emerson, Ralph Waldo 24
Eyma, Xavier
  on American education 45, 46

Ferry, Jules
  praising American education
    system 47
  and separation of Church and
    State 50

Foner, Eric
   on slavery as a metaphor 67
Foote, Edward Bliss
   on celibacy 87–88
Ford, Caroline 15
Foucault, Michel
   on hermaphroditism 116
   on medicalization of sexuality 77
Fowler, O.S. 79, 99, 105
Franchot, Jenny 6, 141

Gallican articles 160
Gardner, Augustus K. 93, 100
   on celibacy 95–6
Garrison, William Lloyd
   on papal infallibility 172
Gender
   as basis of opposition to Catholic Church 13–14
   in writings on anti-Catholicism and anticlericalism 14–15
   see also domesticity, cult of; separate spheres; masculinity
Graham, Sylvester 94
Grandpierre, Jean-Henri 23, 52
Greeley, Horace 108, 119
Griffin, Susan. M. 7, 125

Healy, Róisín 103
Heart, female 135–6
   in convent 136–7
Hecker, Isaac
   on Vatican Council 161
   visit to Father Hyacinthe 169
Herbert, Henry William 32–3
Hermaphrodites, see 'Androgyny'
Hippeau, Célestin
   report on American public schools 45–6
History of the Reformation in the Sixteenth Century 20–1
Hollick, Frederick (Dr.) 81, 87
Hughes, John (Archbishop) 34, 37, 47
Hugo, Victor 70, 75, 76, 137, 151
Hyacinthe, Father
   arrival in New York 1
   career 166, 174–5
   and masculinity 3
   meetings with Americans 168
   opposition to celibacy 3–4
   opposition to Ultramontanism 167
   reception in America 1, 169
   relationship to Emile Meriman 4–5, 171–172, 173
   resignation from Order 2–3
   views of Protestantism 170
Hysteria
   and celibacy 86–7, 97–8
   medical theories on 82–3, 95

Immaculate Conception, Dogma of 11, 14, 73
Infallibility, Papal 160–2, 164–5
   adoption of 172–3
   attitude of Father Hyacinthe to 167
   see also Vatican Council
Inquisition 153–154

Jésuite de robe courte 122–23
Jésuitesse 114–115
Jesuits
   attacks on 29–32, 35, 52
   as authoritarian figures 120–124
   and education system 111, 123
   and masculinity 124–126
   and mob 118–9
   and savagery 119–120
   as submissive figures 108–115
   in Vatican Council 163
   see also androgyny; *Jésuite de robe courte*; *Jésuitesse*; masculinity; Michelet, Quinet, Edgar
Jourdain, Louis 68–9
Le juif errant (Sue) 32–3, 114, 119, 123

Karcher, Théodore 27
Kelso, Isaac 132, 138, 140, 145

Laboulaye, Édouard
   on Channing 41–2, 69
   on origins of American democracy 40
   on separation of Church and State 48–9

Lacordaire, Henri-Dominique 50
Laïcité 14–15
Lallemand, Claude-François (Dr.)
  on celibacy 79, 85
  on *spermatorrhea* 82
Landouzy, Hector 82–3
  see also Hysteria
Laqueur, Thomas 104
Lasteyrie, Charles Philibert de 36
Le Bon, Gustave 118–9
Lea, Henry C. 34, 44
Legouvé, Ernest 105, 136
  on convents 143
Lester, Charles Edward 30–31, 198 (n 34)
Lèvy, Michel 85, 91
Lewis, Dio 97, 99–100, 195 (n 92)
Lincoln, Abraham 4
Longfellow, Henry Wadsworth 1, 24, 168

Masculinity
  and anti-Jesuits 124–6
  and Father Hyacinthe's revolt 3–4
  and public authority 106–107
Le maudit (Michon) 35–36, 139
Mayer, Alexandre (Dr.) 84, 95, 99
McGreevy, John 13
McMillan, James F. 143, 180 (note 29)
Meriman, Emilie 4–5, 171–2, 173, 175
Merle D'Aubigné, Jean-Henri 20–21
Michelet, Jules
  and convent captivity 133, 154
  on French exceptionalism 10
  on gender difference 104–105, 117
  on Jesuits 110, 114, 115, 121–2
  reaction of Catholic Church to 29
  reception in United States 23–31
  see also confessional
Michon, Jean-Hippolyte
  on Carmelites 144
  and convent captivity 133, 137, 139, 154
  on female Jesuits 122
  on Jesuits 123–24

reception of works in United States 35–6
  on slavery 68
  see also Le maudit
Mingrat, curé 76
Monk, Maria 107, 132, 149, 153
Montalembert, Charles 50
Morse, Samuel F.B. 19
Mortara affair
  career of Edgardo Mortara 73
  defense of Vatican 66, 72
  details of 57–8
  and domesticity 62–3
  link to Italian question 61
  reaction to 58–60
  role of slavery in 70–2
  see also domesticity; slavery

Napoléon III (Louis-Napoléon)
  attitude of government to Vatican Council 164
  and Italian question 12
  and Mortara Affair 59
  support from Church 49, 135
Nativism 6, 66
Nichols, Thomas Low 92–3
Nye, Robert A. 90, 124
Nymphomania 86, 87, 97

Onanism
  caused by celibacy 81, 85
  see also Deslandes, Léopold

Palmer, Dr John W. 25–7
Pancoast, Seth 79, 87
Papal States
  and calls for separation of Church and State 49, 51
  in Mortara Affair 59, 61, 71
  and opposition to Catholicism 12
Parkman, Francis 103, 110, 119, 124
Pascal, César 22–3
Pelletan, Eugène 38
  on Channing 42
  on gender difference 117
  on slavery 68
Phrenology 79, 99
  see also Fowler, O.S.

Pitrat, Jean-Claude 111–2, 113
Pius IX 11–12
  and Mortara Affair 59, 60
  opposition to Italian unity 12
  and papal infallibility 162
  and Syllabus of Errors 152, 160
Potts, Mary Engles 21
Protestantism 21
  in American schools 34
  as grounds for national superiority 22–3, 38–40
Proudhon, Pierre-Joseph 44

Quinet, Edgar 10, 42
  on Jesuits 29–31, 110, 113, 124, 125
  on superiority of Protestantism 39–40

Raspail, Francois-Vincent 34–5
Reclus, Élisée 70
Redfield, Justus Starr 37
Reed, Rebecca 107, 145
Rémond, René 7, 22
Renan, Ernest 43
Rodgers, Daniel T. 5, 53
Rodin (Jesuit) 33, 114, 119–120, 123
  see also Sue, Eugène; juif errant
Roger, Philippe 54
Romieu, Madame 107, 136
Roussel, Napoléon 22

Sancton, Thomas A. 53–4
Sand, George
  on androgyny 106
  on Channing 42
Sauvestre, Charles 2, 34, 109
  on America 44, 47, 52
  on convent captivity 133–4
Separate Spheres 15–16
  see also domesticity; gender
Separation of church and state
  condemned in Syllabus of Errors 152
  French praise for America as model of 48–51
Seraine, Dr Louis 79, 86, 136
Simon, Jules 42–3

Slavery
  in anti-Catholic thought 67–9
  French views of American 38–9, 54, 69–70
  as metaphor 66–7
  in Mortara Affair 70–2
Spalding, Martin John 22, 29
Spermatorrhea 85
  and sexual abstinence 81–2
  see also Lallemand, Claude-François
Storer, Horatio Robinson (Dr.) 92, 98
Stowe, Harriet Beecher 69, 109
  meeting with Father Hyacinthe 1, 168
  on Michelet 24
Sue, Eugène 32–3, 114, 119, 175
  admiration for Channing 42
Superior, Mother 107
  hostility to 68, 133, 136, 150
  in Ubryk affair 129, 130, 131
Syllabus of Errors 12, 51, 152
  fears of adoption by Vatican Council 159–62, 164

Torture, see Inquisition
Transnationalism 5–6
  France and the United States 9–10
  and opposition to Catholicism 6–9
Twain, Mark 108, 174

Ubryk, Barbara
  death of 156
  details of captivity 129
  newspaper reaction to captivity 130, 134–5
  physical recovery of 147
  reasons for captivity 131–2, 148–9
  see also convent; captivity; domesticity; torture
Ultramontanism 12, 13
  Father Hyacinthe's opposition to 167
  opposition to 36, 162–3, 165
  and papal infallibility 160, 172

Vacherot, Étienne 43–4
Vatican Council, First 12, 13, 50, 159, 165
    attitude of secular powers to 164
    Hyacinthe's attitude to 167
    Jesuit role in 163
    result of 172–3
    speculation as to purpose of 159–161
    see also infallibility; Ultramontanism; Hyacinthe; Syllabus of Errors.
Veuillot, Louis 13
    on Hyacinthe 167
    and Mortara Affair 59, 66

Walsh, Robert 42

Zeldin, Theodore 15
Zola, Emile 76